THE COCKIN BOOK OF STAFFORDSHIRE RECORDS

DID YOU KNOW THAT... 4

FACTS ABOUT

Lichfield, Burton, Tamworth

A Miscellany of
NOTES, QUERIES, CLAIMS, FOLKLORE,
ODDITIES OF HUMAN LIFE
in the south east corner of Staffordshire.
Volume Four of Five. 2009.

MALTHOUSE PRESS.
GRANGE COTTAGE, MALTHOUSE LANE,
BARLASTON, STAFFORDSHIRE, ST12 9AQ

THE COCKIN BOOK OF STAFFORDSHIRE RECORDS

DID YOU KNOW THAT... 4

FACTS ABOUT

Lichfield, Burton, Tamworth

A Miscellany of
NOTES, QUERIES, CLAIMS, FOLKLORE,
ODDITIES OF HUMAN LIFE
in the south east corner of Staffordshire.
Volume Four of Five. 2009.
Compiled by Tim Cockin.

"All knowledge is of itself of some value.
There is nothing so minute or inconsiderable,
that I would not rather know it than not."
- SAMUEL JOHNSON (1709-84)

MALTHOUSE PRESS.
GRANGE COTTAGE, MALTHOUSE LANE,
BARLASTON, STAFFORDSHIRE, ST12 9AQ

ISBN 978-0-9539018-8-3

Introduction

From time to time local historians and the general public may need to consult a book of claims, firsts, lasts etc for their area. Here is such a book. I have chosen ancient parishes as the chapter perimeters because they are static for when we have statistics. For population ratings Staffordshire had 166 ancient parishes; for dimension ratings 169; for WW1 roll of honour ratings 142. This book is one of five volumes in the series 'The Cockin Book of Staffordshire Records: Did You Know That...' covering the whole of the ancient county of Staffordshire. There are five volumes Volumes 1 (Potteries), 2 (Moorlands), 3 (Stafford, Cannock, Rugeley), 4 (Lichfield, Burton, Tamworth), and 5 (Black Country). For their help with this volume I would like to give my thanks to the local study library staff at Burton, Lichfield, and Tamworth, and in particular to Graham Nutt and his wonderful staff of volunteers at the Magic Attic archive of old newspapers at Swadlincote, Derbyshire.

Contents

Overview of claims

BRITISH/ UK RECORDS

Best: fair for horses *Burton;* regional river regattas, one of (Rowing) *Burton;* family walks *Burton;* Women's Voluntary Service centres, one of the *Burton;* Attraction for Children *Drayton Bassett;* weeping beech (3rd best) *Elford;* kept managed pub 1983 *Handsworth;* large renovation project 2007 *Lichfield;* florist 1994 *Tamworth;* pub (3rd) 2004 *Tatenhill*

Biggest: comprehensive school *Aldridge;* Burmese Python *Drayton Bassett;* vehicle repair and maintenance depots, one of the *Hanbury;* Thai festival outside London *King's Bromley;* Anglo-Saxon hoard ever found (Terry Herbert) *Lichfield;* free County & Western Festival *Lichfield;* motorway service station *Norton Canes;* single haul of farm animals *Weeford* Champion: Brainiest Kid 2002 (Christopher Guerin) *Aldridge;*

women to hold the highest belt in Judo 1959, one of the few *Alrewas;* English Schools' Cross Country only person ever to win four *Lichfield;* Got Talent runner-up 2007 (Connie Talbot) *Shenstone* Earliest: 'Aviation Week' *Burton* Favourite: station for trainspotters *Tamworth* Finest: herds (of pigs) *Lichfield;* church, one of *Tamworth;* entertainment houses, one of *Tamworth;* exam-

ple of herring bone walling, one of *Tamworth* First: ever Ride to the Wall (RTTW) *Alrewas;* canal tunnel built with a towpath *Armitage;* coloured sanitary pottery *Armitage;* wits, one of the (Isaaz Hawkins Brown) *Burton;* registered trade mark *Burton;* town to convert to North Sea Gas *Burton;* comprehensive social centre *Burton;* hospital to introduce a waitress service for patients *Burton;* mainline

steam locomotive to be built for nearly 50 years *Burton*; pilot sessions in ante-natal support group for fathers *Burton*; special wing for the handicapped *Burton*; children's centres, one of *Burton*; Poundland store *Burton*; town with signs to canals for motorists *Burton*; zoo to breed golden pythons 1991 *Drayton Bassett*; zoo to breed SouthAmercian snakes 1992 *Drayton Bassett*; deal with Russian agricultural interests after WW2 *Elford*; man to own his own railway *Lichfield*; church lit by electricity *Lichfield*; place to demonstrate a new 'Black-out' system for air-raid precautions *Lichfield*; (infact 2nd) Cathedral in country visited by a WW2 U.S. Negro Spiritualist choir *Lichfield*; competition against France ever in the history of motor boat racing *Norton Canes;* drive-through pharmacy *Norton Canes*; luxury hospital to be run by a private consortium of part-time NHS hospital doctors *Shenstone*; winners of the co-operative display of handicrafts *Shenstone*; fireproof housing *Tamworth*; reservoir in which the concrete is consolidated by the vibrated shutting principle *Tamworth*; Rural District to sell a council house *Tamworth*; indoor ski slope with real snow *Tamworth;* couple who never met before their wedding, see Cordell *Tamworth*
Greenest: hotel 2008 *Tamworth*
Highest: powered T.V. transmitter 1956 *Hints*
Largest: weeping beech tree *Elford*; cabbage 1953 *Hanbury*; pit

mound *H a n d s - worth*; earliest outbreak of (Mexican) Swine Flu in the 2009 epidemic *Handsworth*; auction centre, one of the *Lichfield*; private housing estates, mid 1980s, one of the *Lichfield*; independent re-manufacturer of power train products 2008 *Tatenhill*; hoard of coins ever found *Tutbury*
Last: royalist Civil War garrison to surrender, one of *Lichfield*
Leading: athletics clubs, one of (Birchfield Harriers) *Handsworth*; brass band 1921-39, one of *Tamworth*
Least: local identity town *Burton*
Longest: serving council chief executive (William Saunders) *Burton*; live-longer-as-a-parish-clerk record *Tamworth*
Most: thundery place *Alrewas*; up-to-date sanitary pottery producer c1966 *Armitage*; famous monastery, one of the *Burton*; sought after jazz drummer (Phil Seaman) *Burton*; famous athletic club 1933 (Birchfield Harriers) *Handsworth*; successful auction centre, one of the *Lichfield*; decorated Non-Commissioned Officer *Rolleston*; successful mobile library *Tamworth*; delightful entertainment houses, one of *Tamworth*; people given a Red Card in football *Tamworth*; haunted castles, one of the *Tutbury*; outstanding herds of British Friesian cattle 1951, one of the *Whittington*
Newest: canal aqueduct, (perhaps) *Lichfield*
Oldest: speed roller skater *Aldridge*; Britain's oldest Tai Chi instructor 2008 *Aldridge;* beer in Britain 2007 *Burton*; Mesolithic settlement

Burton; regional river regattas, one of (Rowing) *Burton*; rugby clubs 2009, one of the *Burton*; known working electrical generator *Burton*; person (reputedly) 1993 (Mrs Daisy Adams) *Burton*; natural history and archaeological societies, one of the *Burton*; village shows, one of the *Hanbury*; disastrous school *Lichfield*; free grammar school foundation of its kind *Rolleston*; sub-postmaster 1946 *Shenstone*
Only: place of worship dedicated in the Millennium Year *Alrewas*; ale brewery *Burton*; school of speech and drama founded and maintained by a local authority *Burton*; standing vertical drop ride *Drayton Bassett*; local authority nationwide literary competition *Lichfield*; county schools sailing centre *Norton Canes*; Britain's? oldest working barber 1955 (Mr B Davis) *Tamworth*; family other than the royal family entitled to own swans *Tamworth*; building society whose directors are unpaid 1951, one of the *Tamworth* Representative: in the European version of TV's 'It's a Knock Out' 1976 *Tamworth* Scariest: woman (Dawn Blake) *Handsworth* Smallest: public park 1998 *Lichfield* Speediest: typist (Albert James Sylvester) *Clifton Campville* Stongest: built house, one of *Lichfield* Tallest: bishop 1954 *Longdon* Top: 10 waterside pubs 2009, one of *Rushall* Widest: panoramas *Aldridge* Worst: baths 1975 *Burton*; explosion disaster *Hanbury*; roads, one of *Rushall*; place to find a single lady to

court *Shenstone*
Youngest: 1st Dan Black Belt in the Wado Ryu discipline of karate, ever *Burton*; person to have a double hip replacement (Simon Edkins) *Burton;* Masters of Hounds, one of *Tatenhill*; Olympian in the men's senior swimming squad to 1984, ever (Paul Howe) *Lichfield;* individual Paralympic gold medal swimmer (Eleanor Simmonds) *Aldridge*

CENTURIANS
Staffordshire's oldest
MEN
1 W Farr of Tamworth, 144
2 James Sands of Harborne, 140
3 Richard Wilson of Maer, 138
4 Joseph Lees (Draycott/Moors), 127
5 William Wakeley, Adbaston, 125
6 A Seighford man, 124
7. William Fasher of Tamworth, 118
8. William Beresford, Ipstones, 116
9. William Hyven of Wednesfield, 115
10.= William Billinge, Alstonefield, 112
10.= _____ Cookey, Kingswinford, 112
12. Thomas Burton, Ellastone, 111
13=.Edward Hall, Alrewas, 110
13=. Thomas Bosley of Longsdon, 110
15.William May of Longdon, 108
15=. William Sefton of Wolverhampton, 108
17=. Henry Lea of Shenstone, 107
17=. Hugh Moore of Tettenhall, 107
WOMEN
1 Mary Clum, Lichfield, 138
2 Elizabeth Powell, Uttoxeter, 132
3 Unknown, Uttoxeter 126
4 Rosamond Cook, Stoke 124
5 Ann Harvey, Ellas-

tone, 120
6 Mary Brooks (d1787), Horton, 119
7 Helen Millard of Long Hurst Hill, Bradley-in-the-Moors, 115 reputedly
8 Eva Morris, Newcastle, 114
9 Daisy Adams, Burton, 112
10 Mrs Nip of Gentleshaw, 109
11 Ann Smallwood of Handsworth, 108
13= Margaret Barclay of Alstonefield? d1731 aged 107 (AVH p9)
13= Lydia Barber, Stoke 107
15= Mary Blood Uttoxeter, 106, a few years prior to 1865 (HOU p244)
15= Priscilla Day, 106, former caretaker at Tamworth old Girls' Grammar School, born 1886, dies 1992 (TH July 17 1992 p11)

CHARACTERISTICS OF THE PARISHES

Obviously claims in themselves do not tell a proper story of the parish, but what was found by chance as information randomly accumulated (and was not searched for) unforeseen themes emerged. For instance:

Aldridge: individuals/ groups succeed to outbid others in great and minor feats
Alrewas: national and human external forces impact on the parish
Armitage: mavericks working in isolation
Burton: in the forefront of innovation, particularly social/ health-care; people are first to die in wars
Canwell: unfazed when confronting celebrity
Clifton Campville: quiet village life occasionally interrupted by scandal; church fabric is pre-eminent in every aspect
Drayton Bassett: human and geographic highs and lows
Edingale: tenacity
Elford: fantasy and sleeping
Farewell: by design or nature that which commemorates a period in the parish's history is left for later rediscovery
Freeford: determined
Hamstall Ridware: individuals obsessively complete most in their particular application
Hanbury: rural life/ craft hub infiltrated by song, poetry, modernity and warfare
Handsworth: the metropolis of endeavour, achievement, polarised attitude, heroism and villainy
Haselour: dormant until blossoming in the C20
Hints: from the very ancient to the very modern
King's Bromley: duty and dishonour
Lichfield: transparent gentility; opaque barbarism
Longdon: trying to curry favour with others; or ultimately not giving a damn
Mavesyn Ridware: parish given to bursts of tragedy/ menace
Norton Canes: getting about in every and peculiar ways
Oakley: thrived until C20, then dormant
Ogley Hay: small-time street villains and heroes
Pipe Ridware: inconsiderable consistency
Rolleston: the established order and those that contest it
Rushall: puritanical zeal
Shenstone: scholarly
Statfold: service
Tamworth: animals
Tatenhill: competition
Thorpe Constantine: squirearchy work for justice beyond the parish, while confusion reigns in it
Tutbury: ignoble, shamed, or scorned women
Weeford: architectural, dangerous, dynastical, funereal, world-wide journeys, through, to and from the parish
Whittington: first to try new middle class diversions
Yoxall: antiquated

ENGLISH RECORDS

Administrative: centre Lichfield
Best: poultry farms, one of Armitage; woman bridge player (Miss Jane Thornehill) Tatenhill; justice of any country gentleman Thorpe Constantine
Biggest: churchyards, one of Lichfield
Champion: trotter of all England 1939 Burton; England County Championship winner 1928 (Carl Bretherton) Shenstone; Heart of England competition winners 1988, 1989, 1991, Best Large Town in Tamworth; Barclays England Schools Girls' under-14 basketball champions 1989 Tatenhill
Coldest: bath Lichfield
Earliest: (2nd) record of bull baiting Tutbury
Finest: cathedral, one of Lichfield; parsonage 'west' region winner Tatenhill; private library of manuscripts owner, c1800 Yoxall, of its kind (Hoar Cross church) Yoxall; example of yew topiary, one of Yoxall
First: 80-barrel vats introduced Burton; religious house to be dissolved Canwell; woman to set foot in the Arctic Circle (Nellie Peel) Drayton Bassett; to lobby for preservation of toll houses (Rev GS Hewins) Hamstall Ridware; (infact 2nd) mill-site of the Anglo-Saxon period found Tamworth
Genteelest: in proportion to their wealth Lichfield
Greatest: 18th Century literary figure Lichfield
Largest: trout ever taken, one of Drayton Bassett; rose tree 1845 Handsworth
Last: toll house built Armitage; Constable of England (Sir William Vernon) Clifton Campville; public sale of a slave Lichfield; person burnt at the stake for heresy Lichfield
Longest: serving postmistress 1935 (Mary Eggleston) Alrewas; serving priest in Church of England by 2006 (Raymond Bristow) Norton Canes
Most: ambitious environmental project Alrewas; beautiful cathedral, one of Lichfield; sober, decent people Lichfield; polluted river Pipe Ridware; beautiful modern church, 1938 Yoxall; beautiful C19 churches 1977, one of Yoxall
Oldest: bellringer in England (David Ward) Alrewas; doctor 1926 (probably) (Dr George Chapman) Armitage; recorded fingerpost Drayton Bassett; alabaster effigy Hanbury; baker 1907 (Edwin Bendall) Handsworth; bell Lichfield; (2nd) floral and horticultural society 1920 Lichfield; signpost Norton Canes; coaching inn, one of Tamworth; village, considered to be Yoxall; cricketer Yoxall
Only: hospital specialising in the care of very young children Canwell; court to keep order over the musicians Tutbury
Poorest: Benedictine monks Burton
Purest: English speak-

ers *Lichfield*

Richest: commoner 1814 *Tatenhill*

Strongest: cricket team 1850, one of *Burton*

Unique: system for ministering to the cathedral parish *Lichfield*; perhaps (churches) *Tamworth*

Worst: hospital 2002-05 *Burton*

Youngest: ever table tennis player to play for their country *Burton*

EUROPEAN RECORDS

Biggest: factory *Handsworth*

Champion: Powerlifting silver 1989 *Tatenhill*: Rowing 3rd 1953 *Burton*: US Kids Challenge runner-up 2008 *Burton*

First: indoor skiing centre *Tamworth*

Only: stand-up rollercoaster *Drayton* Principal: place for brewing pale and other ales *Burton*

Unique: of its type *Burton*

GENERAL ENTRY TOPICS

Animals and their rights *Hanbury, Tamworth*

Archaeology *Drayton;* Anglo-Saxon *Lichfield, Weeford;* Anglo-Saxon and Norman *Tamworth;* Early man *Shenstone;* Mesolithic settlement *Burton;* Mint *Lichfield;* Norman *Tutbury;* Original settlement *Farewell;* Roman *Lichfield*

Awards *Lichfield*

Buildings and the built-environment *Tatenhill, Tutbury;* and housing *Tamworth;* Buildings, bridges, and inns *Burton;* Housing *Edingale, King's Bromley, Lichfield;* Modern expansion *Aldridge;* Pubs *Lichfield, Rushall;* Pubs, dining and entertainment *Tamworth*

Businesses *Lichfield*

Children and families *Burton;* Child Rescue Alert *Clifton Campville*

Civil affairs *Burton, Tamworth;* Municipal affairs *Lichfield;* Shrievalty *Lichfield*

Civil war *Mavesyn Ridware*

Climate *Alrewas*

Communications *Tamworth;* Communications, media and entertainment *Burton;* Communications *Norton*

Community; Centres *Lichfield;* achievements *Shenstone, Tamworth;* and the built-environment *Yoxall;* endeavours *Hanbury;* life *Whittington*

Country pursuits *Burton, Handsworth;* houses *Lichfield;* Countryside *Tatenhill*

Crime *Tamworth;* Law *Rolleston;* Quarter Sessions *Haselour, Lichfield*

Ducal encounter *Canwell*

Endeavours *Armitage, Lichfield;* Personal endeavours *Handsworth, Tatenhill*

Entertainment *Handsworth;* Pubs, dining and entertainment *Tamworth*

Events and festivals *Lichfield*

Farming *Armitage, Hanbury, Lichfield, Tatenhill, Weeford, Whittington, Yoxall;* and the built-environment *Tutbury;* Crop maize *Thorpe*

Fire *Mavesyn Ridware*

Gardening *Whittington*

Glass production *Tutbury*

Health & society *Burton;* Health *Handswort;* Healthcare *Tamworth*

Historical studies *Burton;* old documents *Alrewas*

Hospitality *Shenstone*

Manorial business *Clifton, Edingale, Mavesyn Ridware, Norton;* lordship *El-*

ford; Common land *Handsworth*

Markets and trade *Lichfield*

Mayoralty *Lichfield*

Military *Tamworth;* bases *Hanbury;* defence *Burton, Ogley Hay;* Militia *Lichfield, Whittington*

Mining *Handsworth, Norton;* Mineral extraction *Tamworth*

Natural history *Hamstall, Weeford*

Nomenclature *Lichfield;* Mistaken identity *Norton*

Publishing *Lichfield;* Literary prizes *Lichfield*

Parks and springs *Lichfield*

Public Art *Ogley Hay*

Religion *Tutbury*

Retail *Burton;* Shopping *Tamworth*

Rural pursuits *Drayton, Edingale;* life *Shenstone*

Shows *King's Bromley;* Carnival *Norton*

Slavery *Lichfield*

Social life *Alrewas, Shenstone;* Associations *Handsworth;* Friendly Society *Whittington;* Societies *Lichfield, Tamworth*

Soho Manufactory *Handsworth*

Theatres *Lichfield*

Trade claims *Tamworth*

Trade unionism and exhibitions *Tamworth*

T.V. transmitter *Hints*

Village and built environment *Elford, Hamstall, Hanbury;* Village life *Rolleston*

Utilities *Lichfield*

WW2 *Clifton, Elford, King's Bromley, Lichfield*

MIDLAND RECORDS

Best: animal lovers 1990 *Tamworth,* known medical men 1967, one of (Dr Henry Walter Featherstone) *Yoxall*

Champion: Woman Town Crier 1963 (Mrs G Stott) *Tamworth*

Finest: mansion (Great Barr Hall) *Aldridge;*

village church *Burton;* entertainment houses *Tamworth*

First: Gregory type 'People's houses' *Tamworth;* music and drama festival *Lichfield*

Greenest: towns 2006, one of *Tamworth*

Keenest: agriculturists 1934, one of *Tatenhill*

Largest: Dog shows in the Midlands, one of the *Aldridge;* factory of its type c1960 *Burton*

Last: people to pay 3d. for post *Shenstone*

Most: delightful mansion (Great Barr Hall) *Aldridge;* up-to-date factory of its type c1960 *Burton;* unlikely country ramble *Hints;* modern car washing by 1960 *Lichfield;* historic town *Lichfield;* internationallyminded school 1950 *Tamworth;* delightful entertainment houses *Tamworth;* dangerous road junctions, one of *Weeford;* Oldest: baker 1907 (Edwin Bendall) *Handsworth;* newspaper delivery boy 1956, probably (William J Ward) *King's Bromley;* town *Lichfield;* working barber 1955 *Tamworth*

Pioneer: of cycling *Lichfield*

OVERVIEW COVERING THIS BOOKS AREA

Altitudes: The highest point is Barr Beacon, *Aldridge,* at 745 feet, followed by the boundary at Castle Ring (highest point of Cannock Chase), *Longdon,* at 741 feet. The lowest point is 144 feet near the Dove and Trent confluence in *Burton* parish

Churches (parish): oldest *Tutbury,* 1080; newest *Canwell,* 1911

Distrance to Stafford: nearest *Armitage* and

Mavesyn Ridware, both 9.2m ESE; furtherest *Handsworth*, *Tamworth*, *Edingale* all 19.2m SE

Incumbents: longest serving Nicholas de Rolleston at Rolleston, 1318-1405, 87 years

Parish registers: earliest entry *Burton upon Trent* and *Mavesyn Ridware* both 1538. Latest entry *Lichfield* 1724.

Parish length: longest parish entity Hanbury with 6.5m; shortest Lichfield Friary and Lichfield Cathedral with 0.225m.

Parish size: smallest Lichfield Friary with 11 acres; largest parish entity *Hanbury* with 13,108 acres

Parish width: narrowest parish entity *Lichfield Friary* and *Lichfield Cathedral* at 0.2m; widest parish entity *Hanbury* with 10.8m

Population figures 1801-1901: parish with least *Hopwas Hayes* with between 2 and 6 people; parish with most *Burton-upon-Trent* with between 5,278 and 4,060 people

WW1: most killed *Burton* with 1322; least killed *Freeford* with 1

SPORT

Air racing *Aldridge*

Angling *Alrewas, Tamworth;* Fishing *Mavesyn Ridware*

Archery *Lichfield*

Athletics *Aldridge, Burton, Lichfield, Tamworth*

Barrel-rolling *Burton*

Birchfield Harriers *Handsworth*

Bowling *Lichfield, Tamworth*

Burton Albion Football Club *Burton*

Combat sports *Burton*

Competitions *Aldridge;* Contest *Tamworth*

Cricket *Burton, Handsworth, Lichfield, Tamworth*

Cycling *Aldridge, Lichfield;* Milk Race *Hints*

Dancing *Alrewas*

Endurance *Burton, Lichfield*

Firefighting *Lichfield*

Football *Burton, Handsworth, Lichfield; Tamworth*

Golf *Burton, Handsworth, Shenstone; Tamworth*

Gymnastics *Handsworth*

Horse racing *Burton*

Marksmanship *Alrewas*

Martial Arts *Alrewas, Burton, Handsworth, Lichfield, Tamworth*

Motor cycling *Burton*

Motor-racing *Tamworth*

Mountaineering *Handsworth, Lichfield*

Netball *Burton*

Otter hunting *Armitage*

Pedestrianism *Lichfield*

Power-lifting *Lichfield*

Rowing *Burton*

Rugby *Burton*

Sailing *Burton, Lichfield*

Showmanship *Lichfield*

Skiing *Burton;* Skating and skiing *Tamworth*

Snow Dome *Tamworth*

Sport *Rolleston, Tatenhill*

Swimming *Aldridge, Burton, Handsworth, Lichfield, Tamworth*

Table tennis *Burton*

Tai Chi *Aldridge*

Tennis *Handsworth*

Waterpolo *Burton; Lichfield*

Weight-lifting *Burton*

TRANSPORT

Aircraft *Burton*

Canals *Armitage, Lichfield*

Rail *Burton, Lichfield, Tamworth*

Reliant Robin *Tamworth*

Roads *Aldridge, Alrewas, Burton, Lichfield, Rushall, Tamworth;* by-pass *Hints*

Transport *Tutbury*

Trent, River *Ogley Hay*

Watercraft *Burton, Tamworth*

VILLAINS

Birch, Jacob Ogley Hay's villain

Booth, William Handsworth's villain, 'King of Coiners'

Briggs, Robert H Tamworth's villain (modern times)

Capewell, Charles Thorpe Constantine's villain

Cooper, William Pipe Ridware's villain

Cowland, James William (Amington's villain) *Tamworth*

Doyle, Nicolas (Dosthill's villain) *Tamworth*

Drayton Bassett's villain

Foxall, Rosemary (Brownhills' villainess) *Ogley Hay*

Griffiths, Sandra (Burtnwood's villainess) *Lichfield*

Halliday, Rebecca (Newchurch's villainess) *Tutbury*

Hewitt, John Thomas Norton's villain

Hind, James Elford's villain

King, Agnes Gretta Mavesyn Ridware's villainess

Moon, Ernest Rolleston's villain

Moore, Ann, nee Pegg Tutbury's villainess, Staffordshire's biggest female fraudster

Mycock, Mary Ann Alrewas' villainess

Newberry, Joseph Whittington's villain

Peach, Pte Douglas Rushall's villain

Pry, Paul Alrewas' old villain

Pymme, John Edingale's villain (in Alrewas's eyes!)

Shelley, Jane Hanbury's villainess

Sherriff brothers Anslow's villains *Rolleston*

Statham, Anne First female hung at the New Gaol at Stafford

Stevenson, Edward Shenstone's villain (see Steve Spray)

Stubbings, Christopher (paedophile) King's Bromley's villain

Venables, Piers Tutbury's villain

Westwood, Sarah Chorley's villainess *Farewell*

Weighman, William *Lichfield*

Wright, Robert Tamworth's villain

WORLD RECORDS

Biggest: non-nuclear explosion *Hanbury;* curry *Lichfield*

Champions: Trampolining (male 15-18 age group) 1973 *Handsworth;* Cross-Country Karate (junior) bronze medalist 2008 *Burton;* Natural Strongman 1989 *Lichfield;* Powerlifting bronze 1989 *Tatenhill;* Toe Wrestling 2006/8 (Paul Beech) *Burton*

Deepest: worked seam 1875 *Handsworth*

Fastest: beer lines, one of *Burton;* frankfurter eating *Lichfield*

Finest: herds (of pigs) *Lichfield*

First: newspaper printing *Tamworth;* pit electrically lit *Lichfield;* stand-up tower drop rollercoaster *Drayton Bassett*

Greatest: brewery *Burton;* war hero, one of *Tamworth*

Healthiest: town, one of the *Burton*

Largest: crater to be caused by a gunpowder explosion *Hanbury;* ghost hunt *Tutbury;* maltings belonging to any one firm *Burton*

Longest: train set track *Drayton Bassett*

Oldest: factory *Handsworth;* statuary *Tatenhill*

Only: ale brewery *Burton;* person to lift a Ford Fiesta car etc *Lichfield*

Record: British National Powerboat *Rolleston;* leap frogging *Burton;* longest time on air as a disc jockey *Lichfield;* marathon accompanied singing by a group *Burton;* pulling a BAC 1-11 aircraft farthest unaided *Lichfield;* table football *Burton*

Parishes of South East Staffordshire

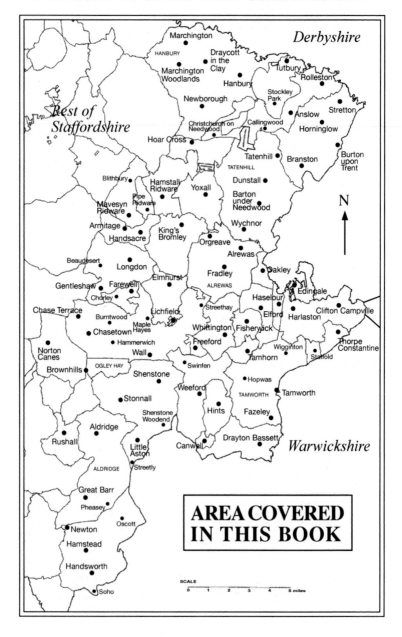

A

Aldridge Aldridge was Staffordshire's 25th largest parish, consisting of 8191 acres; 63rd= farthest parish away from the county town, 15m SSE; extremist length 6.3m, making it 16th longest parish in Staffordshire; extremist width 6.7m, making it 11th widest parish in Staffordshire. The parish's chief settlement is Aldridge, now a large suburban town. The parish is famous for Barr Beacon and its panoramic views.

Air racing *Kings Cup (premier trophy in British air racing) winner 1955, 1963.* Peter Clifford (1914-2003) who was Chief Test Pilot for Helliwells at Walsall Airport in and just after WW2 (TB Sept 18 2003 p15).

Altitudes The highest point is Barr Beacon at 745 feet, and the lowest point is 357 feet by the Tame below Ray Hall. The *highest peak on its longitude before the Urals* is reputedly, Barr Beacon (info Peter Smith). *One of the widest panoramas in country can be seen* from Barr Beacon; Shaw claimed it took in 15 counties (SHOS vol 2 (2nd) p105).

Athletics *First sub-five minute mile female athlete.* Diane Leather of Birchfield Harriers, born Streetly 1933, who achieved a mile in 4.59.6 seconds, at Birmingham in May 1954. She was also one time world record holder for the 1,500 metres in 4 minutes 22.2, and has set world bests in 440 yards and 880 yards (TB Sept 15 2005 p34).

Bonner, Capt Charles George *Aldridge's hero.* (1884/5-1951). Of Aldridge. Born Shuttington, Warws. In the Royal Navy Reserve he won a V.C. for distinguished services on the secret Q-Ship Dunraven in the Bay of Biscay whilst under attack from German U-boat on Aug 8 1917. He received it at Sandringham as a guest of the King and Queen. He was later a salvage expert. His grave is in Aldridge cemetery on the The Green (Walsall Chronicle Oct 30 2003) (TB Feb 8 2007 p15. Feb 22 2007 p20. Feb 21 2008 p27p of his grave).

Cartmel, Rev FW *Fancy that!* Rector of Aldridge in 1946. He made model ships as a hobby. Before coming to Aldridge he built a scale model of the Syrian Prince, a Mediterranean trader, which had no fewer than 724 separate pieces (SA Aug 17 1946 p7p).

The archdruid had his seat on Barr Beacon in Aldridge parish.

Churches *St Mary the Virgin* at Aldridge is one of 23 such county dedications (the most common dedication in the county); 88th= oldest AP county church dating from the C14 or roughly 1350. The most interesting things in the church are the early C14 figures of a priest (Robert Stapleton?) and a cross-legged knight (Nicholas de Alrenzie?). *All Saints'* at Streetly was Lichfield Diocese Best Kept Churchyard winner 2005. *St Margaret's* at Great Barr was Lichfield Diocese Best Kept Churchyard winner 1995.

Competitions *'one of the largest Dog Shows in the Midlands'* was the Aldridge Dog Show, as described in 1975 (Walsall Official Town Guide. 1975 p71). *Only known published quiz on Staffordshire and Staffordshire people* was the "Ask Me Another" series compiled by RD Woodall, JP, published by Norman A Tector Ltd, Aldridge Road, Streetly, c1950 (copy in Walsall Local History Centre, 2006).

Cooper, Rev Thomas *Aldridge's kindest.* Of Aldridge. By indenture dated 1718 gave property for the funding of a free school; he also gave 10s yearly to be paid out on St Thomas' day.

Cycling *One of the first Englishmen to ride in the Tour de France.* Charlie Holland (d1989) of Aldridge in 1937, when he was last of a three-man English team to survive in the race. A biography of him, Dancing Up Hill, has been produced by his daughters (BBC Midlands Today July 4 2007).

Dowell, Mandy *Strange but true!* Mandy, aged in her 40s, from Burntwood, was struck by lightning at Great Barr Leisure Centre on Aug 10 2003 whilst watching a football match, causing her to have a heart attack and stop breathing for five minutes during which time she was classified as dead (Daily Telegraph Aug 12 2003 p5).

Druid's Heath House *Most supernaturally disturbed house in Staffordshire* was Druid's Heath House, according to Thomas Wight in 'Great Barr and its Haunted Environs' (1852) is the (TB July 1987 p23).

Dye, Jane *First girl to be offered a university scholarship by the Midlands Electricity Board.* Aged 18, of Queslett Road, Great Barr in March 1965, head girl at the Hodge Hill Grammar School (Birmingham Post March 12 1965 photo).

Folklore *Aldridge's best.* Legend says the archdruid had his seat on Barr Beacon, or else at the British camp, an oval enclosure of 500 or 600 yards round, on Druid's Heath: This is how Druid's Heath got its name. And that he had his winter camp near Bourne Pool.

Geology Aldridge township is Upper Coal Measures (NW), Silurian (Wenlock) (SW fringes) Bunter (E, Aldridge town), Keuper Sandstones (NE); that of Great Barr township is Bunter (E, Barr Beacon highlands), Permian (W and Great Barr village), Silurian (Wenlock) (SW fringes).

Great Barr Hall *'one of the finest and most delightful mansions in this part of the country....'* was Great Barr Hall, according to Leigh in 1820 (BOE p137). *Fancy that!* Mildred Anne Lady Bateman and Scott (d1909) of Great Barr Hall left to the National Gallery "a miniature portrait of myself by Thorburn, as a work of art and not because it is my portrait" (SA Feb 26 1910 p4 col 4).

Great Barr School *Largest 'human centipede' to move 98 feet five inches (with ankles firmly tied together), biggest comprehensive school in the Country 2001* In May 2001 the school had approximately 2,4000 pupils. The centipede feat involved 1,004 people at the school on May 18 1990 (GBR 1991 p179) (info James Millicip).

Guerin, Christopher *Britain's Brainiest Kid 2002.* Born 1990. Of Yateley Crescent, Great Barr. In the ITV TV contest, achieving 8 points higher than the show's presenter Carol Vorderman. He was then a pupil, with an IQ of 162, at King Edward VI, Aston, Birmingham (E&S Jan 12003 p5).

Hill, John *Worked as a cobbler to age of 100.* Of Great Barr. Was believed to have repaired more than 13,000 pairs of shoes during his working life (Sunday Telegraph Aug 13 2000 p7).

Kilbourn, John *'The Great Barr Nightingale'.* (1838-98). Lecturer, essayist and poet, born Walsall, buried in Ryecroft Cemetery. His poem 'The Nightingale at Great Barr' appears in his 'John Kilbourn: His Writing' (1907), and the first verse goes:-

The sun is chambered in the distant west,
And night has spread her robes across the sky;
Nature is silent in expectancy,
And over all things lies the hush of rest.'

(BCM Spring 2006 pp27-29p).

Lister, Tony *Played a 1,000 organs.* Born 1938. Of Aldridge, native of Derby. Head of music at Queen Mary's High School, Walsall to 1983, associate organist at Rushall parish church. In 2008 he compiled an account of the 1000 organs he had played round the world (E&S Nov 18 2008 p8pc).

Modern expansion The *first sod cut for construction of Pheasey Farm housing estate* was cut on July 13 1937 by Sir Kingsley Wood (StE). The *bungalow legally compelled to have a number* was No. 1198 Aldridge Road, Great Barr, built by Birmingham builder, Sam Crutchley, in 1971. In 1973 he was given a week to put a house number on it or face a 40s. fine under the Towns Improvement Clauses Act of 1847, section 64 and 65 (Birmingham Mail Feb 8 1975 photo). In 2002 the *national home of the British Hyperlipidaemia Association (1986)* was Aldridge.

Morris, PCW Annie *'The Helicopter Girl'.* Birmingham's longest-serving policewoman when she retired in 1969, returning to her native Cwmgors, in Swansea valley, having resided at Great Barr. She was in Cyprus during the Cyprus Emergency (1955-59) and, being female, was used in a Special Branch helicopter mission to 'blow up' a woman with a cache of explosives in a 'hide' in the hills. Thus she was dubbed this by the insurgents, the EOKA (or National Organisation of Cypriot Fighters) (Birmingham Mail Sept 9 1969).

Place-name Aldridge first appeared in Domesday Book, 1086, and means village among the alder trees.

Poorest Those for Aldridge township appear to have used Shenstone workhouse, 1813 (SRO D120/A/PO/1503). After 1834 the poor could be sent to Walsall Poor Law Union workhouse.

Population Aldridge was 38th most-populated parish in 1801 with 1,492 people; 42nd in 1811 with 1,643; 45th in 1821 with 1,583; 45th in 1831 with 1,700; 43rd in 1841 with 2,094; 44th in 1851 with 2,174; 45th in 1861 with 2,254; 44th in 1871 with 2,480; 39th in 1881 with 3,017; 37th in 1891 with 3,594; 37th in 1901 with 3,822. Aldridge could be ranked 37th= worst-affected Staffordshire parish for loss of men in WW1, with 62 lives taken.

Quote *Choicest*. In his Beacon Edge local poet Harold Parry, wrote this, which captures the essence of the parish

'The sunset brims on Beacon Edge,
And leaves are touched with fire;
Somewhere beyond that golden rim
Lies hid our Love's desire.'

Roads *'one of the most horrific incidents that some of the crews have had to face'* was when a car crashed into a lamp post and wall in Erdington Road, bursting into flames and killing the trapped occupants on Sept 8 2003 according to a West Midlands Fire Service spokesman (BBC website).

Robinson, Lydia *Aldridge's most famous old worthy*. Died 1859. Daughter and widow of clergymen (Rev Thomas Gisborne of Yoxall Lodge and Rev Edmund Robinson, respectively), and later wife of Sir Edward-Dolman Scott (d1851) of Great Barr Hall. Mrs Gaskell in her biography of Charlotte Bronte (1857) accused her of being romantically involved with Bramwell Bronte, the ailing brother of the Bronte sisters. The accusation outraged the Scott family so much they threatened libel and Mrs Gaskell was forced to apologise in a letter to The Times.

Smith, Arthur *Inventor of the first automatic weighing and packing machine*. (1870-1960). Of Foley Road, Streetly. The invention led to his becoming a partner in a sheep dip powder manufacturing business. Later he founded a business in

Winson Green, designing and manufacturing weighing and packing machines, which amalgamated with Averys Ltd (Birmingham Mail Dec 15 1960).

Swimming *Great Britain's youngest individual Paralympic gold medal-winner ever 2008, BBC Young Sports Personality 2008, first child ever to receive the MBE, youngest entry in Debrett's People of Today 2009* Eleanor Simmonds of Aldridge, swimmer, born 1994 with achondroplasia, or dwarfism; in the 100 metre freestyle at the 2008 Paralympic Games when aged 13; awarded the MBE aged 14 in 2009. The record for Britain's youngest ever team Paralympic gold was achieved by a 12 year-old in the swimming relay in 1988 (The Times Sept 9 2008 p71) (BBC Midlands Today Sept 9 2008. July 23 2009) (Daily Telegraph Dec 31 2008 p4).

Tai Chi *Britain's oldest Tai Chi instructor 2008* Perhaps Ethel Lote of Aldridge, aged 88; Tai Chi instructor 1956-2008 in which period she had only missed one class (BBC Midlands Today. Oct 16 2008) (E&S Dec 22 2008 p13p).

Alrewas Alrewas was Staffordshire's 6oth largest parish, consisting of 4329 acres; 73rd= farthest parish away from the county town, 14.2m ESE; extremist length 3.8m; extremist width 3.8m. The parish's chief settlement is the large compact timber-framed wattle and daub village of Alrewas by the Trent, and the Trent and Mersey Canal. The parish is now famous for being the home of the National Memorial Arboretum, an area for memorials to those British killed in warfare.

Ainger, Canon *His only curacy*. (1860-63). Was at Alrewas. He was the 'much-loved Master of the Temple' (LGS p72), and composed the hymn 'God is working His purpose out,' and was the author of 'Charles Lamb' in the 'English Men of Letters' series; it was at Alrewas that Ainger began his collection of Lambiana, and first projected the writings which later established his reputation as a biographer; his lectures on Shakespeare attracted people to Alrewas from all parts (E&S Dec 27 1934) (SLM Sept 1951 p21).

Altitudes The parish's highest point is Easthill at 256 feet. The lowest point is 164 feet at the Trent and Tame confluence.

Angling *Alrewas angler in world championship*. Roy Walker of Anson Road, Alrewas, who was selected by his angling club Burton Mutual Angling Association to represent them in the world angling championship on the River Danube in Rumania in Sept 1965. The method used for selection was that the top six clubs in the All-England Championship could nominate one member to fish for the National Federation of Anglers in the world championship (BOb June 10 1965 p11).

Churches All Saints **at** Alrewas is one of 19 such county dedications (of ancient parish churches); 41st= oldest county church dating from 1190. In the churchyard is the grave of Joseph Berrisford who drowned in 2nd lock on Fradley Heath interred 5 July 1785 aged 8. *Staffordshire's 12th earliest commutation of tithes when they were dealt with under a parliamentary enclosure act.* The great and small tithes of the prebend of Alrewas, by allotments of land, 1802.

St Stephen's at Fradley was built in 1861.

Climate *Most thundery place in the country* is Alrewas, with an annual average of 24 thunder days (Daily Telegraph May 9 1998 p34). It was noted in 1953 how thundery and gusty it was over Lichfield. A water diviner who came to Lichfield Cathedral in 1952 claimed that lightning was said to be most likely to come to ground where there was an intersection of streams of water, noting that two streams ran roughly north to south beneath the Cathedral. This might explain why the Cathedral has been struck by lightning more often than most cathedrals (SA June 26 1953 p4 col 5).

Crane, Sharon *Strange but true!* Of Wellfield Road, Alrewas. When aged 45 she went to her wedding to Mark Cassidy, 45, at Wychnor church on May 11 2007 in a narrowboat called 'Sophia Grantham'. The journey was expected to take 30 minutes (Burton Mail May 11 2007 p14).

Crowshaw, Derek *Alrewas' saddest.* Of Mill End Lane, aged 2, who drowned in the Trent, and whose body was not discovered for months after. He went missing on Oct 19 1954 whilst playing with his four-year old brother and others near his home. His body was found on a mud flat at Castle Donnington, Leics, on Jan 8 1955, and was only identifiable from a small Wellington boot recovered during dredging operations. The coroner, unable to establish how the little boy had got into the river, and therefore unable to say for certain the cause of death, returned a verdict of 'Found drowned' (LiMe Jan 14 1955 p3 col 7. Jan 21 1955 p5 col7-8).

Dancing *Imperial Society Teachers of*

Amy Johnson (right) is reputedly the first pilot to land at Fradley airfield. Later, the airfield was said to be haunted by a headless RAF officer (left).

Dancing senior silver medalist. William Burton of Park Road, Alrewas, awarded in 1951; described as one of Burton-on-Trent's best male tap dancers (LiMe Dec 7 1951 p7p).

Documents, old *Staffordshire's oldest manor court rolls* are believed to be those of Alrewas. They cover periods from June 11 1259. *Staffordshire's gossipiest parish register* is Alrewas', telling of who drowned in nearby Trent, a comet sighting Nov-Dec 1585, a damask rose tree in vicarage garden which bore on June 28 1644 two white roses but hadn't been grafted, and an earthquake felt on Jan 4 1675.

Durose, Frederick *Alrewas' bravest.* A scout, who was fishing in the canal when he heard a little girl scream and went to her rescue and saved her from drowning. A Burton newspaper got up a subscription fund and in the presence of a large crowd presented him with a watch on July 7 1929 on the village green (LiMe July 12 1929 p7).

Eggleston, Mrs Mary *Longest serving postmistress in England 1935.* (1844-1935). Born Lullington, Derbys. Came to Alrewas as a bride; became postmistress in 1868; her husband died in 1873; she worked as postmistress until a week prior to Jubilee Day 1935, when she was Alrewas' oldest inhabitant (LiMe June 28 1935 p9 col 1).

Folklore *Alrewas' best.* The former RAF Station Lichfield, on Fradley Common, has several legends; that Amy Johnson was the first pilot to touch down on the airfield, and it is haunted by the ghost of a headless officer walking towards the control tower. The ghost was believed to be a pilot killed in a Wellington Bomber which crashed here in WW2.

Foulkes, Capt Gerard Irvine *Alrewas' WW2 hero.* Of Southlands, Daisy Lane, Alrewas. Awarded the Military Cross after Dunkirk in WW2. On May 15 1963 he saved his 81-year old neighbour in a house fire for which he was presented with an award from the Royal Society for the Protection of Life from Fire (SA &

Chron Oct 3 1963 p15 cols 4-5).

Geology Most the parish is Keuper Red Marls; of the Trent and Tame basins is Alluvium.

Gracey, Eric *Alrewas' WW2 hero.* Formerly of Streethay. Former Lichfield district and Alrewas parish councillor, guilty of a string of fraud and deception charges. In Nov 2006 a court ordered him to pay back £5,000 to a hair salon chain, £24,000 to a finance house he duped and pay £25,000 trial costs. He was given three months to pay back the money, but despite being apparently in a financial position to make the payment, nothing had been paid by March 2007 (LiMe March 1 2007 pp1p,3).

Hall, Edward *13th= oldest Staffordshire man ever.* Of Alrewas. He lived to the age of 110.

Horne, Pte Joseph *Alrewas' WW1 hero.* 1/6th North Staffs, born Alrewas. As a L/Sgt killed in action in Flanders March 21 1918 (ELSONNS p88).

Landers, John *Alrewas' early aviator.* Of Alrewas. He built himself a large glider, capable of carrying himself, in 1913 (BOb Sept 5 1963 p5).

Lister, Miss Helen Margaret *'Alrewas is very proud of her'.* Of Wellfield Road, Alrewas. In 1955 when aged 18, former pupil at The Friary, Lichfield, she was the only one of four to win an £80 open scholarship to Hull University to read English (BA), carrying with it a state scholarship (SA&C June 16 1955 p6).

Marksmanship *RAF Maintenance Command .303 rifle champion 1952.* LACW Myvida Stone, aged 18, daughter of an Alrewas, Burton-on-Trent policeman, at Bisley, beating all comers, including her instructor, Chief Technician JEP Witts, himself an international shot. Miss Stone was a storewoman at 16 M.U., Stafford; she had only visited a .303 range five times before the event, and had only been in the Service eight months (SA May 30 1952 p2p).

Martial Arts *One of the few women to hold the highest belt in Judo in the country 1959.* Mrs Stan Shaw of The Roddige Farm, Fradley. She received her Black Belt (First Dan) on Aug 21 1959, making her one of only about three women in the country to hold such a title (LiMe Aug 28 1959 p4p).

Mycock, Mary Ann *Alrewas' villainess.* Of Alrewas, charged with being drunk and disorderly at Alrewas before Elford Petty sessions on Aug 30 1888, and sentenced to one month in prison with hard labour. There were 16 previous convictions against her (SA Sept 1 1888 p6 col 4).

Nichols, James *Staffordshire's first will proved in a civil District Probate Registry.* Of Fradley. Born Harleston, Norfolk, c1766. His will, proved on Jan 18 1858, has this honour. Wills before Jan 12 1858 were proved in an ecclesiastical court.

Orme, Egerton Edward *'one of the best known and most successful breeders of Shire horses in Staffordshire'.* (1866-1935). Born Scropton, Derbys. He was farming at Ash, Sutton-on-the-Hill, Derbys, 1901; by 1928 at West View House, Alrewas, in 1935 of Hill Brow, Alrewas, died on a bus at Barton-under-Needwood, returning to Alrewas from Burton (LiMe Dec 20 1935 p5 col 1). The quote is from SA Dec 21 1935 p12 col 8.

Place-name The first appearance of the name is in 941, and it means alder swamp. There is no other town, village or hamlet called Alrewas in the world (SA & Chron March 29 1956 p5 col 5).

Poorest Appear to have been sent to Rosliston (Derbys) workhouse. Alrewas overseers accounts show payment to Rosliston 1824-35 (SRO D783/2/3/2-10,13). After 1836 the poor were sent to Lichfield Poor Law union workhouse.

Population Alrewas was 44th most-populated Staffordshire parish in 1801 with 1,312 people; 41st in 1811 with 1,665; 48th in 1821 with 1,492; 49th in 1831 with 1,607; 49th in 1841 with 1,658; 53rd in 1851 with 1,649; 58th in 1861 with 1,633; 60th in 1871 with 1,541; 64th in 1881 with 1,448; 65th in 1891 with 1,410; 66th in 1901 with 1,401. Alrewas could be ranked 68th= worst-affected Staffordshire parish for loss of men in WW1, with 23 lives taken.

Pry, Paul *Alrewas' old villain.* Highwayman who operated from Alrewas (LiMe June 12 2008 p4).

Quote *Choicest.* Someone wrote in 1968 'Alrewas has a wide, unspoilt main street with a remarkable number of 16th century houses, their black beams, white walls and thatched roofs are kept in excellent repair.'

Roads *Staffordshire's first inter-county car chase* is perhaps that involving Mrs Crosswell's stolen car from Allestree, Derby, on Feb 27 1932. Leslie Wilson, 22, and Sidney Braycotton, 20, both of Walsall were spotted in the car in Bridge St, Burton, after the Derby police broadcasted a telephone message. As the police approached the vehicle the occupants drove off at high speed towards Lichfield, even serving round a bus positioned to prevent its passing. The police phoned Ivy Garage, Alrewas, and the proprietor, Mr JT Leavesley, in his most powerful car laid in ambush for them, together with PC Turner. Still, they got away going over the Paul Pry crossroads at 50 mph. They were chased through Alrewas village, over Alrewas Bridge and along Lichfield Road; the men were gradually overtaken at over 70 mph. Realising the chase was up the Wilson and Braycotton abandoned the car and took to the fields, but were caught after a short chase on foot. Each got six months prison (SA March 5 1932 p8 col 2).

National Memorial Arboretum *England's most ambitious environmental project* was the National Forest, which encompasses the National Memorial Arboretum, brainchild of David Childs, 1988, who became the first director of the Arboretum at its opening in 2000 (TH April 10 2003 p14pc) (Lichfield District: The Guide. 2005 p36) (Visit Lichfield 2006). The *first tree planted, first sculpture erected* was 1997, followed by at some time the Polar Bear sculpture, a tribute to 49th West Riding Division, who spent the early years of WW2 in Norway and Iceland before serving in Normandy and Holland (TH April 10 2003 p14pc). *Only chapel built in Britain to celebrate the second millennium* is the National Memorial Arboretum Visitor Centre at Alrewas (Staffordshire County Guide 2006/7 p51). The *country's only place of worship dedicated in the Millennium Year, only place in UK where a Silence is observed on every day of the year* is the Chapel at 11.00am (leaflet, 2006). *First ever national ambulance memorial* in the Garden of Remembrance at the National Memorial Arboretum was unveiled on Sept 16 2004 to 675 UK ambulance personnel. It was the idea of former chief ambulance officer Norman Larkin of Sandy, Bedfordshire (BBC news Sept 12 2004). *UK's first-ever Ride to the Wall (RTTW)* was when bikers from all over the UK rode to the National Memorial Arboretum on Oct 11 2008 to pay their respects, forming a guard of honour on either side of Millennium Avenue before taking part in a service at the Armed Forces Memorial. The event was organised by Nene Valley Harley Owners Group (E&S Oct 13 2008 p15p).

Selvester, Elizabeth *Earliest person*

recorded in the parish register. For her burial on 4 Oct 1547. On the same day is recorded William Courzon was baptised.

Selwyn, John R *2nd Bishop of Melanesia.* (1844-98). Son of George Augustus Selwyn, 1877-94, curate of Alrewas 1869-71 (this was his first curacy), noted oarsman. His wife, Clara, died on Norfolk Island in childbirth in 1877 (VB p37) (DNB).

Shearer, Miss Molly *1st Alrewas Carnival Queen.* In 1939. The last carnival appears to have been in 1956; the following year it was decided not to hold the event due to poor attendance (Burton Mail April 17 2007 p16).

Social life *1st Alrewas Carnival* was Aug 26 1939, held to raise money for restoration of the church tower (SA Sept 2 1939 p10p). *1st Alrewas Show at Bycars Field, Fradley* was 1962, having been held elsewhere since its founding in 1879 (SA & Chron July 26 1962 p12ps). *'one of the finest herb gardens in Staffordshire'* The garden of Christine and David Walker of Old Mill, Mill End Lane, Alrewas (TB Aug 1994 p18). *One of the first organisations to take action on the 'Plant a Tree in '73' campaign* The British Waterways Board who ceremonially planted a tree near the Trent and Mersey Canal at Fradley Junction on Jan 16 1973. This was the Board's first tree planting of 1973, and was watched by pupils of St Stephen's County Primary School, Fradley (BOb Jan 18 1973 p1p).

Stubbs, R Norman *Alrewas's historian.* Of 22 Fox Lane. Deputy headmaster of Alrewas School 1931-58, Senior Master of John Taylor Secondary School, Barton, 1958- (SA & Chron Sept 7 1961 p8p).

Turton, Sir John *Alrewas' most famous old worthy.* Baptised 1637. Died 1707. Prominent lawyer who, according to Staffordshire historian Rev Stebbing Shaw, "was made in the beginning of King William the Third's reign baron of the exchequer, and after some years removed to be one of the honourable justices of the King's-bench, in which place he continued with much honour during the reign of the great prince. He was a person of a most graceful presence, great abilities, and of great probity and virtue; he died at his house in Serjeants-inn, in Fleet-Street, London, March the 15th, 1707, about one or two of the clock in the morning, and was buried at Alrewas, March 22d, being Monday, 1707, anno ætatis 71."

Ward, David *Oldest bellringer in Eng-*

land. (1851-1946). Of Alrewas, native of Liecs. He was claimed this shortly before his retirement from bellringing in 1937, aged 86 (LiMe Feb 1 1946 p2 col 3).

Alrewas Hays Alrewas Hays was Staffordshire's 127th largest parish (extra-parochial), consisting of 1680 acres; 77th= farthest parish away from the county town, 14m ESE; extremist length 2.5m; extremist width 2.5m. First appearance of the name is in 1222. The parish's chief settlement is the prairie-like farm Alrewas Hayes. Alrewas Hays is famous for having the bustling junction of the Coventry and Trent & Mersey Canals. Alrewas Hays was 162nd most-populated Staffordshire parish in 1801 with 12 people; 149th in 1811 with 49; 146th in 1821 with 74; 145th in 1831 with 77; 146th in 1841 with 92; 145th in 1851 with 107; 150th in 1861 with 48; 148th in 1871 with 72; 147th in 1881 with 115; 146th in 1891 with 102; 145th in 1901 with 119.

Amington See Tamworth.

Anslow See Rolleston.

Armitage Armitage was Staffordshire's 120th largest parish, consisting of 1,948 acres; 51st= closest parish to the county town, 9.2m ESE; extremist length 2.9m; extremist width 3.4m. The parish's chief settlement is the straggling large village of Armitage which merges with Handsacre. The parish is famous for Armitage Shanks, sanitary ware producers.

Altitudes The highest point 407 feet on the boundary at Brereton Cross. The lowest point 200 feet by the Trent beyond Bromley Lane Farm.

Bolton, Benjamin *Armitage's kindest*. Along with William Oldacre, both left provisions for the poor. Bolton was living 1731; Oldacre in 1753 (NHOA).

Broughton, James *Staffordshire Local Historians' cruellest critic*. (c1795-c1857), journalist, correspondent under the pseudonym John Smart Bugoe (an anagram of his name) to the SA Nov 13 1841 p2 col 4, and East India Co. employee, Handsacre resident in 1841, who called Stebbing Shaw's 'Staffordshire' history (1799, 1801) 'one of the most unreadable books that ever was compiled'; Simeon Shaw's 'History of the Staffordshire Potteries' (1829) "The contemptible performance of an illiterate sycophant"; and Frederick Calvert's 'Picturesque Views in Staffordshire and Shropshire' (1830) "a pitiful compilation, written in a villainous slip-slop, ungrammatical style, and abounding with the grossest blun-

ders" (WSHL p27).

Chapman, Dr George *Probably oldest doctor in England 1926*. (1824-1926). Member of the Royal College of Surgeons, who commenced his career at Brierley Hill, leaving there in 1883. He subsequently practiced at Armitage, being a surgeon at Rugeley Cottage Hospital. He retired to Hall Green, Birmingham, in 1910 (BPn Jan 4 1926) (BM Jan 14 1926).

Church St John the Baptist at Armitage is one of 11 such county dedications (of AP churches); 46th last AP county church built dating from 1632. It has a quite exceptional organ for a village church as its has 36 stops and was brought from Lichfield Cathedral in 1860. It was built in 1789 (SA & Chron Oct 3 1957 p6 col 4). In the churchyard the *oldest tomb* is that to Edward Westcott d1641 (SA & Chron Oct 3 1957 p6 col 4). Also the grave of John Meredith Eyles, Secretary of the Metropolitan Railway Company d1889 aged 41.

Canals *First British canal tunnel built with a towpath* was the Armitage Tunnel carrying the Trent and Mersey Canal was 139 yards long (Historic Waterways Scenes Series 'The Trent and Mersey Canal' Peter Lead 1980 pl 53 showing illustration from 1910).

Endeavours *Unique name, one of Britain's top 10 waterside pubs 2009*. The Plum Pudding, Rugeley Road, Armitage, by the Trent and Mersey Canal. The first claim was made by its landlord Derek Whipp in 1962, who believed the pub to be 600 years old (SA & Chron Dec 20 1962 p8 col 7). The second claim was made in The Sunday Telegraph's 'Britain's finest attractions' series (The Sunday Telegraph Jan 4 2009 p12). *What Armitage did for the Millennium*. Produce a guide called Armitage with Handsacre 2001.

Farming *Had a 'reputation as one of the soundest farms in the locality'*. Handsacre Hall Farm when occupied by the Boycott family, who left in 1927, according to Neville Wood in 'More Nature Notes' in the Staffordshire Advertiser (SA Jan 17 1931 p3). *'one of the best poultry farms in England'*. The aspiration in 1932 for Armitage Lodge Poultry Farm, owned by Cuthbert Bailey of Armitage Lodge, managing director of Doulton's, Stoke-on-Trent. This farm was one of the earliest to apply mass production to poultry farming, having by early 1932 the only Yankee 'Candee' incubator operating in the country (SA Feb 20 1932 p3).

Gaffey, Thomas *Armitage's saddest.* Aged 74, of Ricardia Terrace, Armitage, former Armitage Sanitary Pottery employee, who was found dead on a seat near his wife's grave, having poisoned himself with aspirin and cyanide of potassium, on April 20 1937. In the 12 months since his wife's death he had 'practically lived in the Churchyard' grieving tremendously for her (SA April 24 1937 p7 col 6).

Geology The Trent valley plain is Alluvian; The Hawkesyard Priory to Brereton Cross area is Bunter; the SE, Handsacre and Armitage (S) village areas is Keuper Red Marls; Armitage (N) village and decline to Handsacre area, and extreme SW pocket is Keuper Sandstones.

Grimley, Mr PJ *National Canine Defence League's silver medalist.* Of Hood Lane, Armitage, for rescuing an Alsatian belonging to Mrs Vale of the Plum Pudding Inn from drowning in the frozen canal by its home in Jan 1958 (SA & Chron Nov 6 1958 p1p).

The Armitage hermit meditates. Left, the first British canal tunnel built with a towpath.

Folklore *Armitage's best.* 'About AD 1100,' says 'The Staffordshire Village Book' by the Staffordshire Federation of Women's Institutes (1988), a hermit came to live among the rocks upon which the church of St John the Baptist now stands. This 'hermitage' eventually gave the village of Armitage its name.'

Hawkesyard Priory *First Dominican house for friars in Staffordshire after the Reformation* was a priory at Hawkesyard (later Spode House). The friars arrived on Sept 3 1894 (LiMe Nov 17 1944 p7 col 4) (HOS 1998 p60).

Lane, Olivia May Allsobrook *A 1st Millennium baby.* Of Handsacre, at Victoria Hospital, Lichfield, at 7.13am Jan 1 2000 (E&S Jan 3 2000 p13).

Lister, Adelaide *Maid of honour to Queen Victoria.* Daughter of Tom Lister

of Armitage Park, by 1839 (SA April 18 1936 p5 col 1).

Oldacre, William *Armitage's kindest.* Of Armitage by indenture dated 1753 left land the rental going to a bread dole for distribution on four Sundays a year (after 25 July, 1 Nov, 2 Feb, 1 May).

Otter hunting *Only revived Staffordshire otter hunting pack* started at Handsacre along the Trent in 1920s and early 1930s before folding (TOS p18) (info County Museum, Shugborough).

Population Armitage was 100th most-populated Staffordshire parish in 1801 with 464 people; 103rd in 1811 with 483; 81st in 1821 with 793; 69th in 1831 with 977; 70th in 1841 with 987; 71st in 1851 with 1,014; 78th in 1861 with 937; 75th in 1871 with 992; 70th in 1881 with 1,283; 69th in 1891 with 1,290; 70th in 1901 with 1,318. Armitage could be ranked 57th worst-affected Staffordshire parish for loss of men in WW1, with 33 lives taken.

Quote *Choicest.* Thomas Pennant in his 'Journey From Chester to London', 1811, passed through Armitage 'IN my road, not far from Blithe field, I again met with the Trent, and the Canal; the last a most fortunate embellishment to the neat seat of Mr. Lister of Hermitage.'

Ratcliffe, Edward Thomas *Armitage's WW1 hero.* (1891-1968). Armitage (Shanks) Ware Ltd employee 1904-58, awarded the MM, & Bar, Croix-de-Guerre (Belgium) (info Doreen Ratcliffe, daughter-in-law). Also Bombdr Jack Johnson of Railway Cottages, Armitage, awarded the Distinguished Conduct Medal for gallant conduct on Aug 28 1918 (SA Feb 19 1919 p3 col 7).

Rayworth, Miss Margaret *Miss Staffordshire 1938.* Aged 16, Miss Armitage 1938; she was the 6th Miss Staffordshire ever (Stafford Pageant: The Exciting Innovative Years 1901-1952. Gordon Henry Loach. 2007).

Roads *Last toll house built in England* was possibly Handsacre Toll House, about 0.25m N of High Bridge, built c1831 (STM June 1969 p32p).

Ruggeley, Richard armig. *Earliest person recorded in the parish register.* For his burial on 6 July 1623.

Place-name The first appearance of the name Armitage is in the C13, and is explained above under Folklore.

Sanitary pottery production *First coloured sanitary pottery in the UK* was produced by Armitage Ware Ltd, Armitage, in 1925 (Staffordshire Handbook c1966 p99). *One of the most up-to-date sanitary ware manufacturers in the UK c1966* was that of Armitage Ware Ltd at Armitage (Staffordshire Handbook c1966 p99).

Spode IV, Josiah *Armitage's most famous old worthy.* (1823-93). 'The last of the four Josiah Spodes of Pottery fame.' He moved with his widowed mother from The Mount, Penkhull, to Armitage Park in the 1830s; re-titled it, Hawkesyard, 1859; converted to Catholicism with his niece and housekeeper, Helen Gulson, 1885, to whom he bequeathed Hawkesyard on condition she transfer it to English Dominicans on her death. But she complied at once, and so, after two years of lying at Stone, Spode's body was able to be brought to a vault at the new Priory, where he now lies beside his niece.

B

Barton-under-Needwood See Tatenhill.

Brownhills See Ogley Hay.

Burntwood See Lichfield.

Burton upon Trent Burton upon Trent was Staffordshire's 30th largest parish, consisting of 7,501 acres; 48th farthest parish away from the county town, 17.1m E; extremist length 5.5m, making it 24th= longest parish in the county; extremist width 4.8m. The parish's chief settlement is Burton upon Trent, a large brewing town which grew out of a Benedictine abbey. Burton is famous for Bass beer and breweries.

Adams, Mrs Daisy *Oldest person in Britain (reputedly) 1993, Staffordshire's 9th oldest woman ever.* Of Burton, aged 112, in 1993 (Daily Telegraph March 18 1993 p7).

Aircraft *Earliest 'Aviation Week' in Britain* was perhaps Burton upon Trent Aviation Week held at Bass' Meadow, Meadow Road, Sept 26 - Oct 1 1910 (EAS pp34-35) (BTOP vol 1 p64p) (ABTOP p104p). It was certainly the first aviation week in England (SA Dec 31 1910 p6 col 4), and the first aviation meeting ever to make a profit (BOb March 21 1963 p7ps). *Fancy that!* A French pilot, M. Mamet, attended Burton's Aviation Week, 1910, and dropped a letter addressed to Mrs GF Reading over Waterloo Mount, which was seized by a small boy, who at first refused to give up his treasured possession from the sky. The letter did finally reach Mrs Reading (BOb Oct 6 1960 p7). *Earliest Staffordshire-built aeroplane to fly* was built by SH Evershed of Burton. It flew for only a 30 yards in June 1910; another private early attempt was made by AE Hartill of Wolverhampton (EAS p15) (TB Dec 1993 p17). First Burtonian to fly in a *passenger aeroplane* was Mr GF Reading of Bridge Street, when he was on holiday at Blackpool, 1910 (BOb Sept 22 1960 p5). *First girl to cross the Channel in a glider* was Miss Joan Meakin in 1934, daughter of Mr H Meakin of Burton; but Miss Meakin was brought up at Repton, Derbys (BOb April 2 1959 p3).

Altitudes The highest points are Burton (Derbys) - 410 feet on the E boundary, E of Winshill. Burton (Staffs) - 384 feet at Rough Hay. Lowest points are for Burton (Staffs) - 144 feet near the Dove and Trent confluence. Burton (Derbys) - 151 feet by the Trent.

Athletics *When a champion pedestrian walked from London to Burton.* George Cummings (b1872) began at Trafalgar Square at 7.50am on Nov 23 1930 and arrived at Burton on Nov 25 1930 (Burton Mail May 12 2008 p20ps). *National Special Athletic Championships discus gold 2005* Matthew Waters, of Pine Close, Branston, born 1989 with hydrocephalus; won Burton Mail's New Year's Honours 2005/6 Child of the Year award; attends Saxon Hill Community School, Lichfield (Burton Mail Jan 31 2006 p28p).

Auden, Rev John *Horninglow's first vicar.* Appointed 1868. His grandson was the poet WH Auden (1907-73), son of GA Auden (d1957), one of the 10 sons of Rev John, and his wife Eliza Sarah Hopkins. In 1966 WH Auden visited St John's as part of the church's centenary celebrations (Burton Mail Feb 15 2007 p16).

Baldwin, David *Burton's self-proclaimed heaviest man 2001.* (c1947-2007). Of Horninglow Road, Burton, weighing more than 30st. In 2001, when of Harper Ave, Horninglow, he protested to Burton Mail that a TV programme, ITV's 'The Fattest Men in Britain', gave fat people a bad name (Burton Mail May 12 2007 p3p).

Barrel-rolling *First barrel-rolling competition at Burton.* May 1933. *First winners of the revived competition* Marston's Brewery team with a time of 5.02 mins along the length of the High Street in July 1975; 16 teams entered; the event had lapsed c1945 (BOb July 3 1975 p14ps). *Barrel rolled from Uttoxeter to Burton* was by Burton Division Young Conservatives on a campaign to increase membership from Uttoxeter to their division HQ at 9 St Paul's Square, Burton, via Tutbury in 7 hours on Oct 22 1966 (BOb Oct 27 1966 p1p). *Barrel hauled 350 miles* was a barrel of beer on a trolley hauled by seven Royal Navy apprentices (of HMS Caledonia) on foot from Alloa, Scotland to Burton to raise money for the Royal National Lifeboat Institution, April 12-27 1970 (BOb April 30 1970 p3p).

Batte, Richard *Fancy that!* A surgeon of Burton, was accused of making wax images of his mother-in-law and her family and sticking pins in them in 1591 (BOb Dec 20 1956 p1).

Beckett, Arthur *Horninglow's bravest.* An abrasive wheelmaker at Pollett Bros Ltd, aged 28, of 45 Rowton Street, Horninglow, dashed into a burning house in Northfield Road on the evening of Empire Day 1950, and rescued Pauline Fletcher, aged five and half months. He was awarded the King's Commendation for brave conduct (BOb Aug 3 1950 p1p).

Blount, Dame Elizabeth *Burton's kindest.* (d1593). Born in Nether Hall, Burton, married firstly Antony Beresford (d1539) of Thorpe, near Ashbourne, secondly Sir Thomas Pope (d1559), Treasurer of the Royal Household, Warden of the Mint, and founder of Trinity College, Oxford, and thirdly Sir Hugh Paulet (d1572), a Somerset knt, by these various marriages she acquired considerable property, the income from rent paid for the schoolmaster and usher of Burton Free Grammar School and almshouses (Market Square and High Street) for five women (BOb June 9 1966 p5).

Brammer, Mr WJ *President of the (national) Clerk of Works 1961.* Of 'Artro', Tutbury Road, Burton, a founder-member and first president of the Burton on Trent and District Clerks of Works and Build-

ers Foremen's Association (formed 1951) (BOb Nov 23 1961 p10p).

BREWING Advertising and consumption. *When Burton ale was historically famous* in King Richard's time according to Sir Walter Scott. *England's 'brewing capital'* (Staffordshire Breaks 2006. Staffordshire Tourism), *'the brewery town'* Burton (Staffordshire Handbook c1966 p35). *First certain reference to Burton beer in London* appeared in the Spectator of May 26 1712 (IHOBT p36). *Britain's first registered trade mark.* Bass brewery red triangle, Jan 1 1876. It was first used as a 'Trade Mark' in 1855. It is No. 1 on the Trade Mark Register, secured by an employee of the firm staying on the steps of the Registrar's Office throughout the night preceding the opening of the Register when the Trade Mark Act came into being in 1875. The Diamond Trade Mark is No. 2 on the Register (Burton-upon-Trent Official Handbook, c1960. p11) (Bass beermat). *"Gone for a Burton"* euphemistic expression meaning something finished, ended, failed, died, possibly from going for a beer (so related to Burton upon Trent), or getting a suit from Burton tailors or other explanations (TB March 21 2002 p4). *Oldest beer in Britain 2007.* Bottles of Harry Ratcliffe's Ale, dating to 1869, found in a deep cellar at the Coors Visitor Centre, Horninglow St, Burton, in Dec 2006. Verification of the claim revealed that the 2nd oldest beer in the country was a bottle from 1900 in the Scottish Brewing Archive, belonging to beer expert and writer Roger Protz (Burton Mail March 22 2007 p8p). *'one of the earliest examples in the UK, if not the World' of a Burton beer label* was a specially brewed ale with the label - "S. Allsopp & Sons' Ale Brewed in 1875 for the Arctic Expedition Burton on Trent" - in the collection of WH Tweddle to be auctioned in 2007 (Burton Mail Jan 12 2007 p13p). The *Titanic 1912 carried Bass* on its maiden voyage the Titantic carried 12,000 pint bottles of Bass for the use of the passengers (BOb March 1 1962 p5). A case of 'King's Ale' was taken on the *Imperial Trans-Antarctic Expedition 1914*. It was brewed by Edward VII on his visit to Burton in 1902, was taken as supplies for this expedition led by Sir Ernest Shackleton (BOb Nov 19 1964 p5).

Auxiliary services. *Marston's last steam locomotive.* Locomotive No. 3, a 0-4-0 saddletank left Marston, Thompson and Evershed Ltd, Shobnall Road, Burton,

on April 12 1967, sold to the Foxfield Light Railway Society; it had served the company for more than 40 years; the last steam engine bought by Marson's was in 1924 (BOb April 13 1967 p1p). *Last tour of the Bass railway tour coach* was on Dec 9 1965, it was used to take guests on tours of Bass's Brewery at Burton. The last passengers were British Railway's officials led by Mr GB Gray, Nottingham Divisional Manager of British Rail. The coach was built in 1889 by the Ashbury Railway Carriage Iron Co. Ltd of Manchester, and was first used by Bass Brewery directors on their regular tours of inspection. It was thought the coach would find a home a museum near Stafford (BOb Dec 16 1965 p7p). *Last train to cross the High Street* was the Bass Sentinel Diesel No. 7 pulling 10 wagons on May 8 1967 shortly after 2.00pm on the breweries service railway which had lines throughout Burton; the line appears to have been first operated in 1861 (BOb May 11 1967 pp1p,6p). *Burton's last cooper.* Eddie Lee, born c1936, employed in 1976 at John Grout and Co. Ltd, but mostly in the Union Room at Bass Charrington. His first job was at Bass. By 1976 he was Burton's only full-time cooper. He and another cooper, Joe Foster, were the models for The Burton Cooper statue, sculpted by James Butler, unveiled in May 1977 on the St Modwen's Walk entrance to Burton shopping precinct (BOb July 1 1976 p8p) (Burton Daily Mail Dec 28 1977 p9).
General. *First Burton bitter brewed* was brewed by Mr Allsopp in 1822 (BOb July 12 1951 p5). *Europe's principal place for brewing pale and other ales* was Burton (Staffordshire County Handbook c1958). *Only ale brewery in the UK, probably in the world* was Bass, Ratcliff & Gretton (essentially later Bass & Co.) of Burton by 1874, with an annual output in excess of 650,000 bar (The Greatest Brewery in the World. Colin C Owen. 1992. p71). *'The Greatest Brewery in the World'* Bass, Ratcliff & Gretton (essentially later Bass & Co.) in the period 1865-75. In 1879 the firm was described as 'a mercantile colossus that has o' erstrided every similar institution in England, if not the world.... a monument to the energy of men' (The British Mercury. June 6 1879) (The Greatest Brewery in the World. Colin C Owen. 1992. p71). *Biggest breweries in the world 1880s.* Bass, and Allsopp (The Times. Weekend Section. Nov 9 1991 p10) (IAS p83). *Largest maltings in the world be-*

longing to any one firm was reputedly, a range at Shobnall belonging to Bass, 1887 (IAS p155). The *'biggest brewery organisation in Britain' 1959* was Ind Coope Ltd on its merger on July 8 1959 with Taylor, Walker and Co, with 5,000 licensed premises (BOb Jan 7 1960 p7). *UK's largest brewery 1996.* Carlsberg-Tetley Burton Brewery (Burton Mail March 22 2006 p12 'On this day'). *Second largest brewer in UK 2000s.* Coors Brewers, whose Burton brewery is the UK's largest brewery (East Staffordshire Official Guide. 2005?).
People *First common brewer of Burton.* Benjamin Printon (d1728/9), who established a small brewery at the western end of the Trent Bridge in 1708 (SHOS vol 1 p13) (VCH vol 2 p243) (NSJFS 1974 p80) (IHOBT p36). *First chemist appointed to a Burton brewery.* Dr Henry Bottinger of

A Burton cooper at work.

Germany for Allsopp and Sons in 1845 (VCH vol 9 p76). *'the prince of brewers' 'the Burton Patriarch'* are references to Michael Thomas Bass (d1884) (The Times 1884) (VCH vol 9 p17). *Highest earning tradespeople in C19 Burton* were the Coopers who made the beer barrels (SLM March 2005 p22). *Strange but true!* Sidney Gilchrist Thomas (b1850) was famous for his discovery of the method of eliminating phosphorus in the Bessemer process of converting pig-iron into steel. He was once offered the post of analytical chemist at Burton, but refused because of his conscientious objection to alcohol in any shape or form (SA Dec 31 1949 p6 col 6).
Production. *First 80-barrel vats introduced into England* were believed to be those photographed at the old Middle Yard of Messrs Allsopp's Brewery, Horninglow, 1907; these giant barrels were made of Slavonic oak by a firm named Bodenheim of Cassels, Germany (BOb Dec 12 1963 p14p). *'Burtonisation'* was a term apparently prevalent in 1933 for the use of gypsum in water used for brewing (SA June 24 1933 p9 col 1). *Last coal-*

fired kiln in a Burton maltings were the Plough Maltings, No. 22 Malthouse, Bass, Horninglow Street, Burton, in Jan 1967 (SP-t Nov 2006). *One of the fastest beer lines in the world* was the Canning Hall, Bass Brewery, commissioned 1989. It can achieve speeds of up to 2,440 cans per minute and a single pallet of empty cans is used every 165 seconds (S-Pt, 2007). *Last brewery to operate the Burton union system* was Marston's Brewery, Shobnall Road, Burton. Still operating their union rooms in 2009 (their oldest has 40 casks and their largest has 144); Bass phased out their giant union rooms in the early 1980s (Marston's: A Brewer of Pedigree. Khadi-ja Buckland & Eric Fower. 1999. p57).

Brown, Isaaz Hawkins *'One of the first wits of this country, got into Parliament and never opened his mouth'*. Dr Johnson on him. Born Burton 1705, MP.

Brown family *Strange but true!* In 2005 Julie Brown, aged 35, and her partner Sean Mizon, of Harper Ave, Horninglow, received a written warning from East Staffordshire Housing Service complaining their son had been riding a scooter, but he was not due to be born for another eight weeks! (BBC news July 13 2005).

Bryan, Denise *Woman who tricked Burton*. She worked fraudulently from 2001 under perhaps as many as 11 false names. She came to Burton in 2003 posing as twins Claire and Chess Elliot, planning to stage a play through her Journeyman Theatre Company at the Brewhouse Arts Centre duping council leaders, Burton MP Janet Dean, a solicitor, a film-maker, Burton College, and Burton Mail, into believing her during her application to the Arts Council for a grant. But the non-existent 'twins' were never seen together, which raised suspicion. In 2005 she moved to Bristol and subsequently went 'to ground' (Burton Mail Aug 14 2006 p3p).

Buildings, bridges, and inns First *gas lighting* in Burton 1832; gas works were established in Station Street in 1832 (BOb July 12 1951 p5). The first town in Britain to convert to *North Sea Gas* was Burton in 1967 ('The Rock and Roll Years' BBC 1 July 9 1993). *Most famous bridge in Staffordshire ever* The former Burton Bridge which was first mentioned soon after 1100. *Unique of its type in Europe* Ferry Bridge over the Trent, built 1899 (SLM Oct 1999 p22pc). *First to drive over Trent Bridge* was William Blyth on the day it opened June 22 1864. He was for '30 years state coachman to King Edward' and at some-

time to Sir Henry de Vaeux of Drakelow Hall. He eventually returned to Burton and lived at Rosemount Road, retiring in 1908 (BOb July 10 1958 p3). *'amongst the finest of their class in the county'* The police station and court in Horninglow Street, according to The Staffordshire Advertiser Dec 31 1910 p6 col 4, when opened in 1910. Burton's *oldest public house* in 1952 was Queen's Hotel, Bridge Street, formerly The Three Queens', and first licensed in 1531. Reputedly frequented by Mary, Queen of Scots, on her journey from Chartley to Fotheringay (Sept 1586), Adelaide, consort of William IV (while travelling to Sudbury Hall on a visit to Lord Vernon), and the third Queen is a reference to Elizabeth I (BOb May 15 1952 p1 il. Feb 2 1967 p1). Burton's *2nd oldest public house* in 1952 was reputedly the Star Inn, High Street. In 1851, according to old maps, it was shown as a brewery, the license being held apparently by Sarah Measom. Many of the outbuildings still existed in 1952, and reached practically down to Friars' Walk, although the house itself had been rebuilt (BOb May 1 1952 p1 il). *'one of the Burton's most interesting old inns' 1951* The Royal Oak, Market Place, Burton. It was built as a lock-up, probably after the Dissolution of Burton Abbey in the C16. Rebuilt in the early C18, remodelled in the earlier C20 (BOb June 21 1951 p1 il). *Worst baths in Britain* Burton Baths in 1975, according to Cllr D Heptonstall (BOb Nov 27 1975 p12). One of the first to receive a *Beautiful Beer Award* was The Bridge Inn, Tatenhill Lane, Branston, awarded by the British Beer and Pub Association in 2006. The award was launched in Feb 2006 to recognise pubs serving excellent beer (Burton Mail May 8 2006 p4).

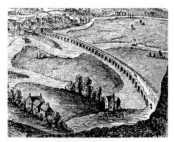

Burton Old Bridge

Burton Abbey *One of the most famous monasteries in the country* (Staffordshire County Handbook c1958), *Staffordshire's* *earliest document monastic house* was Burton Abbey, founded 1004. *Largest monastic community* of any period, most wealthy in Staffordshire was Burton Abbey (HOS p26). *Poorest of all Benedictine monks in England* were the Burton Abbey monks who complained of being so in 1310. *Only Anglian monastery north of the Trent* was Burton Abbey for a time after its foundation (SSE 1996 p24). *Last abbey in Staffordshire to surrender* Burton Abbey on Nov 14 1539. *Prostitute who bedded the monks!* Alice Browne of Lichfield in the 1460s (SHC 1999 p79). *Staffordshire's oldest ghost story* dates to 1090s and was written down by Abbot Geoffrey 1114-50 in his Life of St Modwen. It concerns two of his manorial villeins at Stapenhill (Derbys, but in Burton County Borough from 1894), who fled to the lord of Drakelow manor (Derbys). A feud broke out between the manorial powers. The two villeins then mysteriously died of an illness. Then ghostly savage beasts came at night banging their coffins on house walls. It was thought these were the transformation of the villeins' corpses. In desperation after more ill-fortune their bodies were exhumed, hearts torn out and burnt. Then an evil spirit in the form of a large bird emerged from the flames and disappeared towards heaven (VCH vol 9 p7) (Staffordshire Encyclopaedia).

Burton Albion Football Club *Their first semi-final of a major trophy* Birmingham Senior Cup in 1953, having knocked out Hednesford Town (BOb Nov 19 1953 p7). *Their first ever FA Cup third round tie* Against Charlton Athletic, losing 7-0, in 1956. The second occasion Burton Albion achieved a 3rd round FA Cup tie was when they played Manchester United on Jan 8 2008 with a 0-0 result. In the replay on Jan 18 2006 Burton Albion lost to Manchester United 5-0 (BOb Jan 12 1956 p3) (Burton Mail Jan 6 2006 p3. Jan 9 2006 p40. Jan 19 2006 p1). *Only unbeaten side in the whole of the Premier Division (Southern League) in 1970-71 season by Oct 1970.* Burton Albion after Chelmsford lost at home to Barnet and Burton won 1-0 to Canterbury (BOb Oct 8 1970 p15). *Southern League record for unbeaten runs by 1972* was Burton Albion with 29 successive wins, 18 of which were in the 1971-72 season (BOb Feb 3 1972 p15). *Shortest time ever for a semi-professional football team to score* was when Burton Albion scored three goals from the start of the match in

122 seconds against Redditch United in a Beazer Homes League Premier Division on Jan 2 1989 (GBR 1996 p256).

Carvell, Mrs M *Perhaps Staffordshire person with most living descendants.* (b1845). Of Upper Outwoods who, on 91st birthday on June 17 1936, had 54 living descendants (SA June 20 1936 p4 col 7).

Children and families *'one of the homes of the original chav'.* Burton, according to the website chavtowns.co.uk, which listed Burton as one of the most notorious 'chav' towns in the country 2005, and in 2006 (Burton Mail May 8 2006 p9). *Staffordshire's first grant maintained school* was Anglesey Primary School, Clarence Street, Bond End, in 1996, which allowed a school to opt out of local authority control. Four other Staffordshire schools followed - Chasetown and Rising Brook High Schools, Hollinsclough and Corbett (Bobbington) Primary Schools. Grant Maintained Schools were succeeded by Foundation Schools (info Geoff Crockett, Staffs Education Dept) (Burton Mail May 9 2006 p10). *Staffordshire's largest school 2007* De Ferrers Specialist Technology College, in Horninglow (Burton Mail Jan 13 2007 p1). *One of the very first children's centres in the country* was the East Staffordshire Children's Centre, Waterloo Street, Little Burton. Built by Staffordshire County Council's Early Years and Childcare Unit, 2007, to provide education and childcare to families. It is one of the very first of the 3,500 children's centres the Government was committed to building before 2010 (Staffs CC website). *'one of Britain's best family walks'* 2006 Branston Water Park, making the final list of the country's top rambling locations alongside other favourites, including parts of the New Forest, Hants, and Rutland Water. The list was compiled by the Good Dog Campaign from the views of 3,000 adults (Birmingham Mail. May 24 2006 p7).

Chittim, Nellie Elizabeth *Shobnall's heroine.* (1913-2006). District nurse and midwife, of Henhurst Hill, originally of Manchester, came to Burton in 1938. In WW2 she attended many road accidents in the blackout and also taught home nursing for Tutbury RDC. In 1947 she was presented with a diploma form the NSPCC for saving the life of a little girl who had been dragged out of a cesspit and appeared dead. Using artificial respiration and mouth to mouth resuscitation she revived the child (Burton Mail June

19 2006 p20ps).

CHURCHES St Modwen in Market Place, Burton is the only such county dedication (for AP churches); 43rd last AP county church built dating from 1728. Is 'one of the best examples of Palladian-type Gothic architecture in Britain' (Stafford-shire: Shire County Guide. Peter Heaton. 1986). The most interesting memorial in the church is an alabaster, mutilated figure of a knight in mail, c1560-80, thought to represent the founder of the church - Wulfric Spot. It was in the church in the earlier C20 (LGS p96), but in the town Museum in 1955 (BAST vol 51 p41) (JME part II p21). The organ case is by the 'greatest organ builder of the time' 177, being attributed to John Snetzler; but according to John Martin Robinson in Country Life magazine Dec 20 1973 it was the work of James Wyatt (1746-1813) (BOb July 25 1974 p4).

St Aidan's in Shobnall Rd, Shobnall was Lichfield Diocese Best Kept Churchyard winner 1996.

St Chad's in Hunter St, Horninglow, was built 1907-10, having grown out of the Hunter Street school-church, which opened May 14 1883. It was *one of the last buildings designed by GF Bodley*; Pevsner states it is by far the best building in Burton (BOE p87) (info KL Neal).

St Mary's at Stretton was considered the *'finest village church in the Midlands'* when opened 1897. It was built by John Gretton II (d1899) of Bladon House, Winshill, at a cost of £40,000, a director of Bass, Ratcliff and Gretton brewery (The Greatest Brewery in the World. Colin C Owen. 1992. p71) (VCH vol 9 p195).

Civil affairs *Last of the old Burton parish constables.* Alias 'Dick Roe' died 1853 (BOb July 12 1951 p5). *Last sitting of Town Commissioners.* Nov 6 1878 (BOb July 12 1951 p5). First *mayor of Burton* was WH Worthing, elected Nov 13 1878. Elected *mayor four times* was Alderman JW Clark holding the position in 1937, 1938 and 1952, 1953 (BOb May 21 1953 p6p). *Burton's first town clerk.* Mr TN Whitehead (1837-1911). Burton-upon-Trent's first *civic week* May 5 to May 13 1933, at the suggestion of Councillor William Hutson (Burton Mail March 20 2006 p13). Burton's first civic *Christmas tree* was switched on by the mayor on Dec 18 1951 (BOb Jan 3 1952 p5). *2nd equal highest rated county borough in England and Wales 1950* was Burton, with Merthyr Tydfil (out of 83 county borough coun-

cils) at 24 shillings, 6d. West Ham was the highest at 25 shillings; Bournemouth, the lowest, at 12s. 2d. (BOb April 13 1950 p1). *Burton's first smoke control zone* was conversion of grates in 1,478 houses in the Uxbridge Ward to comply with the Smoke Control Order in 1966, in force from June 1 1966 (BOb May 25 1966 p11). Highest *loan debt* per head for a county borough in the country 1970 was Burton with a loan debt on total rate fund services of £119 per head; there were then 83 count boroughs in England and Wales; Tynemouth had the lowest with £36 per person (BOb Feb 12 1970 p4). *One of the best local authority websites* in country was East Staffordshire BC, voted in top ten, because of its clarity and accessibility (BBC Midlands Today Jan 1 2005).

Combat sports *Burton's boxer 1909.* Albert White, 'Burton's only prominent boxer' of this period, a middle weight-light weight, and welter weight (BOb Oct 29 1959 p11). *British Army of the Rhine Welterweight Champion 1969, 1970* 'Staffordshire' Lance-Corp David Warrier, aged 21, of Short Street, Stapenhill, in the British Army's Minor Units Boxing Championships (BOb May 7 1970 p13p). *World Toe Wrestling Champion 2006, 2008* Paul Beech (b1971), alias 'Toeminator', of Burton Road, Branston. He has won this competition twice before (Burton Mail June 25 2008 p3pc. June 30 2008 p1pc).

Communications, media and entertainment *Burton's first telephone* was installed 1898 by the National Telephone Company who bought a shop in High Street and converted it into an exchange. Burton moved over to STD on March 8 1961 (BOb March 2 1961 p4). *First 'talkie' film in Burton.* 'The Broadway Melody' on Nov 4 1929 at the Picturedome in Curzon Street (Burton Mail June 19 2006 p17). *Burton's first talent competition* was held in the Town Hall, sponsored by the Entertainments Committee on Feb 14 1953 (BOb Dec 31 1953 p5). *First T.V. detector van in Staffordshire* was possibly one of the nine detector vans of the Post Office which toured the Burton postal area in the week Oct 10-7 1955 (BOb Oct 6 1955 p1p). *Burton's first Festival of Arts and Crafts* took place in 1978 (Burton Mail April 25 2008 p18). *BAFTA Best Short Film award 2008* 'Dog Altogether', directed by Paddy Considine (b1975), of Winshill, attended Abbot Beyne School. The film, lasting 20 minutes, also won

Best Short Film at the British International Film Festival, and received the Silver Lion Award at the Venice Film Festival. 'The Bourne Ultimatum' starring Considine, won the 2008 BAFTA Best Sound and Best Editing award (Burton Mail Feb 12 2008 p7p). *Best Regional Production Award for Best Musical 2006* The Mellow Dramatics drama company of Burton for their production of Stephen Schwartz's musical 'Godspell', awarded by the National Operatic and Dramatic Society (Burton Mail April 7 2007 p5).

Cooke, William S *Burton's inventor.* (1850-1936). 'well-known in Burton on account of his numerous inventions' (BOb Nov 9 1961 p5).

Country pursuits *'More fine horses, particularly of the black breed, are usually exposed to sale than at any other fair in the kingdom'* Burton's late October fair (Whitaker's Almanack gives 28 Oct) (COOKE) (THS p45) (SCSF pp98,102). *Burton-upon-Trent's first Floral and Horticultural Society annual exhibition* Probably that in 1852; the 2nd was in 1853 (SA July 23 1853 p4 col 7). *Burton's first hosting of the Staffordshire Agricultural Society Show* was on Sept 20 1860 in Bass's middle yard (BOb Aug 4 1960 p6). *Cruft's Supreme Obedience Champion 1972* was 'Kinder Syde Raven', a 4-year-old Alsatian bitch belonging to Mrs Barbara Collins of Shobnall Street, Burton (BOb Feb 17 1972 p3p). *First place in East Staffordshire to be awarded a Green Flag* was Branston Water Park (BBC Midlands Today Nov 23 2005).

Cricket *'the father of Midland cricket'* Abraham Bass the likely founder of Burton Cricket Club (founded by 1830) and perhaps the first recorded cricket club in the county (Staffordshire Cricket. William G Watson. 1924. p15) (VCH vol 2 p368) (BTIH p115) (MR p71). *One of strongest cricket teams in England 1850* Burton, in whose ranks was the famous fast bowler RC Tinley. Tinley was the only 'pro' in the Burton team which beat Liverpool early in July 1850, and Burton also won the return match in the following month, thanks largely to Tinley's bowling (SA Dec 31 1949 p6 cols 5-6). *First life member of Burton Cricket Club.* Wilfred Rhodes (b1877), great all-rounder of England and Yorkshire cricket, veteran of English Test cricket, elected in 1956, by when he was resident in Ashby Road, Burton; but had moved to Bournemouth in, or shortly after, 1956 (BOb Feb 23 1956 p1. 1966

review of the year). *He challenged MPs to submit four sons who could beat his four sons in any 'phase of sport'.* Sydney Evershed, when MP for Burton, but no one was ever able to put the claim to the test; the eldest son was Herbert (see below), another was Frank,

Sir Herbert Evershed: A noted Burton sportsman

an England International forward (SA Feb 3 1934 p9. March 13 1937 p5). *'Burton's most famous sportsman'*, Midland Counties Challenge Cup winner 1883-4, 1887-8. Sir Herbert Evershed (1861-1937) as long recognised by 1934. He was consummate at rugby (three-quarter), cricket (remembered as one of the hardest hitting batsmen of his generation), gymnastics, tennis, skating, billiards, and boxing (SA Feb 3 1934 p9p. March 13 1937 p5p).

Edkins, Simon *Youngest person in Britain to have a double hip replacement.* Of Stapenhill (in Derbys, but in Burton County Borough from 1894) (BBC Midlands Today July 30 2004).

Endurance *World record for leap frogging* Set by nine boys at Horninglow Secondary School in July 1972 (Burton Mail Remembers 2008 p39). *World record for marathon accompanied singing by a group.* The Burton upon Trent Youth Choir sang accompanied for 25 hours 30 mins on April 18-19 1974, beating a record of 24 hours 3 mins set the week before by Latymer Choir of Edmonton, London (GBR 1974 p230) (BOb May 2 1974 p1p). *Most press-ups (push-ups) ever achieved in 30 minutes by 1981* was 1,845 by Noel Barry Mason at Burton Sporting Club on Nov 16 1979 (GBR 1981 p285). *Most beer mats flipped and caught.* Darren Ault, 18 with a record pile of 67 mats through 180 degrees at the inaugural Ind Coope British Beer Mat-flipping Championships at Brewery Vaults, Burton on May 31 1985 (GBR 1987 p164).

Evans, Mr W *Perhaps attended most National Congresses of the Co-operative Society.* Born 1869. JP, of Burton, railway signalman, later traffic inspector, attending 16 Congresses. Native of Breconshire. A director of the Burton Co-operative Society (founded Feb 1890) 1905. He retired in 1945 (BOb July 12 1951 p5) (Burton Mail Aug 21 2006 p20p).

Evershed, Sir Francis Raymond *90th Master of the Rolls.* (1899-1966). Of Burton, serving 1949-62. He was one of the youngest men ever to become King's Counsel, and was believed to be the first Burton man to achieve the honour of being on the King's Counsel. Sir Clifford Gothard, OBE, presiding at Burton borough magistrates' court, said of him he was 'one of the most distinguished legal personalities the country had ever seen' (BOb Oct 6 1966 p4p. Oct 13 1966 p7 col 6).

Fergusson, Mr *Burton's bravest.* He 'effected a gallant rescue' of a lad from Dale Street who had fallen into the Trent near the St Modwen's recreation ground bridge on Nov 27 1888. 'For a minute or two the lives of both persons were in jeopardy, as the lad clutched hold of his rescuer and almost hindered him from acting' (SA Dec 1 1888 p7 col 4).

Folklore *Burton's best.* Perhaps the legend that a young peasant girl murdered by a monk from Sinai House in the Middle Ages is buried under Sinai House; her ghost is known as the 'Grey Lady'. *Stapenhill's best.* That in the late C16 Thomas Darling or Darby, 15, claimed he was bewitched by one of the two Stapenhill witches, Elizabeth Wright and her daughter Alice Gooderidge. Alice, who, under duress in Derby gaol, admitted she had put a spell on the boy, later died in prison. Darling's fits continued. In his late teens during his testament before an Ecclesiastical court at Lambeth against a reputable exorcisist who had cured him of his fits with prayers he confessed his fits were frauds, and he had never been ill at all (BOb Dec 20 1956 p1).

Fox, George *His first visit to Staffordshire.* The founder of Quakerism preached near Burton in 1651 after his release from Derby gaol (HOS 1998 p66). He was subsequently at Bushell Park, Tutbury parish (see Religion).

Football *First football association to celebrate its centenary.* Burton and District Football Association in 1971; the Association was formed in 1871 when Messrs H Harrison, CF Hill, JW Thompson, W Fellowes, and WH Owen met in the lounge of the Rising Sun, Horninglow Street, Burton (BOb Dec 24 1970 p3). *First time electricity was used to light up a football game in Burton* was a game on the Ind Coope cricket ground, Shobnall Street, to mark the winding up of the Robin Hood football club on March 4 1879 (Burton Mail March 17 2008 p20).

Birmingham & District Football League winners 1927-28. Burton Town (CAd Aug 25 1978 p10). *Highest football pools win by 1981* That won by David Preston, 47, of Burton on Feb 23 1980, when he won £953,874.10 (£804,573.35 from Littlewoods, and £149,300.75 from Vernons) (GBR 1981 p277). *Wales' youngest ever full international player 2006.* Lewin Nyatanga, footballer, born Burton 1988 to a Welsh mother, when playing against Paraguay, aged 17 years 195 days, beating a record set by Ryan Green against Malta in 1998, by 31 days (Burton Mail Feb 28 2006 p32pc). *World record for table football* began in Burton on July 28 1972, finishing 120 hours later; the marathon raised over £400 for charity (BOb review of the year 1972).

Geology The Burton and Trent plain area is Alluvium, with gypsum beds (producing the hard water containing magnesium and calcium sulphates excellent for beer making); Needwood highlands is Keuper Red Marls.

Gerrard, Miss Nellie *Miss Staffordshire 1937.* Of Burton-on-Trent; she made her debut in the role at a local cinema on June 19 1937 (SA June 26 1937 p8 col 2).

Gibson, Ted *Nicknamed 'Trolley Ted'.* (1927-2006). Originally a JCB employee at Rocester. Came to Burton in 1983, where he was known for collecting abandoned supermarket trolleys and returning them to their owners. In 1997 Sainsbury supermarket banned him from their store, after they said he was too scruffy. But after a campaign led by The Mail and supported by thousands of people the company relented and allowed him to carry on his voluntary duties. By 2008 there was a Facebook network group called 'I Knew Trolly Ted' (Burton Mail March 3 2006 pp1pc,4. March 8 2008 p3pc. March 12 2008 p6pc).

Golf *Fancy that!* Mr R Whidborne Clubb (d1949). Member of Burton Golf Club, and was still playing aged 97. He died a year later at his home Oakbourne, Brizlincote Lane, Burton. Coming to Burton from London aged 9, he was manager of Bass's Steam Cooperage from 1895 (SA May 21 1949 p5 col 7). *British Junior Golf Tour champion 2008, US Kids European Challenge runner-up 2008.* Josh Thorley, aged 11, of Winshill, Abbot Beyne School pupil. Also in 2008 he became the youngest ever winner of the Derbyshire Boys' under-16 championship (Burton Mail June 6 2008 p48pc. Aug 21

2008 p37pc. Sept 6 2008 p32pc).

Goodaye, William *Earliest person recorded in the parish register.* For his marriage to Ellen Plant, both of Horninglow, on 9 Nov 1538.

Gorton, Trooper *Staffordshire's first casualty in the Boer War.* Of Burton upon Trent 'one of the first colonials to volunteer for active service in the defence of Natal'. He was twice severely wounded, the second time during the siege of Ladysmith proved fatal; has a memorial in the parish church (SA Dec 29 1900 p4 col 6).

Health & society *One of the best Women's Voluntary Service centres in the country* in 1952 was Burton's W.V.S., according to the Dowager Marchioness of Reading, herself the chairman and founder of the W.V.S in Britain, addressing a large rally of local members following a visit to Burton in 1952, which included inspection of W.V.S. activities in Burton, and a tour of Burton General Infirmary and Andressey Hospital (BOb Nov 13 1952 p5). *One of the earliest sterile syringe services* in the country was when Mr J Knapton, Mrs Joan Pocock of Branston, and one other, set up a syringe service in one small room with a staff of two at Burton Hospital in 1956. It was originally known as the Central Syringe Service, becoming the Central Sterile Supply Department (CSSD) in 1963 (BOb Oct 7 1965 p6). *'One of the healthiest towns in the world'* Burton, according to Sir John Wedgwood speaking to the Staffordshire Society at Burton Town Hall at their annual rally, 1958. This was due to the then infant mortality rate of 20 deaths per 1,000 births which was one of the lowest figures in the world. In 1938 it was 39 per 1,000 births, about one-third less than the national average. Sir John also told the Society Burton was 'the most highly taxed community in the world' on account of the excise duty it paid on beer! (BOb May 8 1958 p11). *First comprehensive social centre in the country* was believed to be Burton's Welfare Centre, Waterloo Street, officially opened by Cllr HL Pritchard on April 7 1959. It accommodated all classes and types of handicapped, including the aged (BOb April 9 1959 p7p). *First hospital in the country to introduce a waitress service for patients* was the 'The Burton Waitress Service' at Burton General Hospital, a fully centralised plated meals system operated by a staff under the direct control of the catering officer. It was first tried the orthopaedic and traumatic ward at the General Hos-

pital in Feb 1963, and by 1965 had been extended to other hospitals in the group (BOb Oct 28 1965 p9). *Worst hospital in England 2002-05* Queen's Hospital, Belvedere Road, Burton, according to The Hospital Guide, published by 'Dr Foster', an independent company which monitors health care quality, Dec 2005. The report found that more 'avoidable' deaths occur at the hospital than at any other in England (Burton Mail March 8 2006 p11). *Tiniest twins ever* born at Queen's Hospital were Alex and Amy Dolman of Swadlincote, born prematurely on Sept 29 2001, weighing a combined 5 lbs (Burton Mail Jan 10 2007 p1). *'only one of its kind in the country, founded and maintained by a local authority'* Burton School of Speech and Drama, founded 1946. In 1966 it had about 100 adult members and more than 200 junior students. During the years as it grew, the school developed until its curriculum included full time training for young actors wanting to turn professional and those wishing to teach speech training and drama (Burton Daily Mail Sept 27 1966 p6 cols 3-4). *First in the country with a special wing for the handicapped* was 'Hillfield', Hillfield Lane, Stretton, Staffordshire County Council's Old People's Welfare Home, opened in June 1969, which included a special wing for six physically handicapped people (BOb June 19 1969 p4p). *First place in UK to pilot 'Hit the Ground Crawling' sessions* (antenatal support group for fathers) was The East Staffordshire Children's Centre, Waterloo Street, Little Burton, as developed by the Fatherhood Institute, and based on a groundbreaking American ante-natal peer support programme for fathers-to-be (BBC R4 'Boot Camp for Dads. Sept 15 2008) (Staffs CC website).

Historical studies *One of the oldest natural history and archaeological societies in the country.* The Burton upon Trent Natural History and Archaeological Society (BTNHAS), formed 1842. *Burton's first museum* was in a room in the Cocoa Cafe, Horninglow Street, Burton, which the BTNHAS took over for their library and museum in 1883. In 1888 the Society moved to a room in No. 46 High St, moving to No. 30 in 1893. Finally the Society's collections passed to Burton Corporation who provided the upper storey of a property being built on the corner of Guild and Station Streets, which opened to the public in Feb 1915. Later this property became Bass & Co.'s Club, and was the Tudor Club by 1968 (BOb Dec 5 1968 p7). *Complete set of parish records from 1538* apparently Burton (Staffordshire: Shire County Guide. Peter Heaton. 1986).

Hobday, Sir Frederick Thomas George *Hon. Veterinary surgeon to the King.* (c1870-1939); attended Burton Grammar School; in 1930s was principal and dean of the Royal Veterinary College, London; knighted 1933 (BOb July 2 1964).

Hollemans, Joseph *One of the greatest alabaster sculptors.* From Holland, settled in Burton by 1599, producing nine church monuments in Staffordshire (BAST vol 71 p1) (VCH vol 2 p202).

Horse racing *Champion trotter of all England 1939.* 'Lucy' a mare owned by Mr G Long of Stanton Road, Stapenhill, who incidentally foaled twins in 1939 (BOb July 2 1964 p5).

Hudson, Mrs Annie *First Staffordshire injury due to WW2 blackout regulations.* Of Johnson Road, Uttoxeter. Knocked down at Burton in the week 2-9 Sept. In a concussed state she recuperated in Burton Infirmary (SA Sept 16 1939 p8 col 8).

Insley, Sergt *Burton's hero, 1st man in Burton area to win a V.C.* Royal Marine Light Infantry, 63 Royal Naval Division, C Company, Machine Gun Battalion, awarded a V.C. on Oct 8 1918 in the action before Niergnies. In Nov 1917 he won the M.M. (SA Dec 14 1918 p5 col 5).

Jackson, David Ian *Had five Grammy nominations between 1979-2001.* Alias Joe Jackson. Musician and song writer, born Burton 1954, though grew up in Gosport and Portsmouth. His 'It's Different For Girls' and 'Steppin' Out' respectively reached Nos. 5 and 6 in UK Hit Charts 1979, 1982 (Wikipedia 2009).

Lapper, Alison *A statue of her in the nude occupied the fourth plinth in Trafalgar Square.* Born Burton with the condition Phocomelia, which is to say she was born without arms and legs; artist; MBE. Between Sept 2005 and at least Feb 2007 a 12-foot high marble statue of her made by her friend and artist Marc Quinn was unveiled on Trafalgar Square's fourth plinth (BBC news Sept 15 2005).

Laurence, Sir Ivan *Longest ever backbench speech in parliament, under present standing orders.* Conservative MP for Burton whilst opposing the Water (Fluoridation) Bill on March 6 1985 which lasted four hours 23 minutes (GBR 1996 p183).

Lomas, Ronald *Staffordshire's first casualty of WW2.* R.N. of 25 Ashbury Road, Burton, aged 36, announced Sept 12. He saw considerable service abroad and after several years absence returned home on leave in July 1939, only to be recalled after a short holiday (SA Sept 16 1939 p8 col 2).

Lunn, Mr LL *Burton's last workhouse Master.* He was subsequently the first and last Public Assistance Officer for Burton, retiring from this post in 1956 (BOb Aug 30 1956 p4p). The last walls of the workhouse was finally demolished in 1892 (BOb May 18 1967 p5).

Martial arts *Gladiators (TV series) runner-up 1997, EMAA (European Martial Arts Association) Open English light continuous (under 85kg) champion 2008, WAKO (World Amateur Kickboxing Organisation) British full contact cruiserweight (85kg) champion 2008.* Adam Stretton (b1978) of Burton, a firefighter and kickboxer (Burton Mail Feb 13 2008 p29pc. Feb 26 2008 p31p). *World Karate Championship (junior) bronze medalist 2008* Josh Lewis of Baker St, Stapenhill, aged 14 in early 2009; pupil at Paget High School (Burton Mail Feb 19 2009 p3pc). *UK's youngest ever 1st Dan Black Belt in the Wado Ryu discipline of karate.* Jordan Smith, aged 8, of Wetmore Lane, Burton, in 2008, and attends John Jepson Martial Arts Academy (Burton Mail Jan 25 2008 p52p).

Mason, Philip B *President of the Conchological Society of Great Britain.* JP, MRCS, FGS, of Burton on Trent had served this office by 1897 (SA Nov 30 1897 p4 col 6).

Mercer, Mabel *Presidential Medal of Freedom award holder, first recipient of Stereo Review magazine's 'Award of Merit'.* (d1984). Internationally renowned singer in the 1940s and 1950s, finding fame in the nightclubs of New York City, born James Street, Burton, Feb 3 1900 daughter of Emily Wadham, but shortly left the town, joining her father, Benjamin Mercer, an African American and the musical theatre company he was in. She is said to have influenced Frank Sinatra during his formative years. The Presidential award was made by President Ronald Reagan. The 'Award of Merit' was 'for outstanding contributions to the quality of American musical life' (an award later renamed in her honour) (Burton Mail March 10 2007 p1p. March 13 2007 pp8-9ps. March 21 2007 p12).

Mesolithic settlement *Oldest in Britain.* Near Gallows Bridge, Branston, claimed by AL Armstrong, after the discovery in 1943 of the skeleton of a woman from 8,000 to 10,000 years old (BOb March 22 1951 p3) (NSFCT 1953 p104) (NSJFS 1964 p16) (IVNF) (BTIH p9).

Military defence *Burton-upon-Trent Rifle Volunteers first meeting* took place on Aug 22 1859 (SA Jan 14 1860 p5 col 4). *Salvation Army's first parade in Burton* was on July 17 1886. Their barracks was erected 1889 (BOb July 12 1951 p5). *First annual ball of the Staffordshire Yeomanry as a unit of the new Territorial Army* was at Burton Town Hall in Feb 1909; hitherto, the force had been the 'Imperial' Staffordshire Yeomanry (BOb Feb 5 1959 p3). *First march through Burton of the Mercian Regt's Third Battalion* was on Feb 19 2009, from Burton Town Hall at 1pm, along Station and High Streets; formerly the Battalion was the Staffordshire Regt First Battalion (Burton Mail Feb 18 2009 p9).

Modwen, Saint *Burton's most famous old worthy.* Traditional 7th Century Irish missionary who reputedly founded a religious community on the Island of Andressey in the Trent at Burton. Her supposed bones were enshrined in Burton Abbey when it was founded in 1002.

Motor cycling *National home in 2008 of the Vintage Motor Cycle Club Ltd (WMCC, 1946)* Allen House, Wetmore Road, Burton. The Club seek to preserve, restore, and use both for competition and pleasure pre-1914 motor bikes.

Mydleton, Thomas *Burton person with the earliest-surviving will.* The will is dated Aug 4 1540.

Netball *Commonwealth Games women's netball bronze 2006.* England against Jamaica 53-52. The England side were captained by Olivia Murphy of Stretton (Burton Mail March 27 2006 p25pc).

Oliver, Noreen *Daily Mirror People's Champion 2006.* Born c1961. Former alcoholic before founding Burton Addiction Centre (BAC) in 1998, originally in two rooms in Cross St, Burton, later moved to Station St, where in 2009 it was one of just two centres in the country to attain full marks after an HC inspection; Noreen was awarded MBE in 2009 (Burton Mail Jan 5 2009 pp4-5pcs. Feb 2 2009 p7).

P_____, Sarah *Strange but true!* She was charged with stealing 20 lb of coals in her apron from the sidings of Boothorpe Sanitary Pipe Co. in 1884. The bench cautioned the old woman and sentenced her to only one hour in gaol; if she appeared

again before the bench she would have to go to prison for a longer period (BOb Jan 1 1959 p3).

Quote *Choicest.* Pearson's Magazine Jan-June 1902, said 'one vast brewery .... a very City of Beer - Beeropolis'.

Place-name The earliest record of Burton, the name, is in 1004, and means 'tun of the fort'. *Unique derivation for a surname* Burton will be from Burton in this parish (PDS).

Population Burton was 10th most-populated Staffordshire parish in 1801 with 5,278 people; 13th in 1811 with 5,891; 15th in 1821 with 6,151; 17th in 1831 with 6,455; 17th in 1841 with 7,759; 17th in 1851 with 9,364; 13th in 1861 with 15,365; 12th in 1871 with 22,286; 8th in 1881 with 34,336; 7th in 1891 with 40,112; 8th in 1901 with 43,060. Burton could be ranked 4th worst-affected Staffordshire parish for loss of men in WW1, with 1,389 lives taken. Burton had a higher proportion of young people than in the rest of Staffordshire, according to 'Sample Census 1966' issued by the Stationary Office (BOb review of 1966).

Rail *The locomotive that preceded Stephenson's 'Rocket'* was said to be one built by Thornewill and Warham of Burton, a picture of which appeared in the Burton Observer 1933 (Burton Mail Jan 15 2007 p20p). *Last day of steam locomotives* being maintained at Burton was Sept 4 1966, at the railway motive power depot, off Moor Street, with the depot going over to servicing diesel locomotives (BOb Aug 18 1966 p4).

Retail *Man who founded Baxters' Ltd, butchers* was Mr GE Lowe, Burton cabinet maker, who went with a butcher friend to met a consignment of chilled meat from America, then an innovation, arriving at Liverpool in summer 1880. Although with no knowledge of butchery Lowe bought some more chilled meat which he sold from a stall at Tamworth market. This enterprise became Baxter's, which by 1970, had more than 420 shops (Burton Mail April 24 2006 p28). *First shop to open* in Burton's new central redevelopment area was Tesco supermarket, Station Street, officially opened by Ronnie Corbett on March 10 1970; this was Tesco's 400th supermarket (BOb March 12 1970 p3p). *First Poundland store.* Burton in April 1990 by Dave Dodd and Stephen Smith, which by 2008 was Europe's largest single-price retailer, selling every item in its stores for £1 (Wikipedia 2008). *Town with* *least local identity* was Burton in c2005, as claimed by New Economics Foundation to be one of ten towns in UK most lacking distinctive shops, and thus dubbed a 'clone town' (BBC Midlands Today June 7 2005). *Burton's first shopping precinct* was The Bargates off High Street, predating Cooper's Square. By 2006 Bargates was known as Riverside (Burton Mail April 24 2006 p13). *'Largest shopping centre in East Staffordshire'* Cooper's Square, Burton, officially opened by HRH Princess Alexandra, the Hon Mrs Angus Ogilvy, on March 24 1970 (Burton Mail April 24 2006 p13) (Staffordshire County Guide 2006/7 p53). *Headquarters of Punch Taverns*. Burton.

Roads *Burton's first tram.* Burton Corporation Tramways ran a service along Horninglow Road from Aug 3 1903 (BOb Aug 18 1966 p12p). *Last tram* of Burton Corporation Tramways ran down from Winshill on New Year's Eve 1929 (SLM Dec 2006 p49). *First bus* on the Burton Corporation Transport Department system operated on an experimental service between the Museum and Derby Road (Wetmore Bridge) on May 1 1924; total takings for the day were less than £3 (Burton Observer Aug 18 1966 p12p). Burton High Street was *first paved* in 1838 (BOb July 12 1951 p5). Burton's first *one-way street* was George Street, from Station Street to Guild Street, 1935 (BOb Feb 4 1960 p9). *'one of the largest and bulkiest loads ever moved out of Burton by road'* Set out during Feb 1948 when the haulage company West Midlands Roadways Ltd took a huge arc furnace body, made by EFCO Ltd (Electric Furnace Company Ltd), to Hull for export to Sweden. It weighed 15 tons, the furnace was 18 feet long by over 16 feet wide, and 8 feet deep (Burton Mail March 17 2008 p17).

Rowing *'Burton's Henley', 'one of the best and oldest regional river regattas in the country' 2008*. Burton Regatta, which was first staged in 1865; the 142nd was in 2008; was not staged in 1966, 1969 and 2007. The first senior eights event took place in 1954. The Len Burman challenge vase for Junior-Senior fours was introduced in 1958. The first riverside fete and regatta was held on July 9 1972, attended by 8,000 (BOb July 12 1951 p5. May 20 1954 p6. Feb 13 1958 p7) (Burton Mail Jan 31 2007 p1. July 11 2008 p15. July 14 2008 p28). *European Rowing Championships 3rd 1953, Thames Cup winner 1953, Reading Rowing Race winner 1954, Head of the River Rowing Race winner 1954* EA 'Tex' Field, oarsman, of Burton. He achieved the first when a member of the RAF (Benson) coxless four in Denmark, 1953, then defeated Thames Rowing Club for the Thames Cup, and then as No. 2 with the RAF Rowing Club eight (Burton Mail June 5 2006 p14p). *British Rowing Championship Open under-23 Sculls Gold 2006* Ashley Prestige of Burton Leander (Burton Mail July 20 2006 p62).

Rugby *One of the oldest rugby clubs in the country 2009* Burton Rugby Club, established 1870 (SLM April 2009 p57). It began in fact as the non-professional Burton Football Club in 1870; they played both Rugby and Association football until 1876, when they adopted Rugby Union rules only (VCH vol 9 p148). *Midland Counties Rugby Union Challenge Cup winners 1888.* Burton rugby team (SA April 14 1888. April 16 1938 p10 col 6).

Sailing *First Sea Cadet Unit to win a Ben Line Challenge Cup (North Eastern Area)* Unit No. 61 Burton-on-Trent (T.S. 'Modwena' Stapenhill Road) in 1960, the year the award was introduced by the Ben Line to encourage Sea Cadets to consider the Merchant Navy as a career. A Ben Line Challenge Cup is awarded in each of the five Sea Cadet Corps areas of the country. In addition, to the award, a medal and coastal voyage is presented to an outstanding cadet. For this Area in 1960 it went to Barry Douglas Harvard of Princess St, Burton, aged 15 (SA & Chron Sept 15 1960 p8). *Thomas Trophy winners 1970* Burton Sea Cadet Corps on Feb 3 1970. The trophy was awarded to the winning unit in the 24-hour section of the National Expedition Competition (BOb review of the year 1970).

Saunders, William *UK's longest serving council chief executive*. Chief Executive of East Staffordshire BC, who retired after 25 years, and gained Freedom of the Borough (BBC Midlands Today Oct 31 2005).

Seaman, Phil *'Britain's most sought after jazz drummer'*. (1924-72). Born Burton. He played with Ronnie Scott and Tubby Hayes with the Jazz Couriers and the tubby Hayes' Quartet. As resident drummer at Ronnie Scott's Jazz Club, he played with the likes of Stan Getz and Joe Harriet. He also appeared as a drummer on several 1960s British pop hits such as Cilla Blacks 'Anyone Who Had a Heart'; died as a result of heavy drink and drug use (www.littledrum.co.uk, 2009).

Shuttleworth, Frank *One of the 28-man crew in the 1937 British Antarctic Expedition.* Of Branston Road, Burton, aged 28, expert mountaineer, one of the founders of Burton Rambling Club, chosen as second engineer, motor and aero engineer. Ex-pupil of Broadway School, Burton. The expedition was led by Commander Ernest W Walker, and sailed in the the the schooner The Wyatt Earp (Burton Mail March 5 2007 p15p).

Skiing *British Ski Championship Ladies Silver 1935* Miss Elizabeth Dobson, of Burton (BOb March 10 1960 p5).

Slater, Tom *Strange but true!* (1925/6-2006). On the night of Nov 26 1944 he and his girlfriend were struck by shrapnel from friendly fire in Waterloo St, Burton; the former in the eye, the latter got burnt stockings. She got compensation from the government, but he nothing because he was a serviceman (Daily Mail Nov 24 2006 p83).

Souster, William Ebenezer Clark 'Bill' *'one of Burton's best known sons' 1964.* (c1887-1964), C.B.E. industrialist magistrate and sportsman (BOb Dec 31 1964 p3).

Steadman, William H *He walked on every railway sleeper between Wychnor Junction and Crewe, via Burton, Derby and Macclesfield.* Of 13 Reservoir Road, Shobnall, in the course of his work as a platelayer 1910-24, permanent way inspector at Stoke 1924-33, at Burton 1933-50; there were 2,112 sleepers to the mile (BOb May 11 1950 p3p).

Stone, Michael *Burton's last resident survivor of the Indian Mutiny.* (1837-1911). Of Grange Street, Burton, serving as a corporal in the Royal Horse Artillery, which he joined in 1857. Buried Stapenhill Cemetery (SA Sept 30 1911 p9 col 2).

Swimming *10th to swim the English Channel, record for English Channel (England-France) swim.* Achieved by Bill Pickering, born Overseal 1921, Derbys, former attendant at Burton Baths, manager of Bloxwich Baths, on Aug 27 1955, in 14 hours 6 minutes (BOb Sept 1 1955 p1p. Jan 5 1956 p5). *She swam with the first Girl Guides to swim the Channel.* Sally Rose of Shobnall Road, Burton, 16, of Burton Girl Guide Rangers, who took part in a relay swim of Girl Guides crossing the Channel on Aug 13 1966. She led the team from Cap Gris Nez, where she was met by French Girl Guides, and carried a message from them, pinned to her swimsuit, for English Guides. The girls swam an hour at a time, and Sally swam in all three hours doing three stints and was the last of the six girls chosen from 12 Guides from all over England (BOb Aug 18 1966 p8 cols 7-8, p11p).

Swindells, Detective Constable Michael *Branston's hero.* (1960-2004). Of Thornescroft Garden's, Branston, whilst serving with West Midlands Police was stabbed through the heart on a towpath underneath the M6 at Aston, Birmingham, on May 21 2004. Glaister Earl Butler, aged 49, was convicted of manslaughter, on the grounds of diminished responsibility and detained under the Mental Health Act (Burton Mail July 1 2008 p7).

Sutton, Robert *Staffordshire's first post-Reformation martyr.* Native of Burton, Catholic priest caught preaching in Stafford and executed 1588.

Table tennis *Youngest ever table tennis player to play for England.* Nicola Deaton (b Oct 29 1976) aged 13 years 336 days when England played against Sweden at Burton upon Trent on Sept 30 1990 (GBR 1995 p296). *British League Women's Table tennis Champions 2005, 2007* Uxbridge Table Tennis Club women's team (Burton Mail Feb 3 2007 p46p).

Talbot family *Burton's saddest.* On March 13 1920 the three year old son of Mrs BM Talbot, a widow of Shobnall Street, was playing in that street with a toy wheelbarrow which ran or fell beneath the feet of a heavy horse attached to a sandcart. In trying to rescue the toy the child fell and a wheel of the cart ran over his head, he died a few minutes later indoors (SA March 20 1920 p8 col 3).

Terry, George *One of Burton's Balaclava heroes.* Died 1881. The other is Joseph Reilly (d1909). Both were born in Yorkshire, both of the 17th Lancers at the Charge of the Light Brigade, Oct 25 1854. They both settled in Burton after finishing their military careers: Terry as landlord of the Saracen's Head, Bridge St (now part of the of the Three Queens Hotel), Reilly in the brewing trade, settling in Derby Road. Samuel Potter (d1888) of Stapenhill, also served in the Crimean War and was said to be at the charge at Balaclava as a Corporal in the 4th Light Dragoons, although there is no evidence. He later worked for Bass (SA Feb 25 1888. Feb 26 1938 p4 col 2) (Balaclava Heroes: Midlands Survivors of The Charge of the Light Brigade. Christopher J Poole. 2008) (Burton Mail May 17 2008 pp1,7).

Watercraft The *Burton-upon-Trent Life-*

boat was launched at Redcar, Yorks on June 20 1867. It was built with money from funds raised in Burton, and worked until 1883. Burton's first Lifeboat Saturday was observed on June 27 1896 (BTOP vol 1 p72p) (Burton Mail July 3 2006 p15). *First town in Britain to have new signs aimed at encouraging motorists* to make the most of the country's canal network was when 10 Trent and Mersey Canal signs were placed at five locations in Burton, 1998. The signs, produced in partnership with East Staffordshire Borough Council and British Waterways (Burton Mail March 22 2008 p6).

Waterpolo *Midland District senior water polo championship winners 1957* Burton, defeating Derby 7-6 (BOb Sept 26 1957 p7).

Weight-lifting *Staffordshire senior champion 1957, English national light-heavyweight champion 1962, 1964, set new British records in 1973, Commonwealth Games Gold 1974* Tony Ford, born c1938, of Main St, Branston; in 1964 he set up a new British and British Empire record with a lift of 364.75 lbs clean and jerk, beating the old record of 359.75 lbs. In 1965 he set a new British native record on the press with a lift of 286 lbs. Before 1965 he was the previous holder of the West Midlands light-heavyweight junior champion, Midlands Lightweight champion, Midlands middleweight champion and Midlands light-heavyweight champion titles. In 1973 at the British Championships he set a weight-lifting record, lifting 666.75 lbs, and for the snatch, hoisting 292.25 lbs. In 1974 he captained the British weight-lifting team for the Commonwealth Games (BOb Dec 10 1964 p15p. Sept 23 1965 p11p. Oct 25 1973 p1. Feb 14 1974 pp6-7ps). *Holder of 78 weightlifting records*. John Humble of Burton, achieved in the period c1966-71 (BOb Aug 5 1971 p1p).

Wheat, Thomas *Burton's 'Jack the Ripper'*. Of Needwood. In the 'Jack the Ripper craze' he pretended he was the Ripper on Nov 27 1888, proclaiming as much with 'much noise and gusto, to the evident delight of a tribe of urchins who followed him about' in Station Street, Burton. Fined 7s. 6d. (SA Dec 1 1888 p7 col 4).

Work (other than brewing) *Largest steam engines of their kind in Staffordshire* those of 1885 at the pumping station at Clay Mills (IAS p196). *Oldest known working electrical generator in Britain* is at Claymills Pumping Station, dating from 1885. One of the country's *largest remaining Victorian steam operated pump-ing stations* is at Claymills Pumping Station, dating from 1885. *Largest number of working steam engines still operating at their original position* Probably Claymills Pumping Station, dating from 1885 (BBC Stoke & Staffordshire Where I Live website, 2006). *'Burton is the town where the good beer and knitting machines come from!'* A German industrialist at the Hanover trade fair 1951 (BOb May 17 1951 p6). *Largest, most-up-to-date factory of its type in the Midlands c1960* The Cyclops Engineering Co Ltd, within the Van Leer group of companies (Burton-upon-Trent Official Handbook, c1960. p39). *Queen's Award for Technological Achievement* was awarded to the building company Conder Midlands Ltd, Wellington Road, Burton, in 1981, for their buildings erected using the Kingsworthy method, for example Bass House, in High Street, Burton (Burton Mail April 22 2006 p7). *First time Bovril bottle label changed in its history* was when a limited one-off edition ironic design was produced to celebrate the Burton Albion verses Manchester United FA Cup match 3rd round on Jan 8 2006. The famous drink produced in Burton, was first produced in the 1870s (Burton Mail Jan 6 2006 p3pc). *500th member of Burton Chamber of Commerce* **was** Pascal Arnoux, of the Old Vicarage Restaurant, Main Street, Branston, in 2006; The organisation was founded in 1936 (Burton Mail June 26 2006 p23p). *Burton's biggest warehouses 2006*. Four at the B&Q depot in Burton Road, Branston. One burnt down on Feb 7 2006 in the biggest fire in the area in living memory (Burton Mail Feb 7 2006 p1pc). *'biggest UK operator in its field' 1996*. Thackers

First time Bovril bottle label changed in its history.

Pet Products, Victoria Crescent, Burton, employing 100 people; its warehouse was devastated in a fire in 1996 (Burton Mail March 6 2007 p10). *First mainline steam locomotive to be built in Britain for nearly 50 years*. Tornado, a Peppercorn Class A1, completed at Darlington in 2008, with an engine with components cast by William Cook Cast Products at their former Lloyds Foundry, Wellington Road, Burton (Burton Mail March 11 2008 p6pc).

C

Canwell Canwell was Staffordshire's 161st largest parish (extra-parochial), consisting of 347 acres; 24rd= farthest parish away from the county town, 19.5m SE; extremist length 0.8m, making it 9th shortest parish in the county; extremist width 1m, making it 10th narrowest parish in Staffordshire. The parish's chief settlement is Canwell, a tiny hamlet off a main road. It is famous for Canwell Priory.

Altitudes The highest point of the parish is 541 feet on the drive leading to Canwell Hall. The lowest point is 384 feet by the mere E of Canwell Hall.

Canwell Hall *Only hospital in England specialising in the care of very young children.* The hall was this for a period sometime between 1921 and 1939 (TH May 6 2004 p14).

Canwell Priory *First religious house in all England to be dissolved.* This was said of Canwell Priory, with Cardinal Wolsey seizing its wealth for the benefit of the new college he was founding at Oxford - Cardinal College, which later became Christ Church (SA & Chron Jan 26 1956 p4 col 5).

Canwell Show *First Canwell Show.* The first show, then organised by Canwell Estate Agricultural Society, appears to have been in 1924 (SA July 4 1936 p2 col 6). *When an Olympic horse competed at the Show.* Nizefela belonging to Wilfred White in 1952, it was one of the team which gained a gold Britain at Helsinki Games (SA Aug 8 1952 p4 col 4). *When the Show hosted the Midlands adult jumping competition of the British Show Jumping Association.* 1953, with Miss Margaret Edgar on 'Jane Summers' an 8 year-old mare, winning (SA Aug 7 1953 p4 cols 1-2).

Church St Mary, St Giles, & All Saints at Canwell is the only treble dedication in Staffordshire (for AP churches); it is the 3rd last AP county church built, dating from 1911.

Ducal encounter *When the 'Hero of England' (Duke of Wellington) joined the Atherstone Hunt at Canwell Gate.* On Jan

The ducal encounter between the Duke of Wellington and a Canwell famer.

28 1836 whilst staying with Sir Robert Peel at Drayton Manor. There is a story of a farmer having placed one of his men at the gate of a wheat field, to prevent the sportsmen riding over it. "Well John," said he to him afterwards, "how did you succeed?" "Succeed," replied he, "Why master I turned the mon that Buonaparte never could turn in all his life." (SA Jan 30 1836. Feb 1 1936 p9 col 4).

Folklore *Canwell's best.* There is a legend the fight between Lord L'Isle and Sir Henry Willoughby (of Middleton S of Drayton Bassett), in the cause of Edward IV, occurred at Canwell, according to a document dated 1417 or 1477. It had arisen out of an alleged breach of Drayton Bassett Park. Other sources say it occurred at Weeford. Sir Henry was wounded.

Geology The north of the parish is Permian; that of the south is Keuper Red Marls.

Lawley, Robert *Canwell's most famous old worthy.* (1768-1834). Son and heir of Sir Robert Lawley of Canwell Hall, and of Spoonhill, Salop. Ensign in Grenadier Guards 1787, returning 1791; succeeded his father as 6th Baronet; sheriff of Staffordshire 1797-8; M.P. (Whig) for Newcastle-u-Lyme 1802-6; sometime Equerry to H.R.H. Duke of Cumberland; created Baron Wenlock of Wenlock, Salop, 1831. After his death without issue at his villa near Florence he was buried at Hints on 19th August, and the barony became extinct.

Lewis, Sandra *Canwell schoolgirl who presented the Queen Mother with a purse.* Aged 9, on Nov 5 1956, at the Albert Hall, London. It was a gift of the children of Canwell C. of E. primary School, collected in aid of C. of E. Children's Society. She was also the first representative of the school ever to represent the school (TH Nov 9 1956 p 9 col 4).

Place-name The first appearance of the name c1120, and means 'Can(n)a's spring' (PNSZ p174).

Population Canwell was the 149th most-populated Staffordshire parish in 1801 with 36 people; 152nd in 1811 with 28; 155th in 1821 with 24; 155nd= in 1831 with 24; 158th in 1841 with 27; 154th in 1851 with 27; 152nd in 1861 with 43; 153rd in 1871 with 47; 156th= in 1881 with 38; 150th in 1891 with 78; 154th in 1901 with 52. Canwell could be ranked 104th= worst-affected Staffordshire parish for loss of men in WW1, with 7 lives taken.

Quote *Choicest.* John Leland in The Itinerary, c1540, 'The priory of Canol a cell of one monke was about halfe a mile from Basset's Crosse. The Bassets were foundars of it, sins the Lisles.'

Chase Terrace See Lichfield.

Chasetown See Lichfield.

Chorley See Farewell & Chorley.

Clifton Campville Clifton Campville was Staffordshire's 53rd largest parish, consisting of 4,871 acres; 31st= farthest parish away from the county town, 19.1m ESE; extremist length 2.7m; extremist width 4.8m. The parish's chief settlement is Clifton Campville, a rural village, recently expanding. Clifton Campville is famous for being the hiding place in the Civil War of the valuable Lichfield diocesan archives.

Altitudes The highest point of the parish is a hill east of The Dale at 323 feet. The lowest point is 187 feet by the Mease near Harlaston.

Browne, Charles H *Perhaps Staffordshire's longest serving headmaster at one school.* He held the headmastership of Clifton Campville School for 46 years 1874-1920, retiring on March 31. He was noted in the neighbourhood in the 1880s as a good all-round cricketer (SA Feb 28 1920 p5p).

Child Rescue Alert *First use of in Staffordshire.* In July 2007 when a 13 year-old Asian boy was snatched from a house in Clifton Campville, by someone he knew. A police negotiator later made contact with the person involved, the boy was taken to Tamworth police station and the child rescue alert cancelled. Child Rescue Alert was launched nationally in 2006 (BBC news July 7 2007).

Church St Andrew's at Clifton Campville is one of 3 such county dedications (of AP churches); 81st= oldest AP county church, dating from 1300. '*the loveliest and noblest medieval parish church in Staffordshire'* Could be claimed of St Andrew's (SA & Chron Aug 30 1956 p6), and the Collins Guide to Parish Churches of England and Wales edited by John Betjeman (1980) p370 says 'perhaps the best medieval parish church in the county'. '*One of the greatest parish churches in England'* St Andrew's - its spire is a landmark for miles around (Staffordshire: Shire County Guide. Peter Heaton. 1986); 'by common concent, St Andrew's, with its well proportioned dimensions, its graceful tower and slender spire rising to a height of 189ft, and set off by flying buttresses at the base, and its general air of quality, is in every respect a thing of beauty' (SA & Chron Aug 30 1956 p6). *Earliest woodwork in a church in Staffordshire* Is of the late C12 in the chancel (BAST vol 68 p42). *Earliest misericords in Staffordshire* are those of C14 on 4 seats on S side and 3 on N side of the chancel (BAST vol 68 p48). *Note* the chest tomb in the S chapel with effigies of Sir John Vernon (d1545) and his wife Ellen. Around the chest is a series of birds, animals and foliage, similar to that on the Egerton monument at Madeley, Staffs (LGS p116) (JME part II pp15-16 pl7) (Alabaster Tombs. A Gardner. p8 pl 68) (BAST vol 48 p136). *Rysbrack's only monumental sculpture in Staffordshire* is the one to Sir Charles Pye (d1721), and another to Sir Richard Pye (d1724) and Sir Robert Pye (d1734); both of 1736, in Clifton Campville church (BOE p33). *The first Staffordshire grant by the Historic Churches Preservation Trust* was possibly the £500 for St Andrew's voted on in 1959; the Trust was created in 1952 (LiMe June 5 1959 p4 col 3).

Cragg, PC John *'Happiest (days) in his life'* were those in Clifton Campville according to PC Cragg in his 30 year police career to a presentation gathering at The Green Man Inn, Clifton. He had served the village c1881-90, and was moving on to Draycott-in-the-Clay (SA Jan 25 1890 p7 col 3).

Folklore *Clifton's best.* Clifton Hall,

nearly a mile east of the village, was built by Sir Charles Pye in the 18th Century. According to tradition he ran out of money half way through its construction and the main centre range was never built. There is another tradition that bricks intended for the unbuilt centre part of the hall were used for the wall around Fisherwick Hall park.

Four Counties Inn, The *Unique pub name.* At No Man's Heath, Warws, once bordering Clifton Campville parish (BBC1 Midlands Today Aug 7 2006).

Geology Most of the parish is Keuper Red Marls; the extreme east of the parish is Keuper Sandstones.

Havilland, Geoffrey De *Founded the aircraft firm De Havilland.* Son of Rev Charles De Havilland and his wife, whose family had bought the Clifton Hall estate in the later C19; Geoffrey was due to be ordained and take up the living at Clifton, but instead with more of a talent for engineering founded the aircraft firm which still bears his name (TH April 11 2002 p14).

Jespersen family *Harlaston's saddest* Thorn Gustavia, aged 9, and Shelia Mary, aged three years and 10 months, children of Mr and Mrs Aage Severin Jespersen of Little Harlaston Farm, lost their lives in a fire in their bedroom on Feb 19 1929. It was perhaps started by a bedside candle. Villagers attended the funeral in large numbers. Eight girls, wearing white veils, acted as bearers, and during the service two childrens' hymns were sung. The two children, who had possibly died from suffocation from the smoke, were buried in the same grave; among the wreaths was one from Harlaston School (TH Feb 23 1929 p5 col 7. March 3 1929 p5 col 5).

Manorial business *Last Clifton Campville Manor Court* was held in 1837 (LTM Jan Feb 1973 p15). *The last Plough Monday* in Clifton Campville was in 1890 (LTM Jan Feb 1973 p15).

Place-name The first appearance of the name, Clifton, is 941, and means 'tun near a cliff'; Campville starts to appear 1293, and is from the manorial lords of the place, the Camvills, originally of Canville in l'Eure-Inferieur, Normandy (PNSZ p196).

Population Clifton Campville was 71st most-populated Staffordshire parish in 1801 with 751 people; 77th in 1811 with 741; 78th in 1821 with 838; 80th in 1831 with 801; 86th in 1841 with 759; 87th in 1841 with 784; 90th in 1861 with 752; 89th in 1871 with 756; 86th in 1881 with 773; 90th in 1891 with 703; 93rd in 1901

with 631. Clifton Campville could be ranked 110th= worst-affected Staffordshire parish for loss of men in WW1, with 7 lives taken.

Pye, Henry James *12th Poet Laureate, and last obliged to write official verse to commemorate both Royal personal and public occasions.* (1745-1813). Lord of Clifton Campville, Poet Laureate 1790-1813, MP for Staffordshire. His poetry is quite mediocre, and it is puzzling why he was chosen as Poet Laureate (LTM Jan/Feb 1973 p15). The second claim is by Wikipedia, 2009.

Quote *Choicest.* John Hadfield in The Shell Book of English Villages, 1980, says 'You are in the Midland plain here, as you can see from the big arable fields with hedgerow trees, and the big barns of scattered farmhouses.'

Sarah, the dairymaid *Clifton Campville's kindest, dairymaid who married the squire.* Sarah, a dairymaid at Home Farm, originally of Doveridge, Derbys, to whom Capt Charles Watkins (1783-1813), of the Dragoons, of Clifton Hall, and a branch of the Pye family, took a fancy to. Firstly they married at Gretna Green, then at Clifton with the blessing of Watkins' uncle, rector of Clifton Campville, on July 14 1810. Her modesty, cheerfulness and kindliness endeared her to the village. After her husbands premature death she married Henry Stokes, son of the vicar of Doveridge, but continued as a benefactor to Clifton, as her memorial in the church testifies (TH April 11 2002 p14).

Capt Charles Watkins with his dairymaid; Clifton Hall is in the background.

Snibson, Thomas *Earliest person recorded in the parish register.* For his marriage to Alice Nightingale on Oct 13 1662.

Stafford, Sir Richard de *Clifton Campville's most famous old worthy.* (c1305-80). Statesman, soldier, diplomat and ambassador. He was so important the sheriff of Staffordshire and other officials wore his livery 1359. Cadet of the Staffords of Stafford Castle, who, through marriage inherited Clifton Campville. Served in

Scotland 1334; Commissioner, Justice of Oyer; frequently JP; Collector of Subsidy 1343-68; fought at Crecy, and Poitiers; seneschal of Gascony 1361; M.P. for Staffordshire 1341; keeper of the peace 1351-5; described as a baron from 1361; summoned to Parliament as Sir Richard de Stafford le Piere 1371; served on the Council of State from 1377.

Sylvester, Albert James *Speediest typist in the country, first secretary to be present at a cabinet meeting.* Born son of a farmer, at Harlaston 1890. His first official job was on a Royal Commission, and following that he was enlisted to keep records of the Cabinet Committee during WW1. He was a founder member of the Secretariat when established by Lloyd George in 1916, and became George's principal private secretary from 1923. His memoirs appeared as 'The Real Lloyd George'. In 1982 he was living at Rudloe near Corsham, Wilts (TH May 1 1998 p26. Sept 29 2005 p36) (Holy Dread. James Lees-Milne Diaries 1982-84. p61).

Vernon, Sir William *Last who held for life the office of Constable of England.* (1416~20-1467). Of Harlaston, Haddon and Tong. (LTM Jan-Feb 1973 p28).

WW2 *Strange but true!* When the old wall garden and farmbuildings of the Rectory were being demolished to make way for the new primary school (opened 1966), nine bombs were uncovered on the site. A bomb disposal squad from Hereford came and decommissioned them. They had been planted by a Home Guard Squad who had their headquarters in the old stables of the Rectory, and had been forgotten after WW2 (TH Aug 18 1972 p21).

D

Dosthill See Tamworth.

Drayton Bassett Drayton Bassett was Staffordshire's 80th largest parish, consisting of 3,368 acres; 17th farthest parish away from the county town, 20.1m SE; extremist length 2.2m; extremist width 4.5m. The chief settlement of the parish is Drayton Bassett, a pleasant village near Tamworth. The parish is famous for being the seat of Prime Minister Sir Robert Peel, Drayton Manor, now a famous amusement park.

Altitudes The highest point of the parish is Carroway Head at 486 feet. The lowest point is 195 feet at confluence of Bourne Brook and Tame.

Archaeology *Staffordshire's earliest evidence of man by 1971.* A hand axe from the Upper Palaeolithic (pre-Ice Age) period found during a potato harvest between Drayton Bassett and Bullock's End Farm (SSAHST 1972-3 pp1,3,4 fig 3) (NSJFS vol 12. 1972. pp1-20) (SL p35).

Basset's Pole *England's oldest recorded fingerpost* was that at Bassett's Pole in 1201 (info John Higgins, Milestone Society). This post, nearly 3m WSW of Drayton Basset, may have marked many boundaries which meet here: viz manorial, county, and forest. *Your Route to a Better Ride project launch site* was at Bassett's Pole, on Aug 31 2004, an online scheme which aims to help motorcyclists avoid accident black spots, such as Bassett's Pole, and is part funded by the Highways Agency. The scheme appears on the 'Handle it or Lose it' website (BBC news Aug 24 2004).

Church St Peter's at Drayton Bassett is one of 15 such dedications in Staffordshire (of AP churches); 29th= last AP county church built dating from 1794.

Cochrane, Ernest Henry *Drayton Bassett's saddest.* Aged 54, a quantity surveyor from Moseley, Birmingham, who was found unconscious in a ditch under a layer of frozen snow at Bassetts Pole in Dec 1964, after being missing for 19 hours, and a widespread police search. He subsequently died of exposure in Sutton Coldfield Hospital. His car had broken down on the Stonebridge-Lichfield road, and he was last seen at the Bassetts Pole Inn; there was a lack of a public telephone box in the area (Birmingham Post Dec 30 1964).

Drayton Bassett's villain The person or persons who maliciously entered the stables on the farm of TL Parsons of Drayton Dairy on Jan 28 1885 and cropped the

tails of five valuable cart horses, and 15 milch cows, in an adjoining shed (SA Jan 31 1885).

Drayton Manor Park *First opening to the public as the current tourist attraction* was at Easter 1950; the zoo opened 1957; the *first ride* was Chairlift in 1964 (SLM July 2006 p8). *Britain's biggest Burmese Python* 'Lucy', 20 feet long, weighing 16 and half stone, who had to be moved to a new pen within the zoo in 1989; there were then just 110 Burmese Pythons in captivity in Britain (TH May 12 1989 p9). *First British zoo to breed golden pythons 1991, first British zoo to breed South Amercian snakes 1992* Probably in both instances Drayton Manor Park. On the first occasion it bred 20 golden pythons, on the second to hatch four rare anaconda (TH March 20 1992 p2) (The Independent May 11 1991 p1p), in addition there were the rare fishing cats, indigenous to south-east Asia, born at the zoo in June 1999 (Daily Telegraph. Aug 17 1999 p7p). *Fancy that!* A woman in her 30s died when her sari became entangled in the axle of a miniature train at the Park on June 20 1988 (The Times June 21 1988). *'Best UK Attraction for Children'* Drayton Manor, voted by Group Leisure readers for three consecutive years (Staffordshire Breaks 2006. Staffordshire Tourism). *Europe's only stand-up rollercoaster, Britain's 10th Best ride 2008* Shockwave (Staffordshire Breaks 2006. Staffordshire Tourism) (The Sunday Telegraph 'seven' magazine July 27 2008). *World's 1st stand-up tower drop* (SLM May 2006 p97), *only standing vertical drop ride in UK* (Staffordshire County Guide 2006/7 p31) was Apocalypse. *Only gyro swing to make you face outwards, Britain's 43rd Best ride 2008* was Maelstrom; huge circular gondolas with the seats turned outwards rise up into the air while revolving at 5rpm (Staffordshire Breaks 2006. Staffordshire Tourism) (The Sunday Telegraph 'seven' magazine July 27 2008). *Unique rollercoaster, most eagerly anticipated*

ride of 2005 **was** G-Force, opened 2005, as voted by the Roller Coaster Club of Great Britain (SLM May 2006 p97) (Staffordshire Breaks 2006. Staffordshire Tourism). *World's longest train set track* was a 1.8 km track built by toy company Tomy at Drayton Manor theme park in 2008; a toy locomotive takes 2.5 hours to travel it. The previous record stood at 1.65 km (The Daily Telegraph Aug 29 2008 p10p).

Folklore *Drayton Bassett's best.* The tanner of Tamworth in the famous old ballad 'The Tanner of Tamworth' may have met and conversed with Edward IV at Bassets Pole in the parish. Bassets Pole was a tall, wooden boundary marker, said

God speede, God speede thee,

Thou art welcome, sir,

The readyest way to
Drayton Basset I
praye thee show to mee.

to have been erected in 1201. According to the ballad the tanner suggested to Edward IV he go through Carroway Head to travel between Bassets Pole and Drayton Basset.

Geology Most of the parish is Keuper Red Marls; the Tame basin is Alluvium.

National home of National Association of Nurses for Contraception & Sexual Health in 2008 was Church Close, Drayton Bassett.

Peel, Robert *'Parsley Peel'.* Of Blackburn, Lancs. Calico printer, and father of the first Sir Robert (SHC 1933 p10) (TH Nov 18 2004 p14pil).

Peel, Sir Robert *'The Millionaire'.* (1750-1830). 3rd son of Robert of Blackburn. Bought Drayton Manor and started a mill in Tamworth c1785; MP (Tory) for Tamworth 1790-6, 1796-1802, 1802-6, 1806-7, 1807-12, 1812-8, 1818-20; supporter of Pitt in Parliament; created baronet 1800 (SHC 1933 p10) (TH Nov 18 2004 p14p).

Peel, Rt Hon William Yates *The Privy Councillor.* (1789-1858), 2nd son of Robert of Blackburn. Of Stratton St, Piccadilly. MP (Tory) for Tamworth 1818-20, 1820-26, 1826-30, 1835-7, 1847; Commissioner of the Board of Control 1826-8; Under-Secretary Home Office 1828-30; a Lord of the Treasury 1830, 1834-5; Privy Councillor 1834 (SHC 1933 p46).

Peel, Rt Hon Sir Robert *'The Prime Minister', Drayton Bassett's most famous old worthy.* (1788-1850), eldest son of Sir Robert (d1830). 2nd bart. MP for Tamworth 1830-1, 1831-2, 1832-4, 1835-7, 1837-41, 1841-7 (as a Peelite), 1847-50; Prime Minister of England 1841-7; married (1820) Julia, daughter of General Sir John Floyd bart; buried at Drayton Basset (SHC 1933 p68) (TH Nov 18 2004 p14p).

Peel, Capt William *Drayton Bassett's bravest, the Royal Navy's youngest commander.* (1824-58), 3rd son of Robert Peel, PM. His bravery was well known, always steady beside his battery to survey the line of fine, even in full view of the enemy. "the hotter the fire, the more bloody polite he became' said one of his men. He was his father's favourite son (TH Jan 9 1998 p24il. Oct 17 2002 p14il).

Peel, Sir Robert *'A Professor of Strong Languages', 'The Gambler'.* (1822-95). Eldest son of Sir Robert, PM, noted for his fine voice and his habit of using it in vehement and irrational argument, earning him the above label. He was also extravagant and a gambler, squandering his inherited wealth; reputedly once 'broke the bank' at Monte Carlo, winning over £12,000 (DM p56) (TH June 11 1999 p14p & il. Nov 18 2004 p14p).

Sir Robert (1822-95)

Peel, Nellie *'first Englishwoman to set foot in the Arctic Circle'.* Granddaughter of Sir Robert, PM, who joined a three-month Capt Joseph Wiggins polar expedition in July 1893 on the SS Yacht 'Blencathra' (TH March 12 1999 p14p).

Peel, Robert *Introducer of Lily Langtry to Edward VII, 'The Playboy'.* (d1925). 4th Bt, married Swiss noblewoman, Baroness Mercedes de Graffenreid (TH Dec 3 1999 p14p. Nov 18 2004 p14p).

Peel, Robert 'Bobbie' *Last Peel to be* buried with his forefathers at Drayton, 'The Bandsman'. (d1934). 5th Bt. Great grandson of Sir Robert, PM. Died of appendicitis; No members of the Peel family, save his wife, son, and lady friend, and Drayton villagers came to his funeral (TH Jan 31 2002 p14ps. Nov 18 2004 p14p).

Peel, Hon Maurice *Killed in WW1.* (1873-1917). Cousin of the 4th Sir Robert. Maurice went to France in 1914 as a chaplain with the Staffordshire and Warwickshire Regiments; twice awarded the M.C., seriously wounded, invalided out and came to be vicar of Tamworth in 1915. In 1916 he returned to the Western Front (TH Nov 10 2005 p40p).

Peel, Robert *Killed on Easter Sunday 1942, 'The Sailor'.* (b1921). 6th Bt. Great great grandson of Sir Robert, PM, when his frigate Tendos was sunk by a Japanese bomber in the Indian Ocean; he never lived at Drayton (TH Jan 31 2002 p14. Nov 18 2004 p14p).

Peel, Beatrice Lillie *Played the villainess in 'Thoroughly Modern Milly'* Canadian actress, wife of Robert 'Bobbie' Peel; married 1920; it was his wife's help Robert started a dance band (TH Nov 18 2004 p14).

Peel, Arthur Wellesley *'Viscount Peel'.* Godson of the Duke of Wellington, created Viscount in 1895 (TH Dec 7 2000 p14il).

Peel, William James Robert *'Man of the Dales'.* (b1947) (great-great grandson of Sir Robert, PM), 8th Bt, Earl Peel, resides at Gunnerside, near the Dales, Yorks, as self-styled; DL in Yorks. He put the final stitch in a tapestry of Tamworth's coat of arms, 1989 (TH Dec 7 2000 p14p).

Place-name The first appearance of the name, Drayton, is in Domesday Book, 1086, and it means 'portage or dray tun'; Bassett had appeared by 1511 (Speed's map), and is from the Basset family, medieval lords of the manor (PNSZ p237).

Population Drayton Bassett was 109th most-populated Staffordshire parish in 1801 with 395 people; 105th= in 1811 with 455; 108th in 1821 with 468; 113th in 1831 with 459; 114th in 1841 with 404; 115th in 1851 with 408; 113th in 1861 with 441; 112th in 1871 with 439; 110th in 1881 with 442; 107th in 1891 with 461; 105th in 1901 with 476. Drayton Bassett could be ranked 110th= worst-affected Staffordshire parish for loss of men in WW1, with 6 lives taken.

Quote *Choicest.* George Peel in The

Private Letters of Sir Robert Peel, 1920, published by John Murray, remembers his ancestor Sir Robert Peel, the Prime Minister 'At the age of ten the boy removed with the rest of his family to Drayton, where, under the worthy vicar, he was adjudged to be "a good boy of gentle manners, quick in feeling and very sensitive."' Guizot, the famous historian and contemporary French Prime Minister, visited Drayton Manor in autumn 1848 and wrote:- "I witnessed a numerous and contented tenantry; great works of agricultural improvement. A beautiful home life, great and simple, well ordered, and on a good scale... The great memories of his statesmanship were consecrated by a gallery of portraits mostly of contemporaries, either of colleagues of Sir Robert in the Government, or the eminent men of whom he had had relations." (SA June 12 1926 p7 col 2).

Rural pursuits *Staffordshire's only enclosure of land* not including some open field arable under the General Acts of 1845 by Provisional Order not needing specific parliamentary confirmation was Fishers Meadow and Wheatley Meadow in Drayton Bassett, Kingsbury and Middleton (Warws); 211 acres Awarded 1852 by Act of 1845 (A Domesday of English enclosure acts and awards. WE Tate. 1978). *One of the largest trout ever taken in England* was one that weighed 21 lbs captured at Drayton Basset in 1848; its skeleton went to the Royal College of Surgeons (LGS p11). *Last thatched cottages in Drayton* were said to be two in one row dating from c1600, earmarked to be rebuilt in 1959 (TH Jan 16 1959 p3 cols 5-6). *Fancy that!* A mysterious corn circle, first seen on July 25 1990, after a natural strange whirlwind appeared in a field at Drayton; locals thought it was a hoax, created by local lads (TH Aug 3 1990 p15).

Stokes, Charles *Earliest person recorded in the parish register.* For his burial on 5 Dec 1559.

Draycott-in-the-Clay See Hanbury.

Dunstall See Tatenhill.

E

Edial See Lichfield.

Edingale Edingale was Staffordshire's 140th largest parish, consisting of 900 acres; 28th= farthest parish away from the county town, 19.2m ESE; extremist length 2m; extremist width 1.4m, making it 22nd= narrowest parish in Staffordshire. The parish's chief settlement is Edingale, a quaint village and peculiarly made up of interlocking portions of Edingale and Croxall parishes. The parish is famous for Breeding champion Shire horses. And is the 'only parish in the Lichfield diocese which is north of the River Mease' as Rev Harold Perrins, vicar of Edingale, noted in 1973 (TH Oct 5 1973 p20).

Altitudes The highest point of the parish is 285 feet N of Edingale Fields Farm. Lowest point is 184 feet by the Mease. The soil is sandy loam of the Trent, to heavy clay of Pessall (E:PP).

Beech, Mr JT *One of the judges in Webb's national root competition 1896.* Of Pessall Pits (TH Nov 28 1896 p5 col 3).

Boydell, George *Edingale's longest serving vicar.* He served 68 years, 1575-1643. He was perhaps related to Alderman Boydell, engraver, Lord Mayor of London who produced the *largest edition of Shakespeare ever.* The book has its 'Boydell Gallery' of extra plates. He is said to be a county native (HS p322).

Church Holy Trinity at Edingale is one of 4 such county dedications (of AP churches); 8th last AP county church built dating from 1880. *First time Edingale choirboys wore surplices* was on Christmas Day 1884 (TH Jan 3 1885 p4 col 5).

Cliffe, George *'one of the best known and respected agriculturalists in the Lichfield and Tamworth districts' 1938.* (1879-1938). Of Edingale Fields, Edingale. He was on Edingale PC; member of Lichfield Branch of NFU; and keenly associated with Alrewas Agricultural Society (LiMe Nov 11 1938 p5 col 6).

Geology All of the parish is Keuper Red Marls.

Gresley, Sir Robert de *Edingale's most famous old worthy.* Died after1360-1.

This younger son of Sir Peter de Gresley, lord of Gresley, Derbyshire, was of Edingale and an outright felon in early life who murdered at Marchington 1320, and Marston, Derbyshire, 1321-2. As a reformed character he served as M.P. for Derbyshire 1340, fought in Scotland 1333, 1335; served in Aquitaine under the Earl of Lancaster 1346; and may have been in the siege of Calais.

Holland, 'Jos' Edward Joscelyn *Edingale's hero, Royal Show winner 1956, 'one of the oldest as well as one of the most successful livestock breeders in Staffordshire' (1976), 'one of the last farmers here (Tamworth area) to specialise in Tamworth Pigs'.* (1890-1986). World famous shire horse breeder, who farmed at Edingale House Farm 1909-86 (E:PP p81); the last claim was made by Mabel Swift in Tamworth Herald Feb 20 2003 p14. He started his stud in 1922, and won the Royal Show in 1956 with 'Edingale Blend' (SN May 7 1976 Farming Newsletter p2).

'Jos' Holland with one of his pigs; the Black Horse Inn behind; the gnarled stumps of trees - a focal point of the village - that used to stand on a tiny green at crossroads, are to the left.

Housing *Oldest house in Edingale village* is School House, School Lane, c1550 (E:PP p67).

Howard, Mary *Edingale's kindest.* (1785-1877). Wife of Col and Hon Fulke Grenville Howard of Elford Hall (also Levens Hall, Cumberland, and Ashtead Park, Surrey), who endowed the Mary Howard School, opened 1915 on the S side of the Croxall road, so actually in Croxall, Derbys (E:PP p62).

Manorial business *Staffordshire's longest dependent manor* is perhaps Edingale which has descended with Alrewas for over 1000 years (E:PP).

Place-name The name Edingale, first appears in Domesday Book, 1086, and means 'the halh associated with Edin's or Eadwine's people' (PNSZ p244).

Population Edingale was 138th most-populated Staffordshire parish in 1801 with 158 people; 137th in 1811 with 162; 134th in 1821 with 224; 136th in 1831 with 177; 137th in 1841 with 197; 139th in 1851 with 190; 138th in 1861 with 208; 135th in 1871 with 217; 140th in 1881 with 181; 142nd in 1891 with 165; 141st in 1901 with 156. Edingale could be ranked 129th= worst-affected Staffordshire parish for loss of men in WW1, with 2 lives taken.

Prinsop, Sarah *First person baptised in Edingale church.* Recorded on Sept 13 1736, even before the tower was finished! (E:PP p43).

Pymme, John *Edingale's villain (in Alrewas's eyes!).* Along with William Browne and Thomas Butler, all of Edingale, who petitioned 1604/5 a JP against the unfairness of having to pay towards a footbridge in Alrewas (the two manors were held together), because Alrewas didn't always reciprocate for things at Edingale (E:PP p65).

Quote *Choicest.* Carmel and Anthony Mason in their Edingale: A Parish in Perspective, 2002, write of the division of the parish between Derbys and Staffs 'One of its many consequences was that, a little more than 100 years ago, on a bright Sunday morning, you would have seen more than a third of the villagers of Edingale walking to Croxall church for their morning service.'

Rowley, Arthur *Longest serving person on Edingale parish council.* He served an unbroken 53 years; the council only formed in 1934 (E:PP p66).

Rural pursuits *One of the last Tamworth Sandies (Pigs) bred near Tamworth* was perhaps that kept by 'Jos' Holland of Edingale in the early 1970s (LTM Nov 1972 p46). *'Jos' Holland's most famous Shire horse champion ever bred* 'Edingale Mascot', see below (SVB p72). *Largest shooting ground in the Midlands* Garlands Shooting Ground, Raddle Lane (Visit Lichfield 2006).

Seal, Matthew and Thomas *Twins who could not be be distinguished one from another.* Of Edingale, 'whom (if cloathed alike) as I am credibly informed' wrote Dr Plot in the later C17 (NHS p312).

Smyth, William *Earliest person recorded in the parish register.* For his burial on June 23 1577.

Elford Elford was Staffordshire's 117th largest parish, consisting of 2,024 acres; 46th= farthest parish away from Staffordshire, 17.2m SE; extremist length 3.3m;

extremist width 2.5m. The parish's chief settlement is Elford, a pretty Tame-side village. It is famous for The Stanleys, lords, who helped secure the Tudor dynasty.

Altitudes The highest point of the parish is 236 feet N of Elford Low. The lowest point is 167 feet by the Tame on the north boundary.

Church St Peter's at Elford os one of 15 such county dedications (of AP churches); 88th= oldest AP county church dating from the C14 or roughly 1350. *Earliest recorded death by a tennis ball* John Stanley, killed by a blow from one, c1460. On a monument to him in the church his effigy has a small ball in his left hand. His right hand is raised to the head and the

Monument to John Stanley, the earliest recorded death by a tennis

fingers point to the place of the injury, the jugular vein or artery behind the right ear. The ball was formerly painted blue, but the colour had disappeared by 1934. At the restoration of the monument in 1852 by Edward Richardson it was confessed by a respectable villager to him that when he was a boy he gouged out one of the eyes of the figures in mischief (SA Aug 18 1934 p11 col 6) (info David Starky, Society of Antiquaries lecture, Potteries Museum, Feb 28 2009). *'the most wonderful of their type in Staffordshire'*. Altar tombs in Elford church (SA July 30 1938 p9 col 8). *'one of the finest churchyards in the Midlands'* Elford (TH Sept 1 1972 p11). *Lichfield Diocese Best Kept Churchyard winner 1972, 1997, 2001.* Elford churchyard (TH Oct 13 1972 p1 col 1-3). *Largest weeping beech tree in the country* (E&S Nov 1 1997 p10p) or *'third best weeping beech in the United Kingdom'*. Elford churchyard (Birmingham Post Weekend Section Oct 21 1995 p25).

Eliot, Margarie *Earliest person recorded in the parish register.* For her baptism on Nov 18 1558; she was the daughter of John Eliot.

Folklore *Elford's best.* That Henry VII slept the night at Elford Old Manor House before the battle of Bosworth Field for Lord Stanley changed his allegiance from Richard III to Henry VII during the battle. Anyhow there were two days in Henry's progress to the battle, between Lichfield and Tamworth, which cannot be accounted for.

Geology Elford village and the east part of the parish is Keuper Red Marls; the Tame plain and the NW and SW part of the parish is Alluvium.

Hind, James *Elford's villain.* Along with Charles Aucote. Both were charged with maliciously shooting at the game keepers of Hon Col Howard at Elford on the night of 14 Nov 1839 with intent to murder. They were found guilty in 1840 and sentenced to death (SA March 21 1840 p2).

Manorial lordship *'So very rapid was the change of family in this place!'* Thomas Pennant in his Journey From Chester to London, 1811, alluding to the turnover of possessors of Elford manor - there'd been the Ardernes, Stanleys, Stantons, Smiths, Huddlestons, Bowes and Craven Howards, all in the space of some 400 years.

Paget, Francis Edward *Elford's kindest.* Of Elford Hall, industrialist, owning brickworks and Royal Crown Works, Derby. After fighting in WW1 he returned utterly obsessed by his vision of a better world. He made great donations to restore St Peter's church, endowed the Royal Masonic Hospital, London, with the gift of the 'Elford Wing', contributed large sums towards the operating theatre and the nurses home, and for years maintained a block of beds for the treatment of cancer in the Middlesex Hospital, bequeathed Elford Hall to Birmingham Corporation in 1936 (TH May 17 2001 p14).

Paget, Rev Francis Edward *Author of the first English fairytale.* (1806-82). Author of theological and children's works. He wrote 'The Hope of the Katzekopfs' (1844), and was rector of Elford 1835-82 (VFC p102).

Place-name The first appearance of the name Elford, is in 1002-04, and means probably 'the ford of Å. Elford (Elelford), the placename, is unique in Domesday Book (SPN p46). *Unique derivation for a surname.* Elford will be from this Elford (PDS).

Population Elford was 112th most-populated Staffordshire parish in 1801 with 383 people; 115th in 1811 with397; 116th in 1821 with 424; 110th in 1831 with 483;

111th in 1841 with 434; 111th in 1851 with 468; 110th in 1861 with 461; 111th in 1871 with 453; 111th in 1881 with 426; 115th in 1891 with 373; 116th in 1901 with 363. Elford could be ranked 100th= worst-affected Staffordshire parish for loss of men in WW1, with 8 lives taken.

Quote *Choicest.* Thomas Pennant in his Journey From Chester to London, 1811, crossed the Tame to Elford 'Elford church, village and house, the seat of the late Earl of Suffolk, form a pretty groupe of objects on the opposite bank. I forded the river, and went by Elford Low, a verdant mount.' In 1934 the author of Random Notes in The Staffordshire Advertiser wrote in his column "Elford is a lovely village, possessing many delightful turns and twists in the landscape, and there is nothing of the strictly formal and parish council controlled urbanisms about the place' (SA Aug 18 1934 p10 col 6).

Ridgeway, William *Elford's saddest.* Of Elford, chauffeur, who drowned himself in the Tame on Oct 18 1931 aged 39. He was gassed in WW1, and in 1928 his wife died leaving him with three little children. He never recovered from her loss and subsequently was involved in a series of minor car and bicycle accidents - in one a steam engine ran into the back of his car in Lichfield. A verdict of suicide whilst of unsound mind was returned (SA Oct 24 1931 p9).

Smythe, Sir William *Elford person with the earliest-surviving will.* The will is dated 1527.

Stanley, Sir Humphrey *Elford's most famous old worthy.* (c1455-1505). Second son of the third wife of Sir John Stanley, lord of Elford. His support for Henry Tudor at the battle of Bosworth 1485 made him very powerful in the county during Henry's reign. He was a Knight of the Body, thrice sheriff of Staffordshire, and often represented the county in Parliament. However, he murdered William Chetwynd of Ingestre, a rival who was increasing in the King's esteem, at Tixall

in 1494. Buried Westminster Abbey.

Village and built environment *Most nucleated settlements in Staffordshire. Are in the Tame Valley* (John Hunt, University of Birmingham). *Staffordshire's first enclosure by Private Act of land including some open field arable* was Elford covering 1,378 acres. Awarded 1766 by Act of 1765 (A Domesday of English enclosure acts and awards. WE Tate. 1978). *'Staffordshire's crowning jewel?'* Title for the feature on Elford in The Burton Observer series 'Our Rural Heritage', written by John Cranage, who wrote glowingly about the village 'situated in the Tame Valley it must rank as one of the loveliest villages in England, least of all Staffordshire' (BOb April 20 1972 p8). *First Staffordshire Best Kept Village winner* (Medium Village category) was Elford, 1958. *An original Staffordshire Conservation Area* Elford in 1969, one of seven approved by Staffs CC Archaeology and Historical Property Subcommittee. In total 51 Staffordshire Areas were created under the Civic Amenities Act 1967. The Act enabled planning authorities to provide for the protection of whole Areas of towns and villages if they were of a special architectural or historic interest (BOb Aug 7 1969 p1) (TH Aug 8 1969 p1 cols 6-9).

WW2 *Where Birmingham's art treasures were kept in WW2.* Elford Hall, but conditions in the bomb-proof cellars were not ideal with damp and water from the nearby Tame often flooding in. After the War the hall became derelict and was demolished in 1964 (LiMe May 10 2008 p22p). *First British deal with Russian agricultural interests since WW2* was when Mr R Wylie of Upfields, Elford, sold his Hereford stock bull 'Masterpiece' in Nov 1947; five other bulls and a number of cows from the herd were also included in the sale; to effect which a Soviet delegation visited the farm (TH Nov 29 1947 p5 col 5).

F

Farewell Farewell and Chorley is Staffordshire's 136th largest parish, consisting of 1,049 acres; 67th= closest parish to the county town, 11.2m SE; extremist length 1.7m, making it 29th= shortest parish in Staffordshire; extremist width 2.1m. Parish's chief settlement Chorley, a hillside village aligned along several triangular roads and greens, but the tiny isolated hamlet of Farewell has the parish church. What Farewell and Chorley is famous for Farewell Priory, which was there.

Altitudes The highest point of the parish is 574 feet on the Longdon boundary north of Dodds Lane. The lowest point is 295 feet on the Lichfield boundary by Bilson Brook.

Ball, Mrs Elizabeth *Farewell & Chorley's kindest.* Of Castle Bromwich, Warws. By will dated 1765 bequeathed 1000L; half the interest was to go to the poor who attend church on Sundays at Farewell in a bread dole. The other half of the interest to Hammerwich parish.

Church St Bartholomew at Farewell is one of 6 such county dedications (of AP churches); 39th last ancient parish county church built dating from 1745. *Staffordshire's 2nd oldest church bell* No. 3 bell at Farewell, according to Charles Lynam in his Church Bells of Staffordshire 1889, being roughly coeval with No. 4 bell at St Chad's, Lichfield, which could mid C13 or earlier (SA July 17 1953 p4 col 4).

St Bartholomew's at Farewell in the late 18th Century. The insert shows one of the unexplainable vessels unearthed in the ruins of Farewell Priory.

Deaken, Sarah *First person in the parish register.* Daughter of John Deaken buried May 22 1695 (the register is the bishop's transcript).

Folklore *Farewell's best.* During the total demolition of Farewell Priory in 1747 a number of curious earthen vessels were found in the south wall. The vessels were laid on their sides, the mouth towards the inside of the church, and were sealed with a thin coat of plaster. Nobody has explained their origin or reason.

Geoffrey *Farewell's most famous old worthy.* A hermit who occupied the hermitage at Farewell by c1140.

Geology Chorley village and west of the parish is Keuper Red Marls; Farewell village, the east, and extreme west of parish is Keuper Sandstones.

Original settlement *The settlement of 'one of the first Saxon tribal communities to infiltrate Staffordshire'.* According to tradition, Farewell. As it has been thought an ideal site for a pagan temple of the period, adjacent to woodlands providing Saxons with unlimited timber and its remoteness (before clearings were made in the forest and marshes drained), together with the name Farewell, perhaps a corruption of 'Ferie-Eifel' meaning the festival place of the (Continental) god Eifel (SA Dec 27 1956 p3 cols 1-3).

Place-name The name Farewell first appears in 1129-47, and 1231 for Chorley, and mean 'clear spring' and 'free peasant's lea' respectively.

Population Farewell & Chorley was 136th most-populated Staffordshire parish in 1801 with 165 people; 135th in 1811 with 165; 136th in 1821 with 202; 135th in 1831 with 200; 136th in 1841 with 203; 140th in 1851 with 189; 137th in 1861 with 209; 138th in 1871 with 200; 136th in 1881 with 218; 141st in 1891 with 182; 132nd in 1901 with 224. Farewell & Chorley could be ranked 129th= worst-affected Staffordshire parish for loss of men in WW1, with 2 lives taken.

Quote *Choicest.* John Leland, 'king's antiquary' to Henry VIII in his The Itinerary, c1540, 'Fayre Well, a small priorie of nunes supressyd by Tho. Wolsey Byshope of Yorke, and gyven to Lichefild in recompence of a pencion that shuld have be geven out of his coledge in Oxford to Lichfefild churche, was impropriat to the chorists of Lichefild.'

Waterloo, Battle of *The last Waterloo poplar tree planted at Spade Green.* Was cut down in 1930; thirteen were planted to commemorate the battle of Waterloo (1815) (LiMe Feb 7 1930 p5) (VCH vol 14 p202).

Westwood, Sarah *Chorley's villainess,*

last female hung at Stafford Gaol. Born Sarah Parker at Chorley. Later moved to Burntwood where, when aged 42 she poisoned her husband, John Westwood, with white arsenic in 'a certain gruel' on Nov 9 1843. She was sentenced to death at the Winter Assizes 1843 and executed Jan 13 1844 (SA Dec 30 1843 p2 col 3).

Fisherwick See Lichfield.

Fradley See Alrewas.

Freeford Freeford was Staffordshire's 162nd largest/ 8th smallest parish (extra parochial), consisting of 280 acres; 55th= farthest parish away from Stafford, 15.9m SE; extremist length 1.3m, making it 15th= shortest parish in Staffordshire; extremist width 1.3m, making it 14th= narrowest parish in Staffordshire. The parish's chief settlement is Freeford, a tiny estate hamlet with two centres - Freeford House and Freeford Manor. It is famous for being the seat of the Dyotts, with their peculiar night-time burial custom. Before which, by c1140, this estate was one of the earliest prebendal foundations of Lichfield Cathedral.

Altitudes The highest point of the parish is Freeford Home Farm at 331 feet. The lowest point is 236 feet by Darnford Brook.

Baxter, Thomas *One of the 'most pushing farmer's' in the district', one of the earliest sugar beet growers in the country, 1st Chairman of the Milk Marketing Board*. Of Freeford (since 1903), sheriff of Lichfield 1913-4, born Cheshire, as described by Arthur Chetwynd, agent to the Marquis of Anglesey at a Lichfield Shire Horse Society annual meeting, for always looking ahead in agricultural and civic matters; Chairman of the Sugar Beet Growers Committee 1924; President of the National Farmers' Union 1927 (SA Jan 24 1920 p2 col 4) (SCP Nov 1950 p24p).

Dyott, Anthony *Recorder of Tamworth, MP for Lichfield 1601*. Of Freeford (SHC 1912 p329. 1917-8 p410).

Dyott, Sir Richard *The staunch Royalist*. (c1590-1660). Son of Anthony. Recorder of Stafford 1624; High Steward of Lichfield and Chancellor of the County Palatine of Durham; knt 1635; JP 1634, by1639; MP for Stafford 1621-2, 1624-5, for Lichfield 1625, 1626, 1628-9, 1640; staunch Royalist, on the Royalist assessment committee for Staffs 1643; taken prisoner temporarily at Shrewsbury 1645; capitulated at the siege of Lichfield Cathedral July 16 1646; bought Fulfen 1638; married (c1615) Dorothy, dau and heiress

of Richard Dorrington of Stafford (SHC 1912 pp330,331. 1922 pp23-4).

Dyott, Capt Richard *In exile with Charles II, but returned before the Restoration*. (1618~24-1678). Son of Sir Richard. Captain of the Company of Loyal Volunteers in Lichfield, and fought on the Royalist side; Captain of Horse at Edgehill; MP for Lichfield 1667-78 (SHC 1898 pp91,251. 1922 p131).

Dyott, John 'Dumb' *Freeford's most famous old worthy, man responsible for the most famous fatality of the Civil War sieges of Lichfield Cathedral Close*. He was a mute and relative of the Dyotts of Freeford. He shot dead the parliamentarian leader, Lord Brooke, in Dam Street, on 2 March 1643.

Dyott, Richard *First president of the original Staffordshire Agricultural Society*. Of Freeford, 1800.

Dyott, General William *The diarist*. (1761-1847). He rose in the army, serving in North America, where he became a personal friend of the later William IV, and North Africa. He returned to take up duties as aide-de-camp to George III in 1804. A 'Tory of the old school' he was against most reform of his day, and died at Freeford after a bout of influenza on 7th May. He was buried at night in the family vault at St Mary's, Lichfield, following a torchlight procession which was a family tradition. His journal was published as 'Dyott's Diary 1781-1845' in 1907. For March 13 1787 he noted the most forward spring ever remembered in the Freeford area.

Dyott, Col Richard *Last Dyott buried at night*. On Feb 19 1891, at 9.00pm.

Folklore *Freeford's top*. The Dyotts of Freeford Hall made a tradition of their right of night burial. Is said to have been

A hearse bearing a member of the Dyott family arrives in Lichfield at night.

granted to John 'Dumb' Dyott, a mute, by Charles I in recognition of his shooting Lord Brooke, parliamentarian leader, in the Civil War. Thereafter, deceased family members were carried from Freeford Hall in procession at night to the family vault at St Mary's church, Lichfield. The cortege was lit by torchlight, and traditionally no relative could be present.

Geology The north of the parish is Bunter; the south of the parish is Keuper Marls.

Place-name The first appearance of the name, Freeford, is Domesday Book, 1086, and means 'ford free from undergrowth or other natural obstruction' or 'Frig(a)'s or known ford' (PNSZ pp30-31).

Population Freeford was 150th most-populated Staffordshire parish in 1801 with 35; 158th= in 1811 with 19; 161st= in 1821 with 14; 160th= in 1831 with 17; 152nd in 1841 with 50; 155th in 1851 with 25; 159th in 1861 with 20; 159th in 1871 with 20; 153rd in 1881 with 53; 156th in 1891 with 46; 147th in 1901 with 100. Freeford could be ranked 135th= worst-affected Staffordshire parish for loss of men in WW1, with 1 lives taken.

Quote *Choicest*. General William Dyott, of Freeford Hall, wrote in his diary for March 24 1827 'On the 24th I at length took full occupation of dear, dear Freeford, where I slept for the first time for fourteen years.'

Webb, Royal Marine Stanley *Lichfield's first WW2 casualty*. Of Freeford, aged 18, on the 'Royal Oak' battleship when sunk by a German U-boat at Scapa Flow, early Oct 1939 (LiMe Oct 20 1939 p6p).

Glascote See Tamworth.

Great Barr See Aldridge.

H

Hamstall Ridware Hamstall Ridware was Staffordshire's 85th largest parish, consisting of 3,124 acres; 69th closest parish to the county town, 11.4m ESE; extremist length 3.5m; extremist width 3m. The parish's chief settlement is Hamstall Ridware, a somewhat straggling rural village just within the commuting belt of Lichfield. It is famous for being the home settlement of the Ridwares and entertaining novelist Jane Austen.

Allestree, Thomas *The man who composed '500 sermons and preached above 5000 times'*. MA. Died 30th June 1715 in his 78th year, as stated on his memorial in the church.

Altitudes The highest point is 344 feet on the N boundary. The lowest point is 200 feet by the Trent at Nethertown.

Bayley, Alice *Earliest person recorded in the parish register*. For her baptism in July? June? 1598.

Cholmondeley, Francis G *Newdigate Prizeman 1872*. For his poem, 'The Burning of Paris'; he was born at Hamstall Ridware on March 23 1850 (PSS pp295-297) (VFC p27).

Cooper, Rev Edward *Perhaps Jane Austen's most boring first cousin*. (b1770). Rector of Hamstall Ridware 1799-1833.

Rev Edward Cooper in Hamstall Ridware Church pulpit with his first cousin Jane Austen in the foreground.

The Leigh family were the lords of Hamstall Ridware and the novelist's mother, Cassandra, was a Leigh. Jane visited him at the Old Rectory in 1806, and is believed to have found him rather boring. He died 1833 and is buried in the transept of the church (HR p34) (LiMe May 26 1989 p11).

Church St Michael and All Angels at Hamstall Ridware is one of 12 such county dedications (of AP churches); 21st oldest county church dating from 1130. *Earliest paten in the Archdeaconry of Stafford* is plate-like paten of C14 in the church (BAST vol 73 1955 p6). *Earliest table tomb with an effigy in Staffordshire* is that in the church for Richard and John Cotton 1502 (?) (BAST vols 69-71 p27).

By the early 1970s the brass on the lid was missing, but against the tomb-chest were shields halved between armorial bearings and figures of the children. Above each a scroll with an inscription about their status in life. One reads 'William died in London at the age of 20 years, clerk to Mr John Clerke, the King's Auditor'. The monument stands under a panelled, four-centred arch between chancel and the S chapel (KES p103) (LGS p201) (BOE p140). In the churchyard are the graves of Esau Smith (1809-1901), headman of the Black Patch gypsies, and his wife was 'Queen' Sentinia alias Henty (1809-1907) (SARA Sept 17 1954).

Deleene, Timothy *Hamstall Ridware's kindest.* Died 1690. Late rector of Hamstall Ridware. Left rental money to the poor to be distributed on the feast of St Thomas the Apostle, and Good Friday, and on Ascension day.

Dickinson, Mr H *'had a champion at every major show in England with the exception of the Royal'.* Alias 'Dicky' in Show circles, could claim this in 1953. He was a Lancastrian who came to improve the stock of Large White pigs in an attempt to produce the perfect bacon at Town End Farm, Hamstall Ridware, in c1958. His partner in the enterprise was a Mr E Haggitt, a Yorkshireman, who was an expert Suffolk sheep breeder (SA & Chron May 19 1960 p6).

Evans, William *The 'Hamstall Giant'.* He lived in the early C19 and was known locally as this for his great strength; he made some body-snatchers take a body back to the churchyard (HR pp10-11).

Farming *Hamstall Heirloom* was a stallion toured to sire with local mares belonging to J & W Froggatt, Hamstall Ridware 1901 (SA May 4 1901 p8).

Fitzherbert, Sir Anthony *'the oracle of the law'* (Stebbing Shaw), *'one of the towering figures in the history of English legal literature'* (Professor Winfield) *'best known English legal writer of the C16'* (DNB), *Hamstall Ridware's most famous old worthy.* (c1470-1538). Of Norbury, Derbyshire, where he is buried and there is a memorial brass figure in judicial robes, parts of which (including the head) were detached in 1842 and lost. His major work, the Magnum abbreviamentum (or La Graunde Abridgment) (1514, 1517) is a massive digest of 13,845 cases for the year-books arranged under alphabetical headings. He married for the second time c1511 Maud, daughter and heir of Rich-

ard Cotton, which brought him Hamstall Ridware; that year he was added to the Staffordshire commission of the peace.

Folklore *Hamstall Ridware's best.* The Rectory was said to be haunted by a poltergeist in the 1930s.

Geology Hamstall Ridware village and the north of the parish is Keuper Red Marls; the Trent plain area is Alluvium.

Hewins, Rev GS *Perhaps first to lobby for the preservation of toll houses in England.* Rector of Hamstall Ridware, who had, in or by 1935, approached the Council for the Preservation of Rural England, and the Society for the Protection of Ancient Buildings for toll houses be saved for future generations. His wife, Elsie Vera Hewins, was a poet, who had verse published in 'The Spring Anthology, 1935' by Mitre Press (SA Nov 2 1935 p5 col 2. Dec 21 1935 p10 col 5).

Natural history A Lily of the Valley or Convallaria Majalis, was found by Rev Gisborne in Rough Park (SHOS vol 1 part 1 p102. vol 1 p66).

Parne, John *Hamstall Ridware's longest serving vicar.* He served 62 years, 1536-98.

Place-name The first appearance of the name, Ridware, is Domesday Book, 1086; for Hamstall is 1236. Ridware means 'people who lived by the ford (or bridleway)'. Hamstall means 'homestead, residence' (PNSZ p459).

Population Hamstall Ridware was 118th most-populated Staffordshire parish in 1801 with 349; 110th in 1811 with 428; 110th= in 1821 with 455; 114th in 1831 with 443; 118th in 1841 with 391; 110th in 1851 with 471; 114th in 1861 with 440; 119th in 1871 with 382; 117th in 1881 with 383; 123rd in 1891 with 316; 121st in 1901 with 305. Hamstall Ridware could be ranked 114th= worst-affected Staffordshire parish for loss of men in WW1, with 5 lives taken.

Quote *Choicest.* SC Woodhouse describing a fascinating journey he made in Staffordshire, by car, in Staffordshire Life Magazine (Nov 1967) entitled 'Ramble Amongst the Ridwares' wrote 'The place was so peaceful that late Summer afternoon when we entered. We found the fine Elizabethan Manor House, now a farm house, at the end of the village along the lane to Blithbury.'

Stronginthearme family *One of the most curious surnames found in Staffordshire.* There was a branch of this (or Strong i' th' arm) family, flC18-19, who have memorials in the church and churchyard at Hamstall Ridware (HR p33, portraits facing p20) (STM July 1966 p29); Mee notes the name was still found in west end of London in the 1930s (KES p103).

Village and built environment *Earliest and largest Ridware settlement*. Hamstall Ridware (SL p57). *The "Cinderella' among the Ridware sisters'*. This was Staffordshire Advertiser's controversial title in their 'My village as I see it' series April 15 1950 p6, for the Ridwares, with reference to Hamstall Ridware, considering that then 'things don't appear to be going too well in this picturesque village of 250 inhabitants, and its remote situation - a bus comes only twice a week - has influenced the people and their outlook' to think negatively of the place. The following week, however, a number of counter views were sent to the paper by local residents, including one from the W.I. secretary K Brown, claiming 'Hamstall is no "Cinderella" but one of the loveliest and most beautiful country villages in God's Kingdom' (SA April 22 1950 p7 col 7).

Hamstead See Handsworth.

Hanbury Hanbury was Staffordshire's 7th largest parish, consisting of 13,108 acres; 67th= closest parish to the county town, 11.2m ENE; extremist length 6.5m, making it 12th longest parish in the county; extremist width 7.5m, making it 5th= widest parish in the county. The parish's chief settlement was Hanbury, a small high village overlooking the Dove Valley, but all the other villages in the parish (most have given their names to the former townships) are now bigger. Hanbury is famous for the explosion which created the Fauld crater.

Altitudes The highest point is 485 feet near New Lodge. The lowest point 164 feet by the Dove at Fauld.

Animals and their rights *'one of the biggest investigations in Staffordshire's history'*. Staffordshire Police's investigation into animal rights' campaign against Darley Oaks Farm, at Newchurch, for breeding guinea pigs for medical research, 1999-2005, in which the force took 2,114 statements, traced and interviewed 698 witnesses and seized more than 3,400 exhibits. Between Jan 2003 and Jan 2006 - when the farm ceased breeding guinea pigs - the police dealt with 460 criminal incidents relating to it. Between 2002-06, 69 people had been arrested for offences connected with the protest; 35 were convicted or received cautions. In Oct 2004, after activists took the body of one of the relatives of the farm, Gladys Hammond from her grave in Yoxall, 50 officers were seconded to work on the case (Burton Mail May 15 2006 pp10-11, describing the case as 'one of the most sickening crimes in modern British history'). *Canine 'Olympic' snooker, gambler, and jumping golds 2006*. Keeta, a 6-year old collie bitch, belonging to Jane Powell of Newborough, held at Oosterhuit, Holland (Burton Mail May 27 2006 p3pc).

Burton, William *Earliest historian of Leicestershire, Hanbury's most famous old worthy*. (1575-1645). Born Lindley, Lincolnshire. Called to the Bar, 1603. He resided at Fauld Hall, Hanbury, almost altogether from 1604 to his death. His 'Description of Leicestershire' appeared posthumously in 1662, whilst some of his manuscript collections on Staffordshire were used by Stebbing Shaw in his 'History of Staffordshire.'

Churches St Werburgh at Hanbury is one of 2 such county dedications; 84th= oldest AP county church dating from 1310. *Oldest alabaster effigy in England*. An effigy, if of Sir John de Hanbury (d1303), then the oldest; the alabaster was mined at Tutbury (LGS p143) (BAST vols 69-71 p2). *Other most interesting memorial*. A wall monument above the vicar's stall, with architectural surrounds containing busts of two Puritan ladies, Mrs Katherine Agard (d1628) and her 3rd daughter Mrs Woolocke (d1657), widow of George Woollocke of Quarndon, Leics. They wear broad, black hats and gowns with white ruffs, and 'they survey the scene with eyes of prim disapproval'. Legend says that before Sir John Egerton (d1662) of Newborough had died he had wanted to be buried in the chancel, but his sister Mary was so appalled at the thought of his lying under the gaze of the Puritan ladies that instead she had him buried in the north aisle (where lies an effigy under a low arch to his memory) (SHOS vol 1 p75) (JME part iii p31 pl 12) (SGS p103p) (St Werburgh's Church guide, Hanbury PPC).

St John at Marchington Woodlands. *The church Pevsner thought fussiest, most irritating*. Built 1858-60, by AD Gough (BOE p41). St Peter at Marchington. In the churchyard is the grave of William Brown died March 25 1835, aged 95, bachelor, who frequently asserted, but a short time previously to his disease, that he was never called before a magistrate upon any charge against himself during his life; that he (using his own words) never had a lawyer's letter in his life; and that he never was in a state of intoxication! (SA April 25 1835. April 27 1935 p9 col 2).

Community endeavours *1st winners of the Staffordshire Musical Festival (Schools Section) 1923, 1st to win the Staffordshire Schools' Musical Festival Challenge Trophy 1924*. Penn Woodfield Avenue Council School, Hanbury. The event, organised by the Staffordshire County Musical Association, was first held on March 23-24 1923 at The Corporation Street Schools, Stafford, at which the Hanbury school won the most 1st prizes (in the schools section), being 3 (SA March 31 1923 p4ps. March 8 1924 p9 col 4. March 15 1924 p4p). *First mass held in Marchington for 400 years* was when the new Catholic chapel was opened in Marchington Hall on Sunday Dec 5 1937, erected by the residents of the hall, Mr R.A.F. Longdon and his sister Miss D Longdon (SA Dec 11 1937 p8 col 5).

Deaville, Leonard J *Shoeing smith Staffordshire County Show 1st prize and Championship prize 1934, 1st prize and Champion of Derbyshire 1934, 2nd prize (open England) at Bakewell 1934, 1st prize at Oswestry 1934, and Championship of Staffordshire winner 1934*. Of The Forge, Hanbury Wood End. The latter prize was won at Rodbaston Farm Institute (SA May 18 1935 p3p).

Emery, Tonileigh *'one of FHM magazine's 100 High Street Honeys' (a beauty contest)*. (b1986). Of Hilsea Crescent, Marchington; attended Thomas Alleyne's High School, Uttoxeter (UAd Aug 9 2005 p3p).

Farming *Staffordshire's 10th earliest commutation of tithes when they were dealt with under a parliamentary enclosure act*. The great and small tithes of Needwood Forest, by allotments of land and yearly money payments, Act of 1801. *Biggest operation of the Staffordshire Enclosure Acts* was the Enclosure of Needwood Forest (9,400 acres), Act of 1801 (HOS 1998 p91). *'one of the largest gatherings of agriculturalists ever seen at a farm sale in the Midland counties'* When an agricultural dispersion sale took place at Houndshill on Oct 29 1929, conducted by Messrs WS Bagshaw & Sons and Messrs Winterton & Sons. An estimated 2,000 people were attracted by the Houndshill stock famed for its excellence

consisting of dual purpose animals of great scale and deep milking propensities; 1,000 cars were parked in one field and over 600 people had luncheon (SA Nov 2 1929 p4p). *'One of the country's oldest village shows'*. Draycott-in-the-Clay Show, founded in C19, lapsed c2000, revived 2006 (UAd Aug 30 2006 p19 - the Show's own advertising feature). *Country's largest cabbage 1953* Perhaps one measuring two feet 8 inches in diameter and 8 feet 6 inches with the leaves extended, as considered by Mr GW Ede of Coton Hall Farm, Draycott-in-the-Clay, who grew it in 1953 (BOb Nov 5 1953 p1p). *'one of the highest yielding herds of cattle in Staffordshire' 1957*. Nineteen British pedigree Friesians, belonging to WB Bullock and Son of Villa Farm, Hanbury. In 1956 one of the cows was top of the county with a yield of 2,246 gallons of milk. The herd, built up from 1943, was transferred in its entirety to Llangain, Carmarthen, Wales, in 1957 (BOb Aug 29 1957 p3ps).

Folklore *Hanbury's best*. Hanbury Priory was founded in the C7 by King Elthelfred, who appointed his niece, Werburgh, daughter of King Wulfere, as prioress. In addition to this she was also associated with other convents. According to a very old tradition at one of the convents a flock of wild geese devoured vegetables from the kitchen garden. Werburgh called the flock to her and preached to them. Despite the flock promising to mend their ways the geese attacked the garden the next

St Werburgh, prioress of Hanbury Priory, makes her truce with the geese plaguing the covent garden.

day. Their reason for doing so was that the convent cook had continued to use geese in pies. Werburgh agreed this was not fair and called the cook and the pie in question before her. Her prayers for the geese in the pie revived the geese. She then ordered that no goose be eaten in the convent, so long as the geese did not raid the garden.

Geology The Agardsley and Forest Banks areas are Rhætic Beds; the Dove plain is Alluvium; Hanbury, Draycott, Marchington, Newborough villages is Keuper Red Marls; Hanbury Park-Coulters Hill is Rhætic Beds.

Hall, Henry *'one of the best-known farmers and cattle dealers in the Midlands' 1970.* (b c1900). Of 'The Watlands' Abbots Bromley, son of RJ Hall of 'Hall Flatts', Draycott-in-Clay; farmed on his own account at Stockley Park, Anslow; buried Hanbury churchyard (BOb April 30 1970 p3).

Hallam, Tracey *English National Badminton Championship women's singles champion 2004, 2006, Commonwealth Games women's singles bronze 1998, silver 2002, gold 2006, Britain's No. 1 Female Badminton player 2008.* (b1975). Badminton player, of Hanbury; she reached the quarter finals of the ladies singles in the 2008 Olympics (Burton Mail Feb 6 2006

Badminton champion, Tracey Hallam of Hanbury

p26pc. March 27 2006 p1pc. March 20 2006 p40pc. March 21 2007 pp18-19p. June 16 2008 p32pc. Aug 2 2008 p3pc. Aug 12 2008 p32pc).

Hartshorne, WF *Hanbury's longest-serving chorister.* (d1934). He served for 68 years from the age of 8, 1866-1934 (SA Feb 17 1934 p10 col 1).

Kiazim, Pte A *Army 100 Challenge Cup winner 1965.* Of the Royal Army Ordnance Corps stationed at the C.V.D. Marchington, won at Bisley in the 40th year of the competition. His final score was 181 out of a maximum of 200. In Aug 1965 Pte Kiazim left for service in Hong Kong (BOb July 8 1965 p1p).

Military bases *'Largest crater in the world to be caused by a gunpowder explosion'* (Staffordshire County Guide 2006/7 p114), largest single explosion of WW2 (GLS p45), UK's worst explosion disaster (GBR 1965 p236), world's biggest non-nuclear explosion (LTD p159) occurred at RAF Fauld on Nov 27 1944. *Provided the stone for Epstein's 'Adam'* The sculptor, Jacob Epstein, made his carving of 'Adam' from alabaster from the mine at

RAF Fauld (SA & Chron July 31 1958 p6 cols 5-6). *Maintenance Command Fire Cup and Proficiency Shield 1958* RAF Fauld for having the most efficient fire section in the whole RAF Maintenance Command (BOb May 8 1958 p3). *'one of the biggest vehicle repair and maintenance depots in the country'* Marchington (Army) Camp in about 1950s-60s, with as many as 300 to 400 vehicles passing in and out of the main gate in the course of a single day. Redundant by 1971 (BOb June 3 1971 p1).

Mundy, Francis Noel Clarke *Author of Staffordshire's rarest poem.* the poem in question is 'Needwood Forest' (1776), published 1811, with only a few copies printed for his friends (SHOS vol 1 pp67-68) (GNHS p145) (W p572) (JAT p70) (BS p321) (APB p43) (YX p21) (LTD p130).

Mynors, John *Perhaps the first man ever described in records as a Gentleman.* Of Marchington. He occurs in the Plea Rolls in 1407 as 'of Marchington jentylman', however, despite being of gentlemanly stock, he was hardly a gentleman going about the county murdering people (UTR p78) (SHC 1917 p195).

Patterson, Sgt Norman *Staffordshire's 3rd fatality of the Iraq War.* Of Draycott-in-the-Clay, in Jan 2004 (E&S March 20 2008 p24).

Place-name The first appearance of the name, Hanbury, is in c1185, and it means 'high burh or fortification'.

Population Hanbury was 36th most-populated Staffordshire parish in 1801 with 1,622 people; 32nd in 1811 with 2,130; 32nd in 1821 with 2,516; 34th in 1831 with 2,448; 35th in 1841 with 2,483; 38th in 1851 with 2,535; 40th in 1861 with 2,638; 42nd in 1871 with 2,605; 52nd in 1881 with 2,411; 50th in 1891 with 2,541; 52rd in 1901 with 2,462. Hanbury could be ranked 39th= worst-affected Staffordshire parish for loss of men in WW1, with 59 lives taken.

Porter, John *Newborough person with the earliest-surviving will.* It is dated March 11 1524/5.

Por_____?, Willielmus *Earliest person recorded in Marchington parish register.* For his burial/ baptism? in 1609.

Quote *Choicest.* Stebbing Shaw in his History of Staffordshire, vol 1, 1798 'Hanbury is a village situated in the same hundred of Offlow, a little to the North of Needwood Forest, upon an eminence that commands a bold view over the rich meadows upon the river Dove, to the moorlands and peak hills, which renders it very cold and bleak in Winter, but delightful in Summer.'

Shelley, Jane *Hanbury's villainess.* Daughter of George Shelley of Foxholes Farm, near Hanbury. Aged 17 when she was committed to trial in 1853 after confessing to setting on fire her father's hay ricks, stating her only motive was that a near neighbour called Archer, whom they all disliked, might get the blame. There had previously been a series of other burnings, but she denied knowledge of them (SA Aug 20 1853. Aug 21 1953 p2 col 3).

Sonkey, Raphe *Earliest person recorded in Newborough parish register.* Son of John Sonkye. For his baptism on June 15 1601.

Stafforde, Thomas *Earliest person recorded in Hanbury parish register.* Son of Thomas Stafforde. For his baptism on June 8 1574.

Village and built environment *'one of Staffordshire's most beautiful and interesting villages'.* Hanbury in the opinion of the author of Random Notes in The Staffordshire Advertiser, 1932 (SA Aug 27 1932 p10 col 4). *'a remarkably perfect example of an early 17th century yeoman house of timber construction'.* Woodroffes, Marchington, according to Burton Observer May 14 1953 p1 il.

Handsworth Handsworth was Staffordshire's 27th largest parish, consisting of 7,752 acres; 28th= farthest parish away from the county town, 19.2m SSE; extremist length 5.5m, making it 24th= longest parish in Staffordshire; extremist width, 5.1m, making it 26th= widest parish in Staffordshire. The parish's chief settlement is Handsworth, once a village; the entire parish is now all Birmingham suburbs, as is the other township, Perry Barr. Handsworth is famous for Matthew Boulton and his Soho Manufactory.

Altitudes The highest point of the parish is 568 feet on Aldridge boundary at Cooksey Lane, Kingstanding, also on West Bromwich boundary on Holyhead Road. The lowest point is 305 feet by the Tame near Witton.

Asbury, Francis *First bishop of the American Methodist Church, 'the Prophet of the Long Road', 'the John Wesley of the Western World'.* (1745-1816). Born at Hamstead, but spent his early years at Newton. He was made one of the two bishops of the newly formed Methodist Epis-

copal Church of the United States of America in 1784. He was accorded the latter title by the Bishop of Hamilton in 1924 (VCH vol 17 p4) (BCM Summer 2005 p80). *His first sermon* was at Manwoods Cottage in Forge Lane, Manwoods, c1763.

Francis Asbury (1745-1816) left the Perry Barr Smithy at which he was apprenticed, to become THE FIRST BISHOP TO BE CONSECRATED IN THE UNITED STATES'.

Associations *Earliest-known co-operative trading association* Handsworth Economical Union Provision Company established by workmen of Boulton & Watt at Soho Foundry and Engine Works in 1830; this predates the first Co-operative Store at Rochdale, 1844. The Company seems to have ceased in or after 1855 (SARA Dec 29 1951). *First English Oratory* was the Roman Catholic Oratation Congregation was established at Maryvale, Old Oscott, by John Henry Newman, 1848 (HOS 1998 p60). *First Staffordshire volunteer corps established* was Handsworth Rifle Volunteers, and thus are called the First Staffordshire Rifle Corps; but their first meeting, on June 3 1859 (SA Jan 14 1860 p5 col 4) (IE p120), took place after the first meetings of the Longton and Hanley corps. *Birmingham's first Sons of Rest branch* started in Handsworth Park in 1928 by Henry Courtney of Grove Lane, Handsworth. By 1937 there were 49 branches in and around the city (Birmingham Mail July 12 1937).

Barlow, Charles Thomas *'Midland 'Wizard of Finance'.* (1876-1951). Of Hamstead Hill, Handsworth Wood, born Aston Manor, Birmingham. Began work aged 12 at 5 shillings a week at a Perry Barr arms factory, and rose to found Accles Tube Syndicate (1899), which later became Accles and Pollock Ltd; co-founded Tube Investments (1919-22), which in 1950 made a profit of £6,250,000. He helped found - Birchley Rolling Mills Ltd (1919-23); British Stampings Ltd (1923-45); British Tube Mills Ltd; (1922-35), London Works (Barlows) Ltd (1932-51), Chase Cycles Ltd (1929-47); George Bate (Gunmakers) Ltd (1934-44); Moat Estates Ltd (1919-51); Brown and Barlow (Carburreters), and Aston Motor Accessories, leaving £156,678 in his will (BPn July 2 1951) (Birmingham Gazette July 3 1951 photo. Nov 12 1951).

Bendall, Edwin *England's?, Midlands', Birmingham's oldest baker 1907.* (1810-1907). Of Hamstall Road, Handsworth, born Dursley, Glous, coming to Birmingham c1877 carrying on several bakeries in the city under the name of E Bendall and Sons (BPn April 13 1907 photo).

Birchfield Harriers *'One of the leading athletics clubs in the UK'* Birchfield Harriers, formed 1877 after a cross-country race organised by Excelsior Football Club at Aston Lower Ground ended in farce. The disgruntled athletes decided to form their own club and named it after the old district where they were based (TB Aug 23 2007 p31). *'the most famous athletic club in the country' 1933, most successful club in the team race of the English Cross-Country Championship* Birchfield Harriers. The first quote is from Birmingham Despatch Oct 6 1933. Between 1880 and 1953 the club had 27 wins with one tie (GBR 1965 p270) (TB Aug 2 2007 p35; their 20th win was in 1929). *London to Brighton Road Relay Race winners 1925, 1926, 1928, 1930, 1931, 1952* Birchfield Harriers, winning the first race in 1925, when they achieved a time of 4 hours 50 minutes 53 seconds over the 54 miles. The race was last staged in 1965 (TB Aug 23 2007 p31).

Archie Robertson: Birchfield Harriers' first Olympian.

Birchfield Harriers most famous athlete by 1933 was William Whiteway Alexander (1852-1933), *see* Brewood. *Their first Olympian* was Archie Robertson who won gold in the 3,200m steeplechase at the 1908 games. Their first Olympian woman was Audrey Kilner-Brown who won silver in the 4x100 m relay in 1936 (E&S Aug 23 2008 p10p; lists all the club's Olympians). *World Cross-Country Champion 1975* Ian Stewart of Birchfield Harriers 1965-76. In 1976 he resigned to join Tipton Harriers (Birmingham Mail Jan 11 1977). *'one of the most successful husband-and-wife teams in athletics' 1975* John and Shelia Sherwood, formerly of Birchfield Harriers. John won Olympic Bronze in the hurdles in 1968, whilst Shelia won Silver in the long jump in the same games; both

received an MBE in 1975 (Birmingham Mail June 14 1975 photo).

Blake, Dawn *'the scariest woman in Britain'.* (b1966). Originally from Handsworth, former pupil at King Edward's Handsworth Girls' School, in Handsworth Wood, as she claimed herself appearing on Channel 4's Big Brother in 2006 (Birmingham Mail May 22 2006 p3).

Booth, William *Handsworth's villain, 'King of Coiners', 'Birmingham or Brummajum' Booth. (1776-1812).* Notorious forger of Booth's Farm, S of Booth's Lane, NNW of Perry Beeches Junior School. Born Ullenhall, near Henley-in-Arden, Warws. As well as forging he sold corpses to Birmingham medics. In 1808 he was tried at Warwick for the murder his brother, John, at his father's farm at Wootton Waven, Warws, but acquitted. He was arrested again in c1811, retried at Stafford, found guilty and famously executed. The corpse was buried in Handsworth old churchyard.

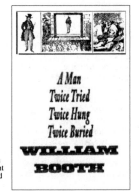

A Man Twice Tried Twice Hung Twice Buried

WILLIAM BOOTH

What a contemporary crime broadsheet for William Booth might have looked like.

Boulton, Matthew *Handsworth's most famous old worthy.* (1728-1809). Manufacturer, engineer and Lunar Society member. Born in Birmingham, the son of a toymaker. With John Fothergill he established the Soho Manufactory, 1762. With James Watt he began manufacturing steam engines, 1774. A coin manufactory was set up in 1788. He retired in 1800 but remained at Soho House, which he had built (it later became a museum to his memory), until his death and was buried in St. Mary's churchyard, Handsworth.

Bowen, Alice *Midland Area Coal Board Queen 1954.* Of Hamstead (SA May 28 1954 p6p).

Church St Mary's at Handsworth is one

of 23 such county dedications (most common dedication in the county); 48th= oldest AP county church dating from 1200. Elihu Burritt, C19 American author and diplomat on Handsworth called the *'a kind of Westminster Abbey to Birmingham, consecrated to the memory of its dead, whose names have won illustrious fame'* (Old and New Birmingham. Robert K Dent. 1879 p618). In the churchyard is the grave of Gypsy Queen Henty Smith (d1907) of the Black Patch gypsy encampment, who is said to have put a curse on anyone who ever builds over Black Patch (Brumroamin. Ted Rudge. 2003).

Clarke, Nathaniel Gooding *He was Crown Counsel at the last case of trial by battle.* KC. (d1833). This was the Mary Ashford Murder Case (1828). He resided at Browns Green House, situated to the rear of what is now a triangle with Handsworth Wood Road and Englestede Close (HPPE p16).

Common land Handsworth Common has been described as 'one of the most barren in England' (MNB p35).

Country pursuits *Largest rose tree in England 1845* was considered to be that grown by Mr C Fletcher of Heathfield Place, Aston Villa, Handsworth, measuring 38 feet in circumference and 14 feet high. In June 1845 when in full bloom it had 700 roses, besides several hundreds of buds (SA June 28 1845). *First National Farmers' Union Market Produce Show at the City of Birmingham Flower Show* was at Handsworth Park Sept 5-6 1958. Hitherto, the NFU's display of British grown fruit had been principally at the Chelsea Flower Show (SA & Chron 28 1958 p6 cols 5-7). *Last and 20th Birmingham Flower* was held at Handsworth Park on Sept 2 1966 (Birmingham Mail Sept 1 1966).

Cricket *She sang the national anthem at the start of the Ashes cricket series 2006.* Amy Pearson (b1985/6) of Perry Beeches, at Brisbane, Australia (BBC Midlands Today Nov 23 2006).

Ebanks, Sharon *First BNP councillor to sit on Birmingham City Council.* When she was elected for Kingstanding, May 2006- (BBC Midlands Today May 8 2006).

Entertainment *The first Odeon cinema* **was** The Odeon, Birchfield Road, Perry Barr, opened 1930, by Oscar Deutsch (1893-1948), 'Napoleon of the cinema', of Birmingham. By the end of 1932 Deutsch had five cinemas; in 1933 another 12 were added. In 1936 he controlled 150 cinemas

(Birmingham Gazette Dec 6 1941) (BPn Dec 4 1941). *First Art Deco style Odeon cinema* was built at Kingstanding, 1935; Oscar Deutsch was so pleased with the design, its architect Harry Weedon was used for Deutsch's later Odeon cinemas (Wikipedia, 2006). *UK Best kept managed pub 1983* 'The Hamstead' Inn, Green Lane, Hamstead, run by Frank and Dorothy Nash, as awarded by Bass, Mitchells and Butler breweries (West Bromwich Midland Chronicle Dec 22 1983 p13p).

Folklore *Handsworth's best.* For the saying that Handsworth's notorious forger, William Booth, was 'a man twice tried, twice hung, and twice buried'. For he had been twice tried at Warwick and Stafford Assizes; twice hung because the noose broke the first time; twice buried because local dignitaries objected to having to pass his grave on their way to church, as it lay at the entrance to Handsworth old church. At night people have heard strange noises during pig farrowing in the vicinity of his farm, Booth's Farm, for which there is no explanation.

Football *Highest score in football between English clubs.* Aston Villa beating Accrington 12-2 at Perry Barr, March 12 1892 (GBR 1995 p252). *The man who won a day with the FA cup.* Martin White, a WBA supporter, of Handsworth Wood, who won the prize of having the FA cup for a day at his house on March 26 2008 (BBC 1 Midlands Today March 26 2008).

Geology Handsworth township is Bunter (Handsworth town and most), Permian (W fringes); Perry Barr township is Bunter (Perry village and Barr Beacon highlands), Permian (Hamstead, Newton and W).

George, Isaac *Last keeper of Handsworth pound.* (1848-1931). Of Churchill Cottage, Hamstead Road, who carried on the blacksmith's shop opposite the parish church. In c1910 the pound was closed due to the widening of Hamstead Road (Birmingham Mail Nov 24 1931).

Gesson, William *Handsworth person with the earliest-surviving will.* It is dated Aug 5 1512.

Golf *One of the historical golf courses of the British Isles 1910.* Handsworth (Historic Golf Courses of the British Isles. Bernard Darwin. 1910. p144). *British Girls' Championship winner 1954, Staffordshire Ladies' Champion 1954 (and 8 more wins to 1967), Midland's Ladies Champion 1954, 1955, 1956, 1957, 1958, 1959, 1960, 1961, England Ladies Cham-*

pion 1956, Curtis Cup Match (England team) 1958, 1964, World Women's Team Championships 3rd 1964. Miss Bridget Jackson of Handsworth; educated at a private school, Handsworth, and Bredenbury Court, Gardenhurst; honorary life member of Handsworth Golf Club (SA & Chron Sept 13 1962 p18 col 1p) (Birmingham Sketch June 1967).

Gretton, Warrant-Officer RH *Birmingham's Battle of Britain hero.* Attended Handsworth Grammar School, continuously engaged in the 'Battle of Britain' Aug-Sept 1940. Joined the Spitfire squadron in June 1940 (Birmingham Gazette Sept 15 1942 photo).

Gough-Calthorpe, Sir Somerset Arthur *The Turks signed the Armistice on his ship.* (1865-1937). Of Perry Hall, Commander-in-Chief of the Mediterranean 1917-19, the flagship was the Agamemnon. Later the first and principal Naval A.D.C. to George V (Birmingham Mail July 27 1937).

Gymnastics *World tumbling (Trampolining) Champion (male 15-18 age group) 1973.* Andrew Farley, aged 15, of Howard Road, Newton, a Churchfields High School pupil (Evening Mail Aug 30 1973).

Hands, Miss Mary *'the grand old lady of Handsworth'.* She died at the age of 101 in 1932 at 119 Leonard Road, Handsworth. She was a native of Atherstone and removed to Handsworth in c1922 to live with her niece (Birmingham Gazette Feb 2 1932).

Haseler, William Hair *Birmingham's oldest manufacturing jeweller 1909.* (1820-1909) of Alinde, Hamstead Road, Handsworth. Founder of the firm of WH Haseler Ltd, goldsmiths and jewellers, Hylton Street, was oldest member of the trade in Birmingham at his death (Weekly Post Oct 26 1909 photo).

Health *Britain's largest earliest outbreak of (Mexican) Swine Flu in the 2009 epidemic* by a long way that concentrated on Welford Primary School, Hamstead Road, which had reached 74 cases by May 29 2009 (BBC Midlands Today May 29 2009).

Heath, Harold *First to show a film in a West End theatre.* Born Handsworth, stage and film impresario, when he arranged a series of film matinees at the London Pavilion in 1914. Just before WW1 he had brought over Florence Turner from America to make films in the UK; she was the first woman who starred in films (Sunday Mercury Feb 7 1937 photo).

Hodgetts, Nicholas *Handsworth's kindest.* Of Handsworth. He gave a number of lands, the revenue from which to maintain bridges in the parish, 1612-13.

Howell, Miss Dorothy *1st Staffordshirian to have their own music composition played on radio.* Born Handsworth, with her 'Lamia' on 5IT's programme in evening of Sept 5 1924. She was studying under John B McEwen, Principal of the Royal Academy of Music, for composition, and under Percy Waller and Tobias Matthy, for piano (Birmingham Gazette Aug 27 1923) (Birmingham Despatch Sept 5 1924).

Hutton (or Hulton), William *Birmingham's first historian.* He had a paper making mill at Bristnels End, later 1750s.

Ishaq, Khyra *Handsworth's saddest.* Aged 7, of 36 Leyton Road, Handsworth, starved to death by her mother Angela Gordon, and her partner Junaid Abuhamza, found unconscious in the house by paramedics in the early hours of May 17 2008. Also allegedly at fault were social workers who failed to visit her, after she was withdrawn from school amid allegations that she and her brothers and sisters were being bullied. Some of these siblings were reduced to eating bread put out by a neighbour for birds (The Daily Telegraph May 23 2008 p5pcs. May 24 2008 p25).

Jacot, Emile *Rome Scholar in Sculpture 1925.* Son of Mr L Jacot of the Hill, Wellington Road, Birchfield. He attended the Slade School of Art 1919-22, winning this most coveted scholarships in the art world in 1925 (BPn Oct 12 1925 photo).

Johnson, Louis *Handsworth's unluckiest.* Newspaper shop proprietor, of Beaudesert Road, Handsworth, 'one of the most experienced members of the South Staffordshire Skydiving Club', killed aged 46 when his parachute failed to open properly on Aug 19 1973 descending at approx 125mph over Halfpenny Green airport, Bobbington. By 1973 the Club was 'the largest of its kind in the country' (Birmingham Post Aug 20 1973 photo).

Kinsey, Joseph Ronald *'a shovel and spade Tory, not a silver spoon in the mouth man from the Right'.* Born c1921. Said of himself. He was the former councillor and alderman, former Post Officer worker and off-licensed, who took the Perry Barr seat for the Conservatives from Labour in 1970 by just 1,266 votes (Birmingham Mail Sept 11 1973 photo).

Labone, Mr OH *Staffordshire Chess*

champion 1897, 1898. Of Handsworth (SA April 23 1898 p5 col 1. Sept 10 1898 p5 col 1).

Locker-Lampson, Commander Oliver *He wrote to Hitler: 'As one Aryan to another'.* (1880-1954). MP for Handsworth

Commander Oliver
Locker-Lampson

worth 1922-45. He had a colourful career embracing the stage, journalism, the law, and military affairs (founding one of the first armoured car squadrons on the Western Front, 1915). His hatred of Communism and Fascism was epitomised in his pre-WW2 toast of 'Death to the dictators' - a toast which brought angry protests from the German Press. He provided refuge and an armed guard to Einstein when in England, 1933, later writing to Hitler "as one Aryan to another" - protesting against Nazi persecution (Birmingham Gazette Oct 9 1954 photo).

Martial Arts *Welsh Open Karate Champion 1974, European Individual Karate Champion (heavyweight) 1975, World Karate Champion 6th place 1975.* Eugene Codrington, aged 21, electrician, of Holly Road, Handsworth (Birmingham Mail June 24 1975 photo. Oct 8 1975).

Mining *World's deepest worked seam 1875* Hamstead Colliery at 1,836 feet (MNB p72). *Largest pit mound in the country* Hamstead Colliery pit mound at 130 feet high, as claimed by a local newspaper in 1930; the mound had been burning since at least c1900 (WBY p39). *'The last man to escape' the Hamstead Colliery disaster* F Jones; the disaster occurred on March 4 1908 (TB May 11 2000 p4p).

Morris, William 'Bill' *First coloured member of the national executive council of Britain's largest union.* This was when he was elected to the council of the Transport and General Workers Union, 1971; he had settled in Handsworth in 1964 (BPn Dec 24 1971).

Mountaineering *First Staffordshirian to conquer Everest, Britain's Men of the Year 1976.* Sergeant John 'Brummie' Stokes, born Hamstead 1946, reaching the summit on May 16 1976. But he lost his toes through frostbite (The Times May 18 1976. Aug 11 1976) (Daily Telegraph. May 18 1976) (Sandwell Evening Mail

June 11 1976. Nov 3 1976).

Sgt John 'Brummie' Stokes, *the first Staffordshirian to conquer Everest.*

National home In 2008 the Society for Italic Handwriting (SIH, 1952) had theirs at 22 Endwood Court, Handsworth Wood Road. The Society promotes the use of Italic handwriting.

Parkes, Frederick *Handsworth's bravest (WW2).* (b1911). Of Robert Road, Handsworth, production hand, awarded the George Medal who entered a burning building adjoining the Birmingham factory where he worked, which had just been bombed in Oct 1940, and succeeded in crawling through a tiny aperture entrance to the cellar to turn off the gas at the mains so preventing an explosion and the destruction of the factory (Evening Despatch Dec 17 1940).

Pepper, Mrs Mary *Direct descendant of John Bunyan.* (b1840). Of Putney Road, Handsworth. Her maiden name was Bunyan, and she was born at Moulsoe, near Newport Pagnell, Bucks, where there have been Bunyans for centuries. Aged 92 in 1932 she could still quote long passages from 'The Pilgrim's Progress' (BPn Oct 18 1932).

Perrett, Mrs Adine *First woman president of The Midland Arts Club.* Of Philip Victor Road, Handsworth, 1962 (Birmingham Mail Feb 12 1962).

Perry Pont House Perry Pont House garden at Perry, when occupied by William Harry Osborn, 1838, has been described as 'one of the most perfect little paradises which any man could desire' (HPPE p93).

Pickup, Mrs Mary Elizabeth *'First woman solicitor'.* (1882-1938). Of Wye Cliff Road, Handsworth, heading the list of successful candidates in the first final examination of the Law Society ever open to women, 1922 (after the Sex Disqualification (Removal) Act of 1919). She subsequently became a partner with her husband in the firm of Redfern & Co of Colmore Row, and was a consultant at the Poor Man's Lawyer Centre at Birmingham

Settlement; Birmingham Soroptimis Club President 1930; President of the British Federation of University Women (Birmingham Mail Nov 24 1938) (Evening Despatch Nov 23 1938).

Place-names The first appearance of the name, Handsworth, is Domesday Book, 1086, and means 'Hun's homestead, or enclosure'. *Only occurrence in Staffordshire of the compound ham-stede in a place name* is Hamstead (PNSZ p26).

Population Handsworth was 24th most-populated in 1801 with 2,719 people; 23rd in 1811 with 3,027; 23rd in 1821 with 3,859; 18th in 1831 with 4,944; 19th in 1841 with 6,138; 19th in 1851 with 7,879; 18th in 1861 with 11,459; 14th in 1871 with 16,042; 14th in 1881 with 24,251; 10th in 1891 with 35,066; 7th in 1901 with 55,269. Handsworth (Perry Barr only) could be ranked 58th= worst-affected Staffordshire parish for loss of men in WW1, with 31 lives taken.

Prem, Dr Dhani *First coloured councillor in Birmingham.* (b1904). Journalist, songwriter, political prisoner and champion of race relations in Birmingham. Originally of India, he became a Labour councillor for Perry Barr in WW2; cofounder of Commonwealth Welfare Council 1955 (BPn Oct 22 1974 photo).

Personal endeavours *Longest ever parachute descent by 1891* Was made by Lieutenant George Philip Lempriere (1855-1949), born London, from a balloon in 1891 for the annual gala of the Lancaster Athletic Association. He surpassed 10,000 feet and was perhaps 2 miles high. His timed descent was 11.15 minutes (perhaps descending at 1000 feet per minute). He is also accredited with making the first leaflet 'raids', dropping leaflets from a balloon to promote himself as the Independent candidate for the Soho Ward on Handsworth Council. By 1926 he was residing at Handsworth; by 1946 at Wilton Road, Handsworth Wood. His private papers were presented to Birmingham Reference Library in 1970 (Birmingham Mail May 15 1926. Feb 23 1945. Nov 10 1970) (Evening Despatch April 30 1945 photo) (Sunday Mercury Feb 24 1946 photo) (BPn Feb 21 1949). *First provincial organ broadcast* was made by Frank Newman, FRCO, on the Wurlitzer organ at the Lozells Picture House in Feb 1927; he later became well known to Midland listeners because of his broadcasts on the famous Foort-designed Christie organ at the Plaza (Granada by 1973), Rugby (BPn

March 30 1973).

Quote *Choicest.* FW Hackwood, teacher, prolific local history author, and 'Wednesbury's Favourite', lived with his family at Comberford Lodge, Bridge St, Wednesbury, until a subterranean fire at the neighbouring colliery forced him out to Handsworth. Here, in his Handsworth Old and New, 1908, he writes of his new home 'Handsworth, not so long ago a pretty Staffordshire village, preserving its freshness and quietude midway between the Black Country and Birmingham, has now grown into a populous suburb of that city.... Handsworth remains almost entirely residential, except that recently a few of the factories typical of Birmingham's jewellery quarter, the adjoining district of Hockley, have begun to stray over the border into the Staffordshire area. It therefore would be hardly fair to compare this congeries of villas, cottages, and private houses with those busier outskirts of the great city....'

Read, Kingsley *Inventor of the 40-letter English alphabet.* (c1888-1975). Born Aston, Birmingham. Attended Handsworth Grammar School and Birmingham College of Art. He worked on the alphabet - the Read System - during air raids in WW2 to break the tedium. George Bernard Shaw declared it 'far and away the best alphabet with the best head at the back of it that has come my way' (BPn Feb 13 1975).

Smallwood, Ann *Staffordshire's 11th oldest woman ever.* Of Handsworth, aged 108, living before 1816 (Directory of Staffordshire. 1816. J Leigh of Manchester).

Soho Manufactory This manufactory was the centre of industry in Britain in its early years, 'arguably the world's oldest factory' (Wikipedia), 'Europa's wonder and Brittania's pride', biggest factory in Europe if not the world and first William Wyatt (b1734) building to be seen by a large public when the manufactory was extended in 1765. *First gas-lit house* Sycamore Hill, Handsworth, 1816, built by William Murdock (d1839), engineer and inventor of coal-gas lighting.

Stephens, Weaver *'one of the best known music teachers in Birmingham'.* (1844-1926). Of 30 South Road, Handsworth, born Tewkesbury. He had at the beginning of the 1887 Session (at Saturday Evening Penny Singing Classes) 734 paid admissions. He became No. 1 on the membership list of the Birmingham Festival Choral Society (Birmingham News Nov 27 1926).

Swimming *Perhaps 1st Staffordshirian to attempt seriously to swim the Channel.*

Frank Holmes of Handsworth Wood Road, Handsworth (1860-1935). His most-noteworthy attempts were in Sept 1898 when he gave up very reluctantly 6 miles from France, and in July 1900 when he swam only 14 miles, giving up because of rough weather. No one had succeeded to swim the Channel after Capt Webb in 1875 until TW Burgess' attempt in Sept 1911. Frank Perks (b1893) of Handsworth, (former winner of the Championship Cup of the All-the-Year-Round Club), attempted the feat in 1923 when he completed 18 miles in 11 and half hours and was only 4.5 miles from France when he gave up due to an attack of cramp. In Aug 1924 he made a second attempt (Birmingham Mail Aug 26 1924. Aug 30 1935). Mrs Ellinor Goderidge, 23 years old, of 161 Kettlebrook Road, Tamworth, was training to swim the Channel in 1951. Another aspirant, Jim Clancy of Lichfield, hoped to make the crossing on or near Aug 20 1951 (SA Feb 16 1951 p1. March 30 1951 p4 col 2. June 29 1951 p2 col 7). Bill Pickering, manager of Bloxwich swimming baths, made a successful crossing in 1955.

Tangye, George *Last of the famous brotherhood of engineers.* (1815-1920). Of Heathfield Hall, Handsworth, last survivor of the famous engineer brothers who came to Birmingham from Cornwall in mid C19, founding the firm of Tangye Brothers (BPn Oct 8 1920).

Taran, alias Hard Kaur *Biggest-selling woman musician in India 2007.* (b1981). Hip-hop star, moved to Handsworth from India aged 11 (Birmingham Sunday Mercury Aug 26 2007 p24).

Tennis *Captained the first Warwickshire lawn tennis team to win the Inter-county championship.* Dr Frederick Augustus L'Estrange (1869-1951), son of Rev RB Burges of St Paul's church, Handsworth, in 1909. In addition, he was thrice winner of the Deykin Cup (subsequently a championship of the area for 50 miles round Birmingham) (BPn July 9 1951 photo).

Ullah, Roupik *Perry Barr's bravest.* When aged 27 and suffering from learning difficulties and a resident of the Birmingham Rathbone Society Supported Home, Perry Barr, he rescued a little girl from drowning as he passed a lake on his way to a pottery class at the Midland Arts Centre in Cannon Hill Park, Birmingham, for which he was presented with a Royal Humane Society certificate (Birmingham Evening Mail. July 9 1998).

Warren, Lieut William George War- ren *Croix de Guerre recipient.* RNVR. Of 123 Copthall Road, Handsworth, native of Normanton, Yorks, awarded 1944; champion swimmer, and sportsman (Evening Despatch June 23 1944) (Birmingham Mail June 23 1944).

Watt, James *"one of the greatest benefactors of mankind".* Of Heathfield, in an obituary by the Staffordshire Advertiser for his improvements to the steam engine on his death in 1819 aged 84 (SA Aug 30 1919 p3 col 3).

Webster, Keith AV *Birmingham's only coloured J.P. 1968.* He served for less than nine months, until he returned to Jamaica in 1968. Apparently he had given up his position on the bench in protest against the Government's immigration policy. He had come to England in 1944; in 1968 his English wife and their son remained at their home in Earlsbury Gardens, Handsworth (Birmingham Mail Sept 9 1968) (The Observer Sept 8 1968).

Weston, Capt John Theodore Spencer *Handworth's bravest (WW1).* Younger son of Dr Darby Weston of The Oaklands, Handsworth, shot in the trenches in France in 1915 aged 23. He was attached to 1st Batt of the Royal Berkshire Regt going to France only a few weeks after WW1 broke out. His commanding officer said of him "he was a splendid soldier, brave and cool, and could be trusted to go anywhere and do anything. We had the greatest admiration for his pluck, which was unlimited..." (BPn Aug 25 1915).

Wright, Thomas Barber *Founder of the Hospital Sunday movement.* Of Quarry House, Hamstead, 1859 (TBS p26).

Zephaniah, Benjamin *Highest honour turned down by a Staffordshirian.* Dub poet. Born Handsworth 1958, turned down an OBE in 2003.

Harlaston See Clifton Campville.

Haselour Haselour was Staffordshire's 155th largest parish (extra parochial), consisting of 586 acres; 34th= farthest parish away from the county town, 18.6m ESE; extremist length 2.3m; extremist width 0.6m, making it 6th narrowest parish in Staffordshire. The parish's chief settlement is Haselour, a small village, and it is famous for the timber-framed mansion Haselour Hall. The name first appears in 1256 (SA July 30 1938 p9 col 8).

Altitudes The highest point of the parish is 236 feet N of Haselour House. The lowest point is 180 feet on the N boundary by the Mease.

De Trafford family *Staffordshire's*

county family who suffered heaviest toll in WW1. Of Haselour Hall. All five sons of Augustus de Trafford had served by late 1915:- Capt Oswald was then of the S. Staffs Regt, taken prisoner at Crefeld; Capt TC was of the Royal Fusilliers, wounded and missing since Nov 1914; Rev R, was a Lieut in the Officers Training Corps; Lieut Edward was of the S. Staffs Regt in France; Pte Herman was in the Canadian Contingent (CL Nov 13 1915 p645).

De Trafford, Augustus *'From the day of his purchase to the last week of his life, he never ceased to beautify the home and its domestic chapel'*. This was said of him after his purchase of Haselour in 1885 (d1904) (LTM Jan Feb 1973 p28).

De Trafford, Capt Edward *Battle of Somme first-day medalist*. He won a M.C. on 1st July 1916.

Dilke, Samuel *First non-feudal lord of Haselour*. He purchased Haselour in 1672 (LTM Jan Feb 1973 p26).

Folklore *Haselour's best*. Haselour Old Hall has a priests hiding-place (KES p106).

Geology All the parish is Keuper Red Marls.

Haselour Hall *One of only two buildings by Sir Edward Lutyens in Staffordshire* An entrance lodge to Haselour Hall (MR2 p167); the other may be Hillcrest in Stone. *'Perhaps the most charming half-timbered house in the county'* Masefield on Haselour Hall (LGS p144).

Haselour Hall

Haselour chapel One of only three undedicated county ancient parish churches; 97th oldest AP county church dating from 1370 and is Staffordshire's smallest chapel (SA July 30 1938 p9 col 8).

Place-name The name first appears in 1256 (SA July 30 1938 p9 col 8), and means 'the flat-topped ridge with the hazels' (PNSZ p303).

Population Haselour was 151st= most-populated Staffordshire parish in 1801 with 33 people; 150th in 1811 with 42; 148th in 1821 with 49; 152nd in 1831 with 36; 156th in 1841 with 29; 157th in 1851

with 22; 155th in 1861 with 27; 158th in 1871 with 21; 159th= in 1881 with 29; 157th in 1891 with 42; 155th in 1901 with 49. Haselour could be ranked 129th= worst-affected Staffordshire parish for loss of men in WW1, with 2 lives taken.

Quarter Sessions *Most extraordinary road case before Staffordshire Quarter Sessions*. Was perhaps that brought by Col Howard of Elford Hall against the whole of Haselour at the Michaelmas Sessions 1840. It was whether Haselour should be made responsible for the upkeep of Salter's street, a Roman road, otherwise called Green Lane. Or as Haselour claimed it had become an obsolete roadway. It caused considerable interest as Haselour consisted of only a handful of inhabitants from two farms, who would certainly be burdened by road rates. The case was adjourned for another whole day, but proved in favour of Howard (SA Oct 24 1840 p2).

Quote *Choicest*. Rev Thomas Harwood in his The History & Antiquities of the Church & City of Lichfield, 1806, notes 'Haselour is a small hamlet, seven miles east of Lichfield. In its chapel, now almost dilapidated, several of the family of Girdler were interred. Divine service has been long discontinued: but at the visitation of Archbishop Laud, in 1624, Thomas Cotton, was curate.'

Hints Hints was Staffordshire's 122nd largest parish, consisting of 1,889 acres; 37th farthest parish away from the county town, 18.2m SE; extremist length 2.7m; extremist width 1.6m, making it 27th= narrowest parish in Staffordshire. The chief settlement is Hints, a tiny village off Watling Street. It is famed for the unexplainable large mound by Watling Street called Gold's Clump and the discovery on Hints Common in the C18 of a 'pig' of lead weighing 180lb bearing the inscription: 'IMP VESP VII T IMP V COS' which gave the date 76 AD in the seventh consulship of Vespasian of the fifth of Titus (SA & Chron Jan 26 1956 p4 col 5).

Altitudes The highest point is Hints Common at 499 feet. The lowest point is 233 feet on Tamworth/ Drayton Bassett boundary by Bourne Brook.

Church St Bartholomew's at Hints is one of 6 such county dedications (of AP churches); 7th last AP county church built dating from 1882.

Badham, Molly *A founder of the 'first Twycross Zoo'*. (1914-2007). Along with Nathalie Evans, had their first menagerie of animals (which became the basis of

Twycross Zoo) at their home, The Bungalow, Hints Lane, Hints 1954-63 (The Daily Telegraph Oct 22 2007 p23).

British Falconers' Club Formed 1924. Their national home in 2002 was Home Farm, Hints.

Floyer, Sir John *Hints' most famous old worthy.* (1649-1734). Physician. Born 3rd March at Hints Hall, 3rd child of Richard Floyer, a barrister. Aged 15 he entered Queen's College, Oxford. He was knighted for local political services, 1684. He recommended young Samuel Johnson be touched by Queen Anne. His is principally remembered for promoting cold water bathing; History of Cold Bathing appeared in 1706. In 1694 he was living in Lichfield with his sister. There he died on 31st January and was buried 'within the shadow of Lichfield Cathedral'; no memorial remains.

Folklore, Hints' top A spring at Hints which never froze, nor did the pool which it fed was noted in the C17 and C18 (NHS p91) (SHOS vol 2 p19).

Geology Hints village (N end) and N of Black Brook is Bunter; Botley House and Mid E fringe is Keuper Red Marls; Hints village (S end) and S of Black Brook is Permian.

Husband, Jo. *Hints' longest serving vicar.* He served 40 years, curate 1681-c1721.

Legg, John *Earliest person in the parish register.* Clerk, buried 17 Jan 1558.

Lucy *Pet chimpanzee who starred with Norman Wisdom.* A West African chimpanzee. One of the original Twycross Zoo animals at Hints. She appeared in the comedy 'Just My Luck' filmed at Pinewood Studios, also starring Margaret Rutherford. When Lucy met Wisdom for the first time she wrapped her arms around his neck and made it quite clear he was her favourite male film star in her life (LiMe Nov 8 1957 p4p).

Lucy, the chimpanzee (or one like her) who met Norman Wisdom; in the background is a television mast of the period of the one originally at Hints.

Milk Race *When the Milk Race passed*

through Hints. In 1991 on the A5 going through Walsall, Shenstone, Weeford, Canwell, Sutton and Lichfield (TH June 7 1991 p9).

Place-name The first appearance of the name Hints is in Domesday Book, 1086, and it means 'road'.

Population Hints was 128th most-populated Staffordshire parish in 1801 with 245 people; 127th in 1811 with 272; 132nd in 1821 with 250; 133rd in 1831 with 225; 134th in 1841 with 213; 136th in 1851 with 218; 139th in 1861 with 200; 139th in 1871 with 193; 137th in 1881 with 214; 132nd in 1891 with 238; 135th in 1901 with 212. Hints could be ranked 100th= worst-affected Staffordshire parish for loss of men in WW1, with 4 lives taken.

Quote *Choicest.* Mabel Swift, the former long-standing local history columnist for The Tamworth Herald, wrote about Hints in a feature on Oct 3 2002, summed it up thus:- 'village of churches, carts, cotton and cold baths!'

Road by-pass *'the most unlikely country ramble in the Midlands'.* When ramblers dressed in fancy dress to walk the new A5 link road between Weeford and Wilnecote in a one-off charity walk prior to its opening in autumn 2005; the road by-passes Hints (Birmingham Sunday Mercury Aug 14 2005 p11).

Sinker Rev Francis Stephen *First vicar instituted by Rt Rev ES Woods as Bishop of Lichfield.* The institution and induction of Rev Francis Stephen Sinker to the vicariate of Hints on Sept 24 1937, two days after his enthronement (SA Oct 2 1937 p5 col 6).

Smith, Leslie *Hints's saddest.* Of School Lane, Hints, aged 84, killed in a blaze at the house of his friend Betty Mosedale, in Commonside, Pelsall, started by a faulty electric blanket on New Year's eve Dec 31 1999; police originally thought he had been murdered (BPn Oct 24 2000 p5).

T.V. transmitter *Highest powered (transmitter) in the country 1956, one of the highest powered Band III stations in the world 1956, first (TV station) built in the Midlands* Lichfield I.T.A. Station, the Independent Television Authority's Midland transmitter, at Common Barn Farm, Hints, which began transmission on Feb 17 1956, with a radiated power of 144 k.w. - extending to Shrewsbury, to Bakewell, to Grantham, to Market Harborough, to Cheltenham, with a potential to reach 6 million people. The original 450 foot mast was replaced in 1960 with a 1,000 foot mast. The station's first engineer-in-chief,

Norman Payne, was awarded an MBE in 1960 for his efforts in bringing television to the Midlands. He was still at the station in 1973 (LiMe Aug 26 1955 p5 il. Feb 17 1956 p4p) (TH Aug 31 1973 p18).

Union, Rev J Hope *He appeared in the Hints team which won a county competition.* Along with Messrs JW Smith, GWS Clarke, and T Tunney, he beat Penkridge in quiz organised by Staffordshire CC on local villages, the county village hall management, and general knowledge, 1958 (TH May 9 1958 p3 cols 3-4).

Hopwas See Tamworth.

Hopwas Hays Hopwas Hays was Staffordshire's 160th largest parish (extra parochial), consisting of 354 acres; 33rd farthest parish away from the county town, 18.7m SE; extremist length 0.9m, making it 10th shortest parish in the county; extremist width 1.2m, making it 12th= narrowest parish in the county. The first reference to the name Hopwas Hays is in 1222. The chief settlement of the place is the solitary property called The Woodhouse, otherwise the rest is wood. It is famous for Nine Limousin cattle from Hints who escaped here in 1999 and the subsequent attempts to recapture them made them national cause celebres. An operation, known as 'Rawhide,' comprising a squad of 100 soldiers from Whittington Barracks, together with NFU representatives, expert marksmen and mounted police, all tried to catch the so-called 'Tamworth Nine' cattle. *Choicest quote.* According to columnist 'Wheelman' writing in Burton Observer Aug 17 1950 p3 "Hopwas is rather more than a 'pocket edition' of Cannock Chase.' *Hopwas Hays' top folklore.* In summer 1834 a human skeleton was found by labourers getting stone near the canal bank at Hopwas Hay. It was believed to have been that of a murder victim, killed c1814 near the spot; the supposed murderer having died c1832 (Dyott's Diaries Aug 6 1834). Hopwas Hays was 166th most-populated Staffordshire parish in 1801 with 2 people; 166th in 1811 with 2; 166th in 1821 with 3; 166th in 1831 with 2; 166th in 1841 with 4; 166th in 1851 with 6; 166th in 1861 with 2; 164th in 1871 with 6; 166th in 1881 with 5; 166th in 1891 with 6; 166th in 1901 with 5.

Horninglow See Burton.

I-K

King's Bromley King's Bromley was Staffordshire's 91st largest parish, consisting of 2,987 acres; 73rd= closest parish to the county town, 11.8m ESE; extremist length 3.1m; extremist width 3.8m. The chief settlement of the parish is Kings Bromley, a pretty, linear timber-framed black and white village. The parish is famous for being the death place in 1057 of Leofric, Earl of Mercia. *First use of a computer in Staffordshire to rearrange parish record data for readers' use.* Perhaps Kings Bromley, 1984 (SHJ vol 1 pp18-25).

Altitudes The highest point of the parish is 266 feet on the SW boundary. The lowest point is 187 feet by the Trent at Lupin.

Butcher, Ivy *King's Bromley's historian.* Long associated with King's Bromley Show; foundress of King's Bromley Historians, 1979, author of 'Snippets from the History of King's Bromley' 2001 (BOb June 17 1971 p1. July 29 1971 pp8,9p).

Church All Saints' at King's Bromley is one of 19 such county dedications (of AP churches); 13th= oldest county church dating from 1120. Most notable thing in the church a stone book rest (a very rare feature) in N wall (LGS p155).

Cooper, Mary *Earliest noted beldam in Staffordshire.* Of King's Bromley, eldest of six living generations. Dr Plot in his

Mary Cooper, beldam, seated far left, and her descendants.

'The Natural History of Staffordshire' (1686) p322, noted she was not long dead, and assumed she must have been a very old woman. She could make the statement he had heard another beldam make: 'Rise up daughter, and goe to they daughter, for thy daughter's daughter hath a daughter'.

Cox, Mrs *King's Bromley's bravest.* Of Kings Bromley, a descendant of Mary Cooper, whose attempt to escape a fire at 60 Grosvenor Street, London, by letting herself down from a forth story window was described by newspaper reports as brave. She had lived in the families of Lord Vernon, the Countess of Jersey, Lord De Vesci, the Earl of Mansfield, the Earl of Wemyss, and the Earl and Countess of Delawarr. As she lay dying of injuries in Middlesex Hospital many enquiries from these families as to her state of health were received. She was buried on Feb 4 1897 (SA Feb 6 1897 p5 col 1).

Folklore *King's Bromley's best.* The coming of age celebrations on Christmas eve of Hugo, son of the medieval lord of King's Bromley, Sir Nigel Corbet, were infiltrated by a strange guest, apparently of noble birth. Finding the stranger cheated at dice, Hugo challenged him to a duel in the grounds, but was slain. His ghost - with sword pierced through his heart - haunted the spot every night until his father avenged the assailant, slaying him through his heart as he tried to escape to a foreign land. It is said Sir Nigel never smiled again, gave up his hunting and festivities, and pulled down the room where the gambling dispute had led to the fatal duel (King's Bromley: A History of the Church and Village. Rev NP Stevens, vicar in the 1950s).

Geology King's Bromley village (S) is Keuper Red Marls; King's Bromley village (N) and Trent plain is Alluvium.

Harold II *King's Bromley was his only Staffordshire possession.* As stated in DB. Harold Godwinson (c1022 –1066), King of England 1066; one of only two Kings of England to have died in battle (the other being Richard III).

Hills, Eileen *King's Bromley's saddest.* Aged 8 she was evacuated to King's Bromley from Margate, Kent, in June 1940 in WW2. She lost her foothold on Trent bank by the cattle bridge to the left of the Yoxall Road, less than 100 yards from the church in Nov 1940 and was swept down river. Her body was recovered 10 days later by PC Bains near to Alrewas Mills. Buried at King's Bromley but her

grave remained unmarked, until villagers led by Mr and Mrs Selby and Joyce Rawlinson, raised funds for a headstone placed on the W wall of the churchyard in 2001 (info King's Bromley Local History Society; Service of Remembrance sheet Sept 2 2001).

Hinckley, J *King's Bromley's longest serving vicar.* He served 1829-67, for 38 years.

Housing *'One of the most beautiful cottages in the county'* Manor Thatch, Manor Road, King's Bromley, according to Michael Raven in his 'A Guide to Staffordshire and the Black Country' (2004) p187 pl 34; Raven used a picture of it on the back cover of the first edition of the book (1989). 'The walls' he writes 'are white-washed and the thatched roof hangs low over the top windows. The gardens, too, are beautiful and a credit to their owner.'

Manor Thatch - 'One of the most beautiful cottages in the county'.

Lane, Jane *Most famous member of the Lane family of King's Bromley Manor.* She helped Charles II escape England, whilst he was a fugitive after the battle of Worcester, 1651 (STMSM Nov 1973 p27). On Sept 10 he famously accompanied her on the same horse from Bentley Hall, Staffordshire (the former seat of the Lanes), disguised as a tenant farmer's son under the alias 'William Jackson'. They were accompanied by Withy Petre (Jane Lane's sister), her husband John Petre, and Henry Lascelles, another related Royalist officer (Wikipedia, 2009). King's Bromley Manor estate passed to the Lanes by marriage in 1794. At the hall they proudly hung her portrait by Sir Peter Lely and displayed a letter from the king to her in a glass case. The hall also contained a portrait of Charles II by Lely.

Leofric *'wise for God and for the world', King's Bromley's most famous old worthy.* (d1057). Son of Ealdorman Leofwine of the Hwicce (died c1023). Founded monasteries at Coventry and Much Wenlock, married Lady Godiva. Earl of Mercia, by at least 1030s to his death. He held and died 'at a good old age' at King's Bromley. Thus described by the Anglo-Saxon Chronicle. Buried at Coventry (Wikipedia, 2009).

Lightwood, Richard *Strange but true!* His twin died of a rare heart condition whilst playing cricket in 1994. Twelve years later Richard died in exactly the same way, then aged 27, collapsing at Kings Bromley Cricket Club on Saturday Sept 11 2006 (BBC Midlands Today Sept 13 2006).

Mulholland, Paul Liam *King's Bromley's rogue.* (b1955). A former insulation lagger from the Manners Estate, Winshill; later a failed Burton tycoon and property developer. Bailiffs booted him out of his home King's Bromley Hall in Dec 2007, which sold for £1.6 million, £1 million less than its original value in a bid to recoup cash for his creditors. He was prosecuted in 2005 by the Dept for Business, Enterprise and Regulatory Reform - formerly Dept of DTI - for 'misappropriating' the 174,512.98 euros grant, which the EU gave to former Burton Albion main sponsor BI Industries (Holdings) Ltd. It is alleged that the money was transferred to the account of Burton-based Shobwood Engineering, another of Mulholland's failed firms, and then 'dissipated'. After moving from the hall Mulholland went to live only yards away in his former home in Manor Road. He was declared bankrupt in 2006 after 12 of his firms went under in 24 months, owing tax worth hundreds of thousands of pounds. He received a driving ban for refusing to give breath test specimen in Yoxall on March 4 2008 (Burton Mail March 4 2008 pp1,3. March 15 2008 p1pc. April 30 2008 pp1,3. June 24 2008 p2).

Place-name The first appearance of the name is 942 for Bromley, 1166 for Kings Bromley. Bromley means 'broom leah' whilst 'King's' refers to the holding of the manor by the king at Domesday and afterwards (PNSZ p153).

Population King's Bromley was 101st most-populated Staffordshire parish in 1801 with 454 people; 96th in 1811 with 527; 92nd in 1821 with 612; 94th in 1831 with 629; 90th in 1841 with 718; 90th in 1851 with 704; 93rd in 1861 with 646; 99th in 1871 with 582; 97th in 1881 with 580; 97th in 1891 with 568; 102nd in 1901 with 500. King's Bromley could be ranked 80th= worst-affected Staffordshire parish for loss of men in WW1, with 14 lives taken.

Quote *Choicest.* Mrs GH Anson of Catton Hall, Derbys, at the 29th annual King's Bromley Show, 1950, said King's Bromley was 'an ideal English village and a model of its kind' (SA July 29 1950 p7).

Riley, Mr JE *First to take over Echills Farm after it was used an aerodrome.* In 1941, farmer at Common Lane Farm. It was derelict. By 1954, when he was elected chairman of Staffordshire NFU, Mr Riley had Church Farm, Kings Bromley (SA Dec 31 1954 p8 col 8).

Shows *King's Bromley Show opened by an 'Archer'* In 1955, when Miss Lesley Saweard, alias Christine Archer (married George Barford in 1979) of 'The Archers' BBC Radio soap opera opened the 34th Kings Bromley Show (SA & Chron July 28 1955 p6 cols 8-9). *'country's biggest Thai festival outside London' to 2008* Sunday Aug 24 2008 at King's Bromley, with 5,000 people expected to attend, organised by the Buddhavihara Thai Buddist Temple based at Eastfields House, once part of the Earl of Lichfield's estate (E&S Aug 23 2008 p5).

Stubbings, Christopher *King's Bromley's villain.* Of King's Bromley, convicted of possession of pictures of child abuse taken from the internet, and sentenced to prison for an indefinite period in 2008, having amassed the largest collection of Level 5 (most explicit grade) pictures in Staffordshire to 2008, and was considered Number 2 in a worldwide on-line paedophile ring (BBC Midlands Today Nov 27 2008).

Ward, William Joseph *'probably the oldest newspaper delivery boy in the whole of the Midlands' 1956.* Born c1875. He was still cycling over 13 miles a day to deliver newspapers in the King's Bromley area in 1956 aged 81. However, this claim was subsequently challenged by William Lacey of Lichfield aged 85 delivering newspapers on foot from a shop in Dam Street (SA & Chron Nov 22 1956 p6 col 2).

WW2 *Readiest Staffordshire village for WW2* was King's Bromley, which had sent four men to serve in the forces by Sept 9 1939 - Mr A Barratt, formerly King's Own Yorkshire Light Infantry, Keith Brentnall, RAF, Mr F Johnson and Mr G Steward, both RAF Reserve. On 3 Sept the vicar preached a rallying sermon from the pulpit to fight for allied liberty and the liberty of ordinary Germans. In addition, A.R.P. arrangements were running smoothly and efficiently, two warning posts were being manned day and night, a first-aid point had been organised at the school, and political activities suspended - inauguration of a branch of the women's section of the Lichfield Conservative Association indefinitely postponed (SA Sept 9 1939 p7 col 6).

King's Bromley Hay King's Bromley Hays was Staffordshire's 137th largest parish (extra parochial), consisting of 1,000 acres; 84th farthest parish away from the county town, 12.9m ESE; extremist length 2m; extremist width 1.6m.

The first-known documentation of the hay is in 1292/3. The parish's chief settlement is the enormous Common Lane Farm. The parish is famous for some of it being personally gifted to a local man by Henry I when hunting in Cannock Forest.

L

Lichfield *Lichfield St Chad* was Staffordshire's 84th largest parish, consisting of 3,182 acres; 81st= closest parish to the county town, 12.8m SE; extremist length 2.9m; extremist width 2.4m. The chief settlement of the parish is the Stowe Hill area of Lichfield. The parish is famous for St Chad and his spring. *Lichfield St Mary* was Staffordshire's 166th largest/ 4th smallest parish, consisting of 58 acres; 67th= farthest parish away from the county town, 14.7m SE; extremist length 0.3m, making it 4th shortest parish in the county; extremist width 0.4m, making it 5th narrowest parish in the county. The chief settlement of the parish is Lichfield's commercial centre, round St Mary's church and the Market Place. It is famous for Dr Johnson and his birthplace, a house overlooking the Market Place. *Lichfield St Michael* was Staffordshire's 9th largest parish, consisting of 12,233 acres; 61st= closest parish to the county town, 10.3m SE; extremist length 3.9m; extremist width 7.5m, making it 5th= widest parish in the county. The chief settlements of the parish are Burntwood, Chasetown, Chase Terrace, Hammerwich; they all expanded at rapid rates in the C19 through mining. The parish is famous for The Roman settlement at Wall on Watling Street and Dr Johnson's school at Edial Hall. *Lichfield Friary* was Staffordshire's 168th largest/ 2nd smallest parish, consisting of 14 acres; 66th farthest parish away from the county town, 14.75m SE; extremist length 0.23m, making it 2nd= shortest parish in the county; extremist width 0.2m, making it 3rd narrowest parish in the county. The parish's chief settlement is the present Lichfield Library built as a girls' school in 1928. Although most of the Friary has long gone a fragment was built into this building.

Altitudes In *St Chad's parish* the highest point is 390 feet at Grange Hill Farm, and the lowest point is 226 feet by Curborough Brook. Most of the old city covering *St Mary's parish* lies below 300 feet (SHC 1950/ 1 pp139-140). The highest point of *St Michael's parish* is 653 feet on NW boundary of Burntwood, on Ironstone Road (in Hammerwich it is Speedwell windmill at 505 feet). The lowest point is 206 feet on Streethay boundary by Mare Brook (in Hammerwich it is 341 feet on Wall boundary by Black Brook).

Anglo-Saxon Lichfield *Earliest-known battle on Staffordshire soil.* 'Battle of Lichfield' fought near Wall in 650 AD between the Kingdom of Powys and King Penda, who was victorious (info Prof Philip Morgan, 2006).

Archery *British archery record highest championship score for Double Round.* 2254 achieved by Steven Hillard at Lichfield on Aug 8-9 1987 (GBR 1992 p224). *Under-16 British Archery Champion 1988.* Jamie Gillespie of Lichfield; he was also the only junior ever to take the Staffordshire under-18 indoor and outdoor titles and county adult outdoor title (LiMe Jan 6 1989 p60).

Ashmole, Elias *'the greatest virtuoso and curioso that ever was known or read of in England before his time'*, one of the 'Seven sons of Staffordshire'. Herald and immortalised in the fabric of Oxford's Ashmolean Museum, born in Priests' Hall by St Mary's church, 1617. Edited a work of the famous alchemist, Dr Dee (adding a treatise of his own) in 1650 (SA Dec 31 1949 p6 col 6. Jan 5 1952 p2 col 2) (Staffordshire Handbook c1966 p25). The *first keeper of the Ashmolean Museum* was Dr Robert Plot, secretary of the Royal Society and author of Natural History of Staffordshire, 1686.

Athletics *Only person ever to win four English Schools' Cross Country Championships.* Spencer Duval of Dam Street, Lichfield, born 1970; one being the English Schools Cross Country championships, March 1988 (becoming only the 2nd person in history to win the championships at all levels); the fourth being the Senior Boys' Race at the Hertford Championships in 1989 (LiMe Jan 6 1989 p60. March 10 1989 p72. July 14 1989 p72). *First Lichfield Dash* 1998, but no winner recorded. A race round the Cathedral Close. Subsequent winners are 1999 Carl Warren (Birchfield Harriers); 2000 Mark Anslow (Tipton Harriers); 2001 Anthony Jones (Tamworth AC); 2002 James Thie (Cardiff AC); 2003-06 Steve Blagdon (Lincoln Wellington AC), probable record-holder for fastest time; 2007 Chris Taylor (Hallamshire Harriers); 2008 James Trollope (Birchfield Harriers); 2009 Jimmy Watkins (Cardiff AC) (LiMe July 16 2009 p2). *First person with Down's Syndrome to complete the London Marathon.* Simon Beresford (b1967) of Lichfield in 2007 in 6 hours 15 mins 27 secs, raising over £10,000 for the Down's Syndrome Association (LiMe June 12 2008 p2pc).

Awards *National Cat Club best in show 1951, Midland Counties Cat Club Championship Show best long-haired cat 1951.* Champion Carreg Cracker, an orange-eyed white Persian belonging to Mrs D Herod of Muckley Corner (LiMe Oct 26 1951 p3 col 2. Dec 7 1951 p7p). *One of the best B&Bs in Britain* Old Rectory Cottage, 21 Gaia Lane, Lichfield (The Good Bed and Breakfast Guide: Over 1000 of the best B&Bs in Britain. 1990. p299). *UK's best large renovation project 2007.* Renovation of a former granary mill into the residence Leamonsley Manor, by DJ Construction (Staffs) Ltd of Rugeley in the Master Builder of the Year awards, completed in a year at a cost of £350,000 (Cannock & Lichfield E&S Nov 12 2007 p19p). *Best Small Company to Work For 2009.* Christians Against Poverty (CAP), a charity with a debt counselling centre in Burntwood; the award is sponsored by a national Sunday newspaper (LiMe March 5 2009 p19).

Ball, Mrs Elizabeth *Lichfield St Michael's kindest.* Spinster, of Castle Bromwich, Warws. The interest of her gift helped education in the various townships as well as the free school at Burntwood, erected in her lifetime; also some further payments were made to the poor of Hammerwich under her will.

Benson, Hon John R *First Staffordshirian to visit Pitcairn Island.* Sheriff of Lichfield 1933, son of Lord Charnwood of Stowe House, planned to visit the island on a round-the-world voyage on a 40-foot ketch, with two others, in 1938 (LiMe Aug 19 1938 p6 col 7).

Bowling *First Bowling League in the district.* One for Brownhills urban district based at the Sankey Working's Men's Club, Lichfield Road, Brownhills, founded 1943 and affiliated to the West Midland Branch Clubs Union (LiMe April 30 1943 p2 col 5).

Bridgeman, Miss Frances Evelyn *Lichfield's bravest (woman).* Second daughter of Cllr JH Bridgeman, who received a Distinguished Service Bar for devotion to duty and bravery controlling an out-of-control tractor as a Land Girls on Smithy Brow, Lancashire, awarded in late 1919 (SA Nov 1 1919 p9p).

Brockhurst, Cpl Edward *Brownhill's hero.* Of Church Street, Brownhills, who enlisted in South Staffs Regt in 1904. He was awarded the M.M. during the battle of Polygon Wood 3-6 Nov 1917. He was a keen footballer and before WW1 he played for Brownhills Albion. He played in the army and was captain of the team that won the army cup in France, he himself scoring the winning goal (ELSONSS pp97-98).

Brookes, Sergt Dennis *Hammerwich's hero.* Coldstream Guards, of 'Sundown', Hall Lane, Hammerwich, was awarded the Military Medal for 'magnificent personal courage and offensive spirit as platoon sergeant to his platoon' at the front of St Martin de Besaces on Aug 1 1944. He fought in hand to hand combat with the enemy, spraying the oncoming force with a Bren gun, so that it withdrew (LiMe Nov 17 1944 p3 col 4. March 15 1945 p2 col 5).

Businesses *Lichfield City's first new post-war factory.* Built on the Trent Valley Estate, the foundation stone for it was laid on Sept 9 1946, for the firm of Messrs Dolphin and Co Ltd, of Harborne, cabinet makers, wood machinists (LiMe Sept 13 1946 p7). *'one of the largest and most successful auction centres in the country' 1991.* Wintertons livestock auction centre of Lichfield. By 1991 pig sales had increased dramatically to nearly 27,000 making Wintertons 9th largest pig centre in the country and 3rd biggest in the Midlands (TH Jan 18 1991 p23).

Butler, John *Earliest person in Lichfield St Chad parish register.* Along with An

Hall, whom he married on April 26 1635. Also on the same day Joan, daughter of Thomas Hunt, buried.

Canals *Newest canal aqueduct in Staffordshire, perhaps in the country.* That carrying the Lichfield Canal over the M6 Toll Road, 2003 (Visit Lichfield 2006).

Carr, Mr LA *'an honour practically unknown in England'.* Of White House, Lichfield, a well-known naturalist in Staffs and Lincs, for having a genus named after him by Continental specialists, having discovered no fewer than three species of insect in Britain - 1) Carria Paradoxa, genus et sp., nov: teste. Prof Dr O Schmiedcknecht. 2) Exochus Carri, sp. nv, teste. Prof Dr O Schmiedcknecht. 3) Barichneumon Carri, sp. nv; teste. Prof H Habermehl (SA Feb 25 1922 p11 col 5 p).

CATHEDRAL & CLOSE Administration *Earliest surviving statutes for any English cathedral.* Lichfield; whose laws for its governance date from the late C12 (VCH vol 3 p142. vol 14 p9). *One of the last secular cathedrals to secure the right of electing its own dean.* Lichfield (English Secular Cathedrals. Edwards. p122) (VCH vol 3 p145 note). *Unique system in England for ministering to the cathedral parish.* Lichfield, where in medieval times prebendaries appointed stipendiary chaplains to minister to the parishes of Lichfield. *First Lichfield Diocesan Directory* Appeared in 1856 and was known as Lichfield Diocesan Church Calendar, published by F Crewe of Newcastle-under-Lyme; TG Lomax of Lichfield took over publication in 1877 (*First Diocesan Festival of Choirs at Lichfield Cathedral.* 1856 (SA Oct 11 1862 p7 col 1. SA & Chron Nov 1 1956 p4 col 3).

Bishop's Palace *First occupant of the bishop's house situated on the site of the present Bishop's Palace.* Probably Bishop Clinton (Friends of Lichfield Cathedral 69th annual report, 2006). *One of Christopher Wren's best masons.* Edward Pierce, architect, who built the present palace, 1687 (BOE p188) (SSAHST 1985-86 pp57-63).

Broadcasts *First service broadcast from Lichfield Cathedral* was that on Sunday Nov 7 1937. The Bishop of Lichfield took as his subject 'I believe in the Communion of Saints' (SA Nov 13 1937 p10 col 6). *First broadcast of Evensong from Lichfield Cathedral* was on Wednesday afternoon May 10 1939, when apparently the service took the place of the usual mid-weekly service from St Paul's Cathedral, London.

Rev D Stuart-Fox intoned the prayers. Lessons were read by Canons Hammond and Stockley (LiMe May 12 1939 p6 col 4). *A.B.C. T.V.'s 1000th outside broadcast* was from Lichfield Cathedral, 1964 (TH Dec 11 1964 p11 cols 1-3).

Gatherings in the Cathedral *Place where the Order of the Garter was envisaged.* Possibly at The Hastiludes in Lichfield Cathedral in April 1348 attended by Edward III. In July 1348 he ordered the building of St George's chapel, Windsor - the chapel of the Companionship of the Order of the Garter, and it is possible he conceived the Order when at Lichfield (LTM March April 1972 p28). *First annual gathering of Anglo-Catholics in Lichfield Diocese.* Took place at Lichfield Cathedral on July 18 1929, with upwards of 200 people attending (LiMe July 19 1929 p5 col 4).

Lichfield Cathedral 's west front in the 19th century

Close, The *Staffordshire's earliest known school.* A song school attached to Lichfield Cathedral, c1190 (HOS 1998 p130). *First bishop buried in the Close after the Norman Conquest.* Bishop Muschamp (d1208) (VCH vol 14 p9). *Probably one of the best surviving examples in England of what a cathedral close would have looked like in the middle ages.* Lichfield Cathedral Close, 2006. *Fifth or sixth largest bishop's palace in England c1315* was that at Lichfield. *Last recorded time someone took sanctuary in the Close* was in 1532, for a thief; but he was found in one of the Canons' houses and since sanctuary was only granted in the cathedral or graveyard, he was able to be arrested (MCC). *First Parliamentary suc-*

cess of the Civil War in Staffordshire was the capture of the Close March 5 1643 (HOS 1998 p73). *Last watchman of the Close.* Albert Haycock, who held the office until his death in 1956. When aged 71 and he had been in post 40 years, never taking a holiday, and only having a few days off for illness, he had his photograph taken for a newspaper; which cutting appears in Wilks' Scrapbook, WSL D1863, vol 2, p41. *St Chad's Cathedral Choir School's first Foundation Scholarship.* The Bostock Scholarship, in memory of Henry John Bostock (1871-1957) of Stafford, CBE, founded Feb 1959, whereby the head chorister receives an increased grant during his education at the school; the school was founded in 1942 (LiMe Feb 27 1959 p3). *St Chad's Cathedral Choir School's first headgirl.* Vanessa Hibbs (b1969) of Radford Rise, Stafford, from Sept 1980 (SN July 25 1980 p5p, the report says the school is one of the country's top preparatory schools). *Last conduit in the Close* worked to 1969 (VCH vol 14 p96). *Sandford Award winner 1991 (for excellence in Heritage education), 1996.* Lichfield Cathedral Visitors' Study Centre (Friends of Lichfield Cathedral 69th annual report, 2006 p35).

Exterior of the Cathedral. The Cathedral Church is dedicated to St Mary and St Chad. *Earliest and principal cathedral of the Mercians.* Lichfield cathedral (PNSZ p11) (MR2 p198; the 'Cathedral of all Mercia'). *Unique among English cathedrals.* Lichfield cathedral because it has three spires, and because it lies beside a pool (BOE pp21,174). *England's smallest cathedral 1953.* Lichfield (SA Jan 23 1953 p4 col 4). *'the cathedral's most spectacular architectural feature'.* The West Front, according to Henry Thorold. It was built from c1280 in red sandstone, and is adorned with a wealth of statues and arcading, of trefoils, quatrefoils, cinquefails; at the centre a geometrical window, at the base three sumptuously carved porches (BOE p179) (SGS p118). *'triumphant ladies of the vale'.* Reference to the three spires of Lichfield cathedral by Francis Mundy in his poem Needwood Forest 1776. *'one of the finest and most beautiful (cathedrals) in England'.* Daniel Defoe on Lichfield (VCH vol 14 p3). *'the building equals any in England for elegance and grace'.* Messrs Hutchinson in their '1,001 Wonderful Things' (1935 ed), taking into account the three spires and the rich and tasteful decoration of the facades (SA July 13 1935 p11

col 1). *First siege of Lichfield Cathedral (royal) garrison in the Civil War* began on 2 March 1643. *Last royalist Civil War garrison in Staffordshire to surrender and one of the last in the country.* Lichfield Cathedral, July 10 1646 (VCH vol 14 p18).

Interior of the Cathedral *Oldest part of the present cathedral.* The Consistory Court, with above, the Chapel of St Chad's Head, dating from c1200-20 (BOE p175). *Most beautiful glass in England* is that of c1540 in the Lady Chapel from Herckenrode Abbey, nr Hasselt, nr Liege, Belgium (KES p134). *'still the most popular monument in the cathedral' 1974.* 'The Sleeping Children' or 'Snowdrop' monument in the

Lichfield Cathedral's most popular monument: Chantrey's 'The Sleeping Children'.

S choir aisle at the E end, to Misses Robinson, according to Pevsner; here, says Masefield, 'pathos is indeed perfectly free from sentimentality'. The white marble figures on a chest tomb are of the children of Prebendary William Robinson, sleeping; they died in a fire in 1812. It was one of the earliest works of sculptor, Sir Francis Chantrey, completed 1814, and firmly established his fame. It was inspired by T Banks' sculpture of Sir Brooke Boothby's daughters, of 1791, in Ashbourne parish church (AAD p66) (W pp498-499) (LGS p173) (SOSH p302) (BOE p185) (BCGB pp379-380) (COS p45p). *'A masterpiece of High Victorian Art'.* Pulpit and chancel screen by Gilbert Scot and Francis Skidmore (Staffordshire County Guide 2006/7 p74). *Thomas Scheemakers' only monumental sculpture in Staffordshire.* That to Lady Mary Wortley Montagu (d1789) (BOE p33). *Probably oldest surviving pieces of dramatic literature in English* are excerpts known as 'The Lichfield Fragments', were produced at the cathedral c1430. *James Wyatt's first plans for a cathedral restoration carried out.* Lichfield, 1788-95; the architect was from Weeford. *'one of the finest and most complete medieval examples to have survived' of late C13 floor tiles.* Discovered behind bookcases in the library at the cathedral, 1992 (CL April 30 1992 p75pcs). *First grant awarded by the Staffordshire Environmental Fund.* £88,500 for the creation of a Chapel of Prayer and storage space within the Cathedral, made in 1998, towards the total cost of the project £118,000; the Fund was created in 1997 (info Staffs Environmental Fund).

Parish of Lichfield Cathedral and Close was Staffordshire's 167th largest/ 3rd smallest parish, consisting of 16 acres; 69th farthest parish away from the county town, 14.6m SE; extremist length 0.23m, making it 2nd= shortest parish in the county; extremist width 0.2m, making it equal narrowest parish in the county. The earliest appearance of a Staffordshire parish name is the 4th century for Lichfield. The chief thing is the Cathedral, famed for its three spires, whilst the Close is famous for being a classic medieval/ Georgian-looking cathedral close. For the fact that the Cathedral had been struck by lightning more often than most cathedrals see Alrewas.

Population The Cathedral and Close was 132nd most-populated Staffordshire parish in 1801 with 200 people; 132nd in 1811 with 241 people; 135th in 1821 with 220; 132nd in 1831 with 247; 138th in 1841 with 190; 133rd in 1851 with 246; 135th in 1861 with 235; 133rd in 1871 with 251; 133rd in 1881 with 232; 137th in 1891 with 212; 131st in 1901 with 249.

Cecilia _____? *Lichfield prostitute who bedded the most royals.* She boasted 'she had made six royals during the visit of the duke of Clarence and had been known fourteen times by day and night by members of the duke's household, 1460s (SHC 1999 p79).

Chad *First Bishop of Mercia to reside at Lichfield, 5th bishop of Lichfield since Diuma, 'most gentle and kindly man by repute'.* Northumbrian Benedictine monk, serving as first bishop from 669 to his death in 672 (Staffordshire Handbook c1966 p15).

CHURCHES Christ Church Junction of Church Road and Farewell Lane, Burntwood, was built 1819-20. *Notable memorial* To Rifleman David Walker of The Royal Green Jackets killed in Belfast 12 July 1971, the emblem of The Royal Green Jackets is in stain glass in one of the doors.

Primitive Methodist Chapel George Lane, Lichfield. *Staffordshire's place of worship which had to wait longest for its first marriage.* Perhaps this chapel erected 1847, which did not have a marriage solemnised in it until 1920 when Elisie

Elizabeth Dale of Leomansley and Ernest William Matthews of Swinfen, superintendent of the Sunday School married there on March 17 1920 (SA March 20 1920 p8 col 3).

St Anne Church Street, Chasetown, was built in 1865. *First church in the country to be lit by electricity.* Reputedly, St Anne's. It had its supply from nearby The Fly pit in 1883; the device installed in 1938 to make the church bell ring electrically is also claimed to be the first in the country (LiMe Oct 15 1886 p5) (BCM vol 9 No. 3 pp5-57) (VCH vol 14 p222).

St Chad St Chad's Road by Stowe Pool is one of 4 such county dedications (of AP churches); 61st= oldest AP county church dating from the C13 or roughly 1250. *England's oldest bell* No. 4 bell at St Chad's, discovered c1886, but remained undated until 1926, when it was believed to date to 1033, or another authority has dated it to 1255. The Saxon inscription on the bell reads - 'O-A BE-1 M-R-A PR" which has been translated as 'ORA BEATA MARIA PRO NOBIS (Pray Blessed Mary for us) (LiMe April 23 1926 p5. Aug 29 1947 p5 col 3). *Staffordshire's oldest church bell* Charles Lynam in his Church Bells of Staffordshire 1889 thought the bell dated to the mid C13, which would make it one of the earliest bells in England (Lynam pviii). But it bears no date or an identifiable founder's mark, and he based his conclusions on its unique character (SA July 17 1953 p4 col 4).

St John *Last stained glass window by John Piper.* That in the E window of St John's Hospital chapel, St John's Street, erected in 1984, and depicting Christ in majesty. It was paid for out of a bequest of Samuel Hayes, a resident of the hospital, and by hospital trustees (VCH vol 14 p153) (additional info).

St John the Baptist On the west side of Green Lane, Wall, built 1843. *First use of electric light for church service at Wall* Sunday evening service on July 19 1936 (LiMe July 24 1936 p6 col 4).

St Mary Market Place, Lichfield. Is one of 23 such county dedications (most common dedication in the county); 44th last AP county church built dating from 1717.

St Michael Church Street, Greenhill, Lichfield, is one of 12 such county dedications (of AP churches); 61st= oldest AP county church dating from the C13 or roughly 1250. *Most interesting memorials* An early C13 effigy of a Civilian praying (BOE p190). In c1800 two incised slabs with effigies near the entrance into the chancel were noted: 1) Thomas Streethay (d1521) and his wife Elizabeth (d1500), under the man are five sons, under the woman are four daughters, 2) John Streethay (d1523) and his wife Anna (d1534) (SHOS vol 1 pp338-339) (HOL p518). *One of the biggest churchyards in England.* St Michael's, Lichfield (Staffordshire: Shire County Guide. Peter Heaton. 1986).

Chadwick, Ruth Felicity *Most GCE exams passed whilst at school.* Born Birmingham 1951; living in Lichfield in 1970, 17 'O' Levels and 6 'A' Levels, totalling 23 between summer 1966 and summer 1969 (GBR 1970 p219).

Chichester, Arthur *Lichfield St Michael's most famous old worthy.* (1739-99). Most famous resident of the most famous country house in St Michael's parish, Fisherwick Hall. 5th Earl of Donegal; Baron Fisherwick 1790; Earl of Belfast and Marquess of Donegal 1791. He bought Fisherwick 1761, rebuilt the hall and remodelled the park.

Claims for the city *Staffordshire's first town made a city, or incorporated.* Lichfield. *Daniel Defoe's best town in Staffordshire.* Lichfield, which he is believed to have visited by 1723. *The administrative centre of England.* It was suggested by Monsignor Ronald Knox in WW2 that after the war Britain should reorganise on United States lines, make Lichfield the administrative centre and London the commercial centre. His views were aired in the 'Sunday Express' in 1941. The Mayor of the time CH Averill, thought '... Lichfield is the right place. We *speak the purest English*, we are historically and architecturally suitable to take over the traditions of England' (LiMe March 21 1941 p6 cols 6-7). *Staffordshire's premier heritage city.* Lichfield (Staffordshire Breaks 2006. Staffordshire Tourism). *'one of the most desirable places to live' 2004.* Lichfield, in a survey by Halifax Building Society, 2004 (BBC news Oct 2004).

Clinton, Bishop Roger de *39th and most famous bishop of Lichfield*, serving 1129-48. Died 1148. He created Lichfield town on a grid pattern; he fortified the Close; added to the Cathedral; reorganised its clergy as a secular chapter c1130s; founded many of its prebends, the hospital of St John at Lichfield, and Farewell Priory. He reputedly died on a Crusade.

Clum, Mary *Staffordshire's oldest woman ever.* Of Lichfield, who lived to 138, later C18 (WOb Dec 3 1887 - Annals of Walsall).

Collins, Pte SC *Lichfield St Chad's hero.* Of the Royal Artillery, of No. 21 Wheel Lane, awarded the M.M. in 1941 for his bravery at Dunkirk in keeping his guns in action again low-flying aircraft. 'Collins was untiring in his efforts, and as first-aid orderly to the troops he assisted in attending to wounded men under heavy shellfire on several occasions (LiMe March 28 1941 p3 col 4).

Community Centres *'one of the best (community centres) in Staffordshire'.* The Centre, which opened on Sept 17 1953 with the conversion of an R.A.F. dining hall, on the Curborough housing estate. It was Lichfield's first community centre (LiMe Sept 25 1953 p4).

Cooper, Sir Richard Ashmole *Kindest person of Lichfield Friary.* (1874-1946). Bart. Son of Sir Richard Cooper (d1913), 1st Bart of Shenstone (created 1905). In 1920, following his late father's wishes, he purchased the Friary estate and then donated it to the City of Lichfield, to help relieve traffic congestion. In 1928 he supplemented the gift with £6,650 to defray the cost to the city of the new arterial roads through the estate (LiMe March 8 1946 p7 col 6).

Country houses *'Most disastrous school in Britain'.* Dr Johnson's academy at Edial Hall, which ran from spring 1736 to Feb 1737, having only had three pupils - David and George Garrick, and Lawrence Offley (BBC Stoke & Staffordshire Where I Live website, 2006). *'One of the stongest-built houses in the kingdom'.* Stebbing Shaw considered Elmhurst Hall was; it was demolished in 1804 (SHOS vol 1 p351).

Cricket *Staffordshire's longest running 20-over (knockout) competition 2009* Probably Lichfield's CC's Chauntry Cup, inaugurated 1936 with Pelsall CC winning, scoring 86 over Burntwood MH CC's 50 (LiMe March 5 2009 pp92-93).

Crow, Benjamin *British Army's tallest soldier.* He signed on at Lichfield, Nov 1947, seven feet one inch tall (GBR 1980 p185).

Curtis, George *Chasetown's 'Jack the Ripper'.* American, so described when aged 30 charged before the bench at Brownhills with vagrancy at Chase Town on Oct 9 1888. He was in the High Street about 10pm the previous night wearing a black mask and declaring he was 'Jack the Ripper'. Several people were alarmed at his behaviour. He is believed to have been an inmate of Dudley Workhouse, subsequently earning his living 'tumbling' in public houses, carrying with him a live cat. On promising to leave the neighbourhood he was discharged (SA Oct 13 1888 p6 col 7).

Cycling *'pioneer of cycling, not only in the Midlands, but throughout the world'*, *'father of cycling'* John Urry (d1927/8) of Lichfield City Cycling and Athletic Club (LiMe Jan 27 1928 pp col 1). His son Francis John Urry (1879-1956), founded the Centenary Club, to mark the centenary of the bicycle, and was elected its first president in 1938 (Evening Despatch June 2 1956 photo). *First Lichfield-Newport (Salop)-Lichfield and Back race cyclists* Messrs C Lord and Angrave in 1930; C Lord won with 2 hours 49 mins. This record was beaten by L Hanslow with 2 hours 31 mins 11 3-5 seconds in 1933 (LiMe Oct 20 1933 p10 col 3). *Olympic team pursuit cycling gold medalists 2008*. Paul Manning of Burntwood, captaining his fellow team members Ed Clancy, Geraint Thomas, and Bradley Wiggins (BBC Midlands Today Aug 18 2008).

Darwin, Eramus *First person to "fully understand and explain the process of photosynthesis in plants, and the first to describe the formation of clouds"* (1731-1802). Physician and botanist. By 1758 he was occupying a house on the W side of the Close, now known as 'Darwin's House' (TB June 26 2008 p13).

Dickin, Rifleman Leslie *Possibly Staffordshire's last combat death in Europe in WW2*. Of Walsall Road, Muckley Corner, 6th Airborne Division, killed in action over the Rhine on April 2 1945 (SA April 28 1945 p4 col 8).

Dillon, Siobhan *3rd in 'How Do you Solve a Problem like Maria?'* When aged 21, a fashion student of Lichfield, in BBC's talent contest to win the part of Maria in a West End production of 'The Sound of Music', Sept 16 2006.

Diuma *First known bishop of Lichfield.* Enthroned after 655.

Emery, Albert Eric *Boney Hay's unluckiest.* Of 218 Chorley Road. When aged 17 killed by lightning whilst playing football with friends on Gentleshaw Common on Aug 21 1939. A direct bolt of lightning struck his head and split his cap to pieces (LiMe Aug 25 1939 p4 col 5).

Endeavours *'most modern car washing by' in Midlands 1960*. Messrs JT Leavesley (Lichfield) Ltd, Beacon Street, Lichfield, at cost of over £3,000, and in-

cluded a Victoria automatic gantry washer made by Laycock Engineering Ltd, Sheffield (LiMe June 3 1960 p4ps). *World's biggest curry.* A 10-tonne chicken tikka masala made by Abdul Salam, originally from Bangladesh, of the Eastern Eye restaurant, Lichfield, with dozens of helpers in July 2005. The curry was made in a 36 feet long stainless steel vessel at Beacon Park, for the Lichfield Arts Festival. It had it in six tonnes of vegetables and chicken, one tonne of spices, two tonnes of water and one tonne of oil and batter, and was sold to raise funds for a Bangladeshi charity. This beat his own record for a 3.1 tonne curry, set in 2000. In 1999 Salam won the UK Curry Chef of the year contest (Birmingham Sunday Mercury July 17 2005 p9) (GBR).

An imaginery scene of the World's biggest curry made by a Lichfield restaurant.

Endurance *World record for fastest frankfurter eating.* Reg Morris who ate 30 frankfurters in 64 seconds at Burntwood in Dec 1986 (GBR 1999 p60). *World record for flame exhalation.* Reg Morris who blew from his mouth fire 31 feet at the Miner's Rest Inn, Chasetown, on Oct 29 1986 (GBR 1992 p75). *Racing pigeon who flew across the Channel 26 times.* 'The Marquis' alias 'Top Box', owned by Billy Higgs of Burntwood. The bird is thought to have set the local record, his photograph and that of his hen 'Naomi' hung on a wall at the West Cannock Inn (CAd March 2 1984 p4). *World record for longest time on air as a disc jockey.* Roy Broke Sandbrook, presenting a show on Streaming Radio at Lichfield for 122 hours Nov 2004 (BBC 1 Midlands Today Nov 23 2004).

Events and festivals *'first of its kind in the Midlands'.* The Lichfield Festival of Music and Drama, when it first took place Sept 10-22 1951, organised by the Garrick Theatre (founded 1949), with performances staged at the Cathedral and at the Garrick, allowing the theatre to claim it was the first theatre in the country to have founded a festival within two and half years of its inception (LiMe Aug 17 1951 p7 col 1). *Lichfield's first Walk of Witness.* Took place on the evening of Good Friday March 27 1959, the route covered by Anglican and Free Churches of the city, was from the Market Place to the Friary, and then to the Cathedral (LiMe April 3 1959 p1ps). *Strange but true!* On May 30 1983 Andy Rawson landlord of Nelson Inn, Cresswell Green, left to become a leisure balloon pilot. Exactly 25 years later to the day the wind took his Wickers World balloon from Shugborough to land near the Triangle Inn, junction of Boney Hay and Highfield Roads, Burntwood, a mile SW of Nelson Inn (E&S May 31 2008 p4pc). *UK's biggest free County & Western Festival.* The Blue Rodeo Festival at Lichfield, Aug 10-11 2002 (BBC Midlands Today Aug 10-11 2002). *Only the 2nd Speakers' Corner to be created outside London.* That in Dam Street, Lichfield, opened on about May 6 2009 (E&S may 7 2009 p13pc).

Farming *'one of the finest herds (of pigs) not only in this country but in the whole world'.* Herd of pigs at Manor Farm, Wall, founded by the Ryman family in c1910. In 1950 the herd numbered 350-400, 320 of which were then Clun ewes, and about 50 head of polled Irish bullocks (SA Aug 27 1949 p2) (SLM Feb 1950 p107p). In 1951 Mr WJ Ryman was described as 'one of the best known breeders in Britain of Large White pigs'. Between 1929-53 the herd had won 227 championships, 132 reserve championships, 488 first prizes, and 249 seconds (LiMe Dec 7 1951 p3 col 5. Aug 14 1953 p8 col 3). *First stables of the South Staffordshire Hunt.* Moat Bank House, Wall Lane, Wall.

Firefighting *Staffordshire Extrication Challenge winners 2008, 2009.* Lichfield Fire Fighters (E&S April 30 2009 p9pc).

Folklore *St Chad's parish's best.* There are several legends associated with Stowe House, a Georgian property on Stowe Hill by Stowe Pool. That Selwyn House was deliberately built, across Stowe Pool, to spoil it's view of the Cathedral; and that here after 1770 Thomas Day attempted, unsuccessfully, to educate a foundling girl

Thomas Day. It was at Stowe House in Lichfield he tried unsuccessfully to educate a foundling girl on Rousseausque lines.

on Rousseausque lines in the hope of turning her into a perfect wife for himself. *St Mary's parish's best.* A real event which has become legendary is that in the Civil War on March 2 1643, a mute from a local royalist family, John 'Dumb' Dyott of Freeford, shot dead parliamentarian leader, Lord Brooke, standing outside a house in Dam Street. He was some 200 yards away from where Dyott was on the central tower of the Cathedral in the royalist garrison in the Close. The house in Dam Street has become known as Brooke House, and the event is alluded to in Walter Scott's epic poem 'Marmion'. *St Michael's parish's best.* According to tradition in c286 AD St Amphihalus after the death of his spiritual pupil or teacher, St Alban, left Verulam (St Albans) and fled along Watling Street until he came to the Lichfield area where he held weekly Christian seminars. During his reign 284-305 Emperor Diocletian decreed their execution. It was carried out by a Roman legion, under Maximian. Various

Followers of St Amphihalus were traditionally massacred by the Romans at Lichfield.

sites have been given for the massacre, St Michael's churchyard, and Borrowcop Hill. The number massacred is said to have been 999 or 1000 Christians.

Football *Lowest ranked club to reach 3rd round of the FA Cup final.* Chasetown FC (British Gas League Midland Division One - four divisions below the Football League) when they beat Port Vale 1-0 at Chasetown on Dec 11 2007. In the 4th round (Jan 5 2008) they lost at home 3-1 to Cardiff - 153 places ahead of them in the League! Even then Chasetown led for 45 minutes, scoring the first goal; the Scholars Ground had a record 2,420 spectators (BBC Midlands Today Dec 12 2007. Jan 7 2008) (The Sunday Telegraph Jan 6 2008 Sport p5). *Minute Maid under-13s Schools Cup winners (girls football) 2008.* The Friary School, Lichfield beating Frances Bardsley School, Romford, 3-2 (LiMe May 22 2008 p112).

Garrick, David *One of the 'Seven sons of Staffordshire'.* (1716-1779). Actor. Born Hereford. Spent the first 20 years of his life in a house in Beacon Street, Lichfield, which was pulled down in 1856 and the probate court built on the site. He accompanied Dr Johnson to London (Staffordshire Handbook c1966 p25). *His stage debut* was as Sergeant Kite in Farquhar's 'The Recruiting Officer' at the Bishop's Palace, 1727, when aged 10 (VCH vol 14 p165).

Gibbs, Lieut *Staffordshire's first decorated pilot*. Of Chasetown. Former pupil of Walsall Grammar School, of the S. Staffs Regt and Royal Flying Corps awarded the Military Cross on Sept 27 1917 'for conspicuous gallantry in attacking enemy aircraft and engaging hostile troops from the ground. He has in all driven down five enemy machines, which were destroyed, and one other completely out of control. He has also attacked and silenced a hostile battery with machine-gun fire, displaying on every occasion the same dash and determined offensive spirit.' He gained his pilot's certificate in the RFC in Oct 1916 (SA Jan 19 1918 p3 col 5p).

Gledhill, Rev Jonathan *105th bishop of Lichfield since Diuma, believed the execution of Saddam Hussein to have been 'just'*. In his belief about the execution he caused national controversy. Saddam Hussein was hung in Dec 2006 (LiMe Jan 4 2007 p1. Jan 11 2007 p10).

Geology The Curborough and Elmhurst areas are entirely Keuper Marls. The central Lichfield area is Bunter (S fringe), Keuper Sandstones (City and Cathedral), Keuper Marls (N). Burntwood is Middle Coal Measures (W), Keuper Sandstones (rest); that of west Hammerwich is Middle Coal Measures; that of Hammerwich village and the rest is Keuper Sandstones. Pipehill and Wall township is entirely Keuper Sandstones. Streethay township is Keuper Marls (Streethay village and N), Keuper Sandstones (S fringe).

Gregory, William *Earliest person in Hammerwich parish register*. Along with Dorothy Billing of Lichfield who he married on Nov 7 1724.

Griffiths, Sandra *Burntwood's villainess*. Born 1957. Of Thorpe Ave, Burntwood, who fraudulently collected charity money from the general public in pubs and clubs in Penkridge and Rugeley, between July 1998 and Jan 2007, and collected money using false ID for the Staffordshire Air Ambulance Service between Jan and March 2007, only part of which she handed to the Service. She was sentenced to 20 weeks prison in 2008 (SN Sept 4 2008 p9).

Guise, Sergt Alan George *Burntwood's hero*. Of the Rifle Brigade of Cannock Road, Burntwood, awarded a D.C.M. for gallantry in action at the battle of Knightsbridge, Africa, on June 14 1942. He was also mentioned in despatches and awarded the Oak Leaves for gallant conduct on Jan 25 1945, for going to the rescue of a comrade seriously injured by a mine explosion on Symi island, in the Dodecanese (LiMe March 29 1946 p3p).

Headquarters *UK centre of the Mormons 1972-77* Lichfield (info Catherine Cartwright. Jack Leighton Seminar, Keele University. 2009). *National home in 2008 of the National Dance Teachers' Association (NDTA, 1988)* Lichfield. *National home in 2008 of the Institute of Leadership & Management (ILM, 1947)* Stowe House, Netherstowe. In 2008 Brooke House, 24 Dam Street, Lichfield was the *national home of the Institute of Automotive Engineer Assessors* (IAEA, 1932); *Institute of Science Technology* (IST, 1954); *Institute of Management Services* (IMS, 1978). Whilst 33 Market Street was the national home of the Motor Vehicle Dismantlers Association of Great Britain (MVDA, 1943). The *National home of the Guild of Straw Craftsmen (1989)* was at No. 82 Manor Rise, Chasetown, in 2008.

Herbert, Terry *He found 'The Staffordshire Hoard' - the biggest Anglo-Saxon hoard ever found 2009*. Born c1954. Of of Scott Way, Burntwood. Member of Bloxwich Metal Detector Group. The discovery, made whilst metal detecting in July 2009, just off the A5 near Brownhills, will apparently make Herbert very rich (The Daily Telegraph. Sept 25 2009 p7pc).

Hiskins, Hubert Campbell *'One of Lichfield's greatest pioneers in the local business world' 1910-60*. (1885-1960). Of 'Overdale' Nether Beacon, Lichfield, coach builder and later customised motor production and retail (LiMe April 29 1960 p2 col 7).

Hodgkins, John *Earliest person in Lichfield Cathedral parish register*. Along with Catherine Woodward whom he married on 5 July 1665.

Housing *Lichfield's worst C19 slums*. Probably by the end of the century the triangle of houses at Greenhill (Church Street, Greenhill, Bower Court, Rotten Row) earmarked for clearance in the 1930s, when labelled 'Lichfield 's biggest slum clearance scheme' (LiMe May 8 1936 p6. April 23 1939 p5 col 1). *Lichfield City Council's 500th Post-war house*. No.

17 Friday Acre, Stowe, which was opened by Julian Snow MP on April 8 1953 (SA April 3 1953 p1). *Lichfield RDC house 1,000th Post-war house*. No. 8 Birch Ave, on the Oakdene Estate, Chasetown, a semi-detached property, completed early May 1953 (SA May 8 1953 p6 cols 3-4). *Lichfield City's first house to be occupied under the overspill agreement with Birmingham City*. No. 3 Windmill Lane, on the Wheel Lane estate, to be occupied by Mr & Mrs SJ Facer and family of California, Birmingham, who were ceremonial handed the key on Sept 25 1957 (LiMe Sept 27 1957 p6). *Lichfield City's first block of flats*. A five-storey building in Dimbles Lane, on the Wheel Lane estate, officially opened on afternoon of Dec 10 1959. The first tenants were a Mr & Mrs TJ Derry (LiMe Nov 27 1959 p5. Dec 11 1959 p1p. Dec 18 1959 p3 col 5). *One of the largest private housing estates in the country and among the top 10 in Europe mid 1980s*. Boley Park, begun by the late 1970s (LiMe Nov 28 1986 p3) (VCH vol 14 p35).

Hubbard, Nick *Made Hazel's Blears' brooch*. Jeweller of Hubbard Jewellery in Burntwood. When Hazel Blears resigned as Communities Secretary in the Labour Government in June 2009 she famously wore a brooch made by his company. It bore the inscription 'Rocking The Boat', said to be a rallying cry to others unhappy with Gordon Brown, P.M. to resign from the Cabinet, to bring about his downfall (E&S June 9 2009 p13p).

Hurst, Dr James Edgar *'Pioneer in the casting of metals and invented his own well-known method of centri-fugal casting'*. (1894-1959), CBE, of 'Tregonatha', Gaia Lane, metallurgist, Stubbs Medalist and EJ Fox Medalist; Sheriff of Lichfield 1945-46; Master of the Worshipful Company of Smiths 1953- (LiMe June 26 1959 p1 col 1).

Jerrard, Lieut Alan *First member of the Staffordshire Territorial Association to gain a V.C*. (1897-1968). Of Sutton Coldfield. He originally joined the 5th South Staffords (Territorial) Regt, before transferring to the RAF. He was the son of the headmaster of Bishop Vesey Grammar School, Sutton Coldfield (SA Jan 18 1919 p4 col 6).

Johnson, Malcolm *6th in National Town Criers' Championship 1955*. Lichfield's Town Crier and Sword Bearer (LiMe Aug 26 1955 p7 col 5).

Johnson, Norman *Lichfield St Chad's bravest*. Of 91 Gaia Lane was on a stroll round Stowe Pool on August Bank Holiday Monday 1960 when he heard cries for help from the water. Using an umbrella found on the bank side he waded out to help save a father and son from drowning; the pair were visiting Lichfield for the day and were going to attend evensong at the Cathedral (LiMe Aug 5 1960 p5 col 1).

JOHNSON, DR SAMUEL General *One of the 'Seven sons of Staffordshire', 'Ursa Major', Staffordshire's most famous old worthy, Lichfield St Mary's most famous old worthy*. Lexicographer. He was born in a house in the Market Place, 1709; St Mary's parish register records his baptism. England's greatest 18th Century literary figure, producing 'Dictionary of the English Language' (1755). He left for London in 1737. Died 1784 (Staffordshire Handbook c1966 p25), Ursa Major was his alias (SLM Winter 1954 pp9,26). *'landmark in English literary history'* (Michael Greenslade in HOS 1998 p20), *first English dictionary* was his dictionary compiled 1747-55 (Staffordshire Breaks 2006. Staffordshire Tourism). *Anne Oliver's best pupil*. Johnson who attended her dame school (Young Samuel Johnson. James L Clifford. 1955 1962 ed. pp23,42,107). *His first love* was Ann Hector (1711-88), daughter of Edmund Hector. *His first desire on revisiting Lichfield* was to see a certain willow tree on the N side of Minster Pool. *Johnson's favoured Lichfield inn*. The Three Crowns, Breadmarket Street, which he called a 'good old-fashioned inn'. Here he and Boswell stayed on

David Garrick and Samuel Johnson leave for London on March 2 1737.

their visits to the city (SA Feb 18 1947 p5 col 7). *First to bring a copy of Fanny Burney's novel 'Evelina' (1778) to Lichfield*. Johnson. *'the most sober, decent people in England, the genteelest in proportion to their wealth, and spoke the purest English'*. Johnson on his fellow Lichfield citizens, March 23 1776. *When the Johnson Museum was debated in the House of Commons.* On Feb 26 1960 by Julian Snow, MP for Lichfield, in his attempt to initiate a major debate asking for more Government help for the fine arts (LiMe March 4 1960 p3 cols 1-2).

Johnson Societies *First invitation of ladies to Johnson Society annual Supper.* Sept 1939, but the meal was cancelled due to the declaration of war. By tradition the supper has to take place by candlelight (LiMe July 28 1939 p2 col 4) (SA Sept 21 1951 p5). *National home of the Johnson Society.* Johnson's birthplace museum. *First televisation of the Johnson Supper.* 20th Sept 1952 (LiMe Sept 26 1952 p5 col 1). *Largest attendance at the Johnson Supper by 1972.* A record attendance in 1972 (Lichfield & Tamworth Magazine Oct 1972 p37). *First woman president of the Johnson Society.* Miss Mary Lascelles of Somerville College, Oxford, who held office elected in 1951 (LiMe Feb 23 1951 p5 col 5). *First joint meeting of the Johnson Society (of London) and the Staffordshire Society.* Afternoon of Friday March 28 1947 at the headquarters of the Royal Empire Society in Northumberland Avenue, London (LiMe April 4 1947 p2 col 4). *Other notable Staffordshire Samuel Johnsons.* A Dr Samuel Johnson attended the murder victim Mary Ann Wood at Stoke-upon-Trent in 1882, shortly before she died (SA Nov 11 1882 p5). The prominent Burslem pottery (tea pot) manufacturer and public figure (1855-1934) (SA Jan 27 1934 p5 col 5), probably the same Samuel Johnson who made 'Rockingham and Jet' at the Swan Bank Pottery in 1892 (notice at excavation site, 2009).

Jones, Cyril *Patentee of a device for aiding fire brigades.* Of Trent Valley Road, Lichfield, aged 31, fire officer, in 1938 with a device which enables many operations to do with the fire engine to be controlled in one operation (LiMe Nov 25 1938 p3 col 4).

Kempthorne, Rev John Augustine *The first to marry in Christ's College chapel, Cambridge since the Reformation, 100th bishop of Lichfield since Diuma.* He and his bride who wedded there in 1890. Bishop of Lichfield 1913-37 (SA Feb 10 1934 p9).

Lamb, John *His second and last lodge.* Was at Lamb's Warren; he was a rabbit warrener and Lichfield coach maker (AFT pp190, 220-236) (LOU p72) (VCH vol 14 p267).

Lane, Olivia May Allsobrook *Lichfield's 1st Millennium baby.* Born at Victoria Hospital at 7.13am Jan 1 2000 (E&S Jan 3 2000 p13).

Langton, Walter *26th & 30th Lord High Treasurer, 54th bishop of Lichfield since Diuma.* Serving as High Treasurer in 1295-1307, and 1312. Bishop of Lichfield 1296-1321 (Wikipedia 2008).

Literary prizes *Britain's only literary competition organised and sponsored by a local authority and competed for on a national basis.* The biennial Lichfield Literary Prize, founded 1988. *First Lichfield Literary Prize winner.* Valerie Kershaw with Rockabye, 1989.

Loder-Symonds, Mrs Mary Josephine *Lichfield's heroine.* She was awarded an OBE in 1920 for services at the refreshment buffet at Lichfield Station in WW1 (SA April 3 1920 p5 col 3).

Lonsdale, John *96th bishop of Lichfield since Diuma, his daughter caught the eye of Charles Kingsley.* Bishop of Lichfield, 1843-67. His daughter Margaret was very charming and attracted the attention of the young men of the city to such an extent that the jocular remark was often made that the stream of Margaret's lovers was so constant to her home at Lyncroft that the road to it ought to be kept in repair by her father! She caught the eye of the famous Charles Kingsley at a ball at Trinity College, Cambridge, and on the following morning he remarked to a group of friends: "for beauties give me that Miss Lonsdale, I never saw such lilies and roses" (SA Aug 1 1936 p5 col 2).

Markets and trade *Earliest granting of a market by charter in Staffordshire.* A Sunday market for Lichfield, 1153 (HOS 1998 p119). *Earliest reference to a smith in Lichfield.* The shop of Tharold the Smith, 1177, as recorded in the Great White Register of the cathedral (SA March 21 1952 p5 5). *Oldest recorded Lichfield fair.* The Whitsun fair, 1293. *Britain's 4th finest historic town square.* The Market Square, Lichfield, the site of markets since 1161, as chosen by Visit Britain in the Snapshot Series on Britain's Finest Attractions in The Sunday Telegraph (The Sunday Telegraph Aug 10 2008 p15).

Martial Arts *National Jujutsu Kumite championships silver 2008.* Jack Bayliss of Lichfield, representing West Midlands (LiMe Dec 4 2008 p72pc). *Junior tae kwon do world champion 2009 (in his grade and weight)* Michael Patterson (1994-2009) of Park End, Boley Park, Lichfield; John Taylor High School, Barton-under-Needwood, pupil (LiMe May 7

2009 p1).

Mayoralty *First female mayor.* Mrs Stuart Shaw, in 1928, and as such was the first woman to make the 'proclamation' of the old fair on Tuesday, Feb 21 1928 (TH Feb 25 1928 p6 col 3).

Matthews, Rev Bert *The 'Sporting Parson'.* Vicar of St Anne's, Chasetown, 1939-56. Billiard player, footballer, and often on the tennis courts in Hednesford Park (CAd Aug 24 1984 p4. Aug 31 1984 p4).

McClean, John Robinson *First man in Britain to own his own railway.* (1813-73). Civil engineer. After he applied for the licence to lease the South Staffordshire Railway for himself, shortly after it opened 1849. It runs through the parish and his colliery concerns developed the whole of the western part of the parish (TB Sept 12 2002 p21p).

Militia *Earliest Staffordshire regiment raised.* Col Luke Lillington's at the King's Head Inn, Lichfield, 1705. *First meeting of the Brownhills and District Rifle Volunteers.* Took place on Jan 9 1860 (SA Jan 14 1860 p5 col 4).

Mint *'one of the most famous rarities in the entire English series (of coins)'.* The Short Cross Penny, alias Lichfield Penny, minted at Lichfield c1190. The only known specimen was held at the BM, until 1971 when another was found in an American collection. In 1988 a clipped half of another specimen was found (St Mary's Centre, Lichfield, 2008).

Moss, Leading-Aircraftman T Clive *Hammerwich's first WW2 casualty.* Of Suffolk House, Hammerwich. When aged 20 lost his life as a result of enemy action somewhere in Wales on April 15 1941 (LiMe April 25 1941 p5p).

Mott, Edward Spencer *He had the non de plume 'Nathaniel Gubbins'.* (1844-1910). Second son of William Mott JP, DL, of Lichfield, when writing for the 'Sporting Times'. He contributed to the 'Pioneer' of India in the first year of its publication. He subsequently contributed to the Pall Mall Gazette, 'Bailey's Magazine' and many other publications. His books include 'Clear the Course', 'My Hostesses', 'Cakes and Ale', 'A Mingled Yarn', 'The Flowing Bowl', 'The Great Game', and 'Dopes, Bits of Turf' (Who's Who) (SA Jan 15 1910 p4 col 5).

Mountaineering *First to cross Europe's largest glacier on foot in winter.* Karrimor British Icelandic Expedition, organised by John Hughes of Oak Tree Rise, Beaudesert, Burntwood, of Lichfield Mountaineering Club. Three men succeeded, including Dave Calmers of Peaks Road, Rugeley. They took 21 days in March 1989 to cross 110 miles of Vatnajokull, Iceland (LiMe Jan 13 1989 p1. April 7 1989 p1).

Municipal affairs *Finest silver-gilt maces outside London.* The rare examples of Lichfield corporation according to Queen Victoria (STMSM April 1979 pp10,11). *Lichfield Rural District's first Civic Sunday.* May 8 1938; the procession began at the Colliery Sports Field and proceeded up High Street, Chasetown, to Trinity Methodist Church, Chasetown, where a service was held (LiMe May 13 1938 p6p). *Best local authority in the country for amount of rubbish recycled.* Lichfield DC, for nearly 50% of all its waste (BBC Midlands Today Jan 14 2005). *Record in local government.* Possibly when members of the same family had four seats on Lichfield City Council in 1958. There was FM Tayler, senior alderman and member, with 38 years' service; his son, John, Mayor-elect; his daughter, Mrs ME Halfpenny; and Councillor F Halfpenny, his son-in-law (SA May 29 1958 p10 cols 3-4). *Largest Staffordshire civil parish for councillors 2008, Staffordshire's first 'Quality' Town Council.* Lichfield City Council with 29 councillors; and awarded 'Quality' status by Staffordshire's County Accreditation Panel. The scheme was launched in March 2003; as well as Lichfield three Staffordshire parish councils received Quality Status; there are only a hundred other councils with Quality Status in the country (info Mary Booth).

Nomenclature *'Lichfield'* was a stallion in the Longhouse Farm Stud of Cannock Agricultural Company Ltd advertised in Staffordshire Advertiser to pregnate local mares (SA April 14 1888 p8 col 6). *'Lichfield'* is a noun amongst funeral directors. A 'Lichfield' is an expensive type of funeral ('In Excess' BBC Radio 4 Dec 27 1994). *'City of Lichfield' engine* was an LMS engine No. 6250 so named at a ceremony at Trent Valley Station on July 20 1944. It was one of the 'Coronation' class, and one of the modified non-streamlined type, weighing 161 tons 12 cwt, and with an overall length of 74 feet. The tender carried 10 tons of coal, and 4,000 gallons of water (LiMe June 23 1944 p3p). *'City of Lichfield' ship* was a 7,279 ton Liberty ship, part of the Merchant Navy fleet, was launched at the Bethlehem Fairfield shipyard Baltimore, Ohio in 1943 under its original name 'Samuel H. Ralston'. It was transferred to the British Government under the Lend-Lease agreement, and renamed 'Samois'. It was renamed again 'City of Lichfield' when Ellerman Lines Ltd purchased it in 1947 (LiMe March 28 1952 p5p).

Norman, Rev Denham Rowe *England's oldest acting clergyman 1923.* Born Chichester, Master of St John's Hospital, Lichfield, 1898-1925, who celebrated his 95th birthday by 1923. He was ordained in 1855; Rector of Stafford 1875-98. He lived to at least the age of 100 (TH May 26 1923 p5 col 2. May 1926. May 1928 p3).

Oxford Blues hoaxer, The A good looking man, dressed in the uniform of a private of the Oxford Blues came through Lichfield on July 2 1833 and called on one of the High Constables and requested him to prepare billets for 200 of the regiment, which he said would pass through on the next day, and to be followed by 200 more with the band. A billet was given for himself, and he took up quarters at the Admiral Nelson Inn. In the course of the day, he visited many of the inns in the town under the pretence of looking at the stables, and was treated liberally. the next day he decamped and was seen leaving on the Burton road. Many publicans and innkeepers made considerable preparations for their expected guests (SA July 6 1833).

Parks and springs *Britain's smallest public park 1998.* Princes Park, Burntwood, 1840s-, measuring 29 feet by 15 feet (ITV. Central News. March 24 1998 10.30pm). *Coldest bath in England.* Unite Well spring at Abnalls, yet it never froze (STMSM May 1978 p20).

Pateshull, Hugh de *8th Lord High Treasurer, 50th bishop of Lichfield since Diuma.* Serving as High Treasurer 1234-40. Bishop of Lichfield 1239-41.

Pedestrianism *7th in London-Brighton-London walk 1951.* CG Evans (b1913), of Ivanhoe Road, Lichfield, Man completing the 103.75 miles in 20 hours 49 minutes and 8 seconds (LiMe July 13 1951 p7).

Penda *His last fight.* **Was** at Gayfield (Gaia Lane) according to Appendix to Nennius (NSFCT 1908 p140).

Place-name *One of only two places in county with a Roman name.* Lichfield (the other is Penkridge) (PNSZ p17). *Earliest reference in the Anglo-Saxon Chronicle to any place within Staffordshire.* Lichfield (PNSZ p14 note). *First Anglian name for Lichfield.* Lyccidfelth or Licidfelth. First attempts to explain the name Lichfield c1250s. *Earliest surviving written Welsh*

inscription. The Chad Gospels, of ?740-50 AD (Three Spires: Friends of Lichfield Cathedral Newsletter. Spring 2006). *Unique derivation for a surname.* Lichfield will be from Lichfield in this parish (PDS). Chasetown the name, is first mentioned by 1867, reputedly by Elijah Wills, master of the boys' department at the school from 1863 (Found Ready. Mason p48) (LHSB 38. p58) (BCM vol 9 No. 2 p26) (VCH vol 14 p199).

Population *Staffordshire's largest populated town 1563.* Lichfield, with Wolverhampton next and Stafford next (SL p155). *Lichfield Friary* was 157th most-populated Staffordshire parish in 1801 with 20 people; 156th= in 1811 with 20; 158th in 1821 with 20; 158th in 1831 with 20; 163rd in 1841 with 14; 163rd in 1851 with 9; 165th in 1861 with 8; 161st in 1871 with 12; 163rd in 1881 with 9; 163rd in 1891 with 9; 165th in 1901 with 7. *St Chad's parish* was 42nd most-populated Staffordshire parish in 1801 with 1,357 people; 44th in 1811 with 1,634; 38th in 1821 with 2,066; 39th in 1831 with 2,193; 40th in 1841 with 2,263; 39th in 1851 with 2,351 48th in 1861 with 2,145 49th in 1871 with 2,270 51st in 1881 with 2,446; 52nd in 1891 with 2,171; 55th in 1901 with 2,252. *St Mary's parish* was 25th most-populated Staffordshire parish in 1801 with 2,422 people; 28th in 1811 with 2,382; 28th in 1821 with 2,721; 31st in 1831 with 2,780; 33rd in 1841 with 2,634; 37th in 1851 with 2,659; 39th in 1861 with 2,683; 39th in 1871 with 2,784; 42nd in 1881 with 2,832; 49th in 1891 with 2,555; 54th in 1901 with 2,281. Lichfield (City, St Chad's, St Mary's) could be ranked 18th worst-affected Staffordshire parish for loss of men in WW1, with 229 lives taken. *Lichfield St Michael* was 30th most-populated Staffordshire parish in 1801 with 2,088; 30th in 1811 with 2,270; 31st in 1821 with 2,568; 30th in 1831 with 2,869; 28th in 1841 with 3,202; 28th in 1851 with 3,425; 21st in 1861 with 5,092; 21st in 1871 with 8,570; 22nd in 1881 with 11,253; 22nd in 1891 with 12,441; 22nd in 1901 with 13,755. Lichfield St Michael could be ranked 25th worst-affected Staffordshire parish for loss of men in WW1, with 138 lives taken.

Power-lifting *World record for pulling a BAC 1-11 aircraft farthest unaided, only person in the world to lift a Ford Fiesta car off the ground using a special harness for his neck, 'The World's No. 1 Natural Strongman' Sept 1989.* Dave

Wilkins, strongman, of Ferndale Close, Burntwood. The first feat was 75 feet, achieved in 1986. Wilkins earned the last title (from power lifting governing bodies in USA and Germany) for pulling a train, an articulated truck, a 300-ton ship, and a transport plane, unaided, all in one week of each other. These feats earned him his third entry in GBR (LiMe July 14 1989 p3p. Sept 8 1989 p10p).

Publishing *First novel published in Birmingham* 'Life of Fanny Brown' by Edward (alias John) Piper of Lichfield, 1760, who claimed in his preface that the nicest lady whatever, though she be a Methodist, a Holy Sister, or a Spotless Nun, would be able to read his book without the least offence (BS) (SA June 29 1935 p9 col 3). *Longest continuous subscription to The Staffordshire Advertiser.* Perhaps the Hodgskiss family of The Old Farm, Hammerwich, readers from at least Feb 22 1806 - with a copy of the paper surviving in 1937 - to at least 1937 (SA Aug 28 1937 p6 col 5).

Pubs *Unique pub name in Britain.* Perhaps the Scales Inn, Market Street, so called after scales used weighing jockeys at Lichfield races on Whittington Heath (VB p14). *Oldest building in Burntwood.* The Nag's Head Inn, called the Stag's Head in C18 (CAd March 2 1984 p4). *Lichfield's oldest licensed house 1940.* The Windsor Castle, Dam Street, dating back as an inn to somewhere between 1540 and 1640. But in 1940 it became a private dwelling (LiMe April 12 1940 p5 cols 6-7). *Fancy that!* In 1979 Jane Rossington, alias Jill Harvey in the soap-opera 'Crossroads, which was set in a motel, lost her battle to stop a real-life motel being built near her home, a development for Aldershawe Farm, Wall, by travel magnate and Aston Villa director Doug Ellis. "Although 'Crossroads' is fictitious, I see enough of motels at work,' she said. Four rival hoteliers also objected, but Lichfield Council's planning committee granted permission (E&S April 4 2009 p8).

Quarter sessions *First Recorder of Lichfield.* The Duke of Somerset (LTM Jan Feb 1972 p34). *Maiden sessions.* There were no cases for trial at Lichfield midsummer quarter sessions 1879 (SA July 26 1879 p7 col 4). *Last Lichfield Quarter Sessions.* In 1971 (LTM Jan Feb 1972 p34).

Quotes *The walls of Lichfield are biographies in miniature'* (Staffordshire County Handbook c1958). *'Athens of the Midlands'* (Staffordshire: Shire County Guide. Peter Heaton. 1986). *'the Mother of the Midlands'* (SA & Chron Feb 20 1958 p6 col 7). *'one of the oldest and probably one of the most historic towns in the Midlands'* Lichfield, according to a former 'well-known 'Mercury' contributor' in 1951 (LiMe Aug 10 1951 p4 col 1). The *choicest quote about the Cathedral.* In A Tour Through The Whole Island of Great Britain (1724-6), Daniel Defoe noted: 'three beautiful spires, the like of which are not to be seen in one church, no not in Europe.' The *choicest quote about the city.* In Walks in the Black Country and its Green Border-land (1869), Elihu Burritt, US consular agent in Birmingham wrote: 'Lichfield looks like a little city of steeples on approaching it from any side.' The *choicest quote about the natives* is probably Dr Johnson's famous remark: 'We are a city of philosophers: we work with our heads and make the boobies of Birmingham work for us with their hands'

Rail *Lichfield's worst railway disaster* was perhaps that on Jan 1 1946 when at 6.55pm a fast fish freight train from Fleetwood, Lancs, travelling to London crashed into the rear of local passenger train running from Stafford to Nuneaton stationary on the down line at Trent Valley Station. Nineteen people were killed and 20 injured (LiMe Jan 4 1946 p7. Jan 11 1946 p5). *2nd prize in British railways (Rugby and district) gardening competition 1951.* Trent Valley Station, equal with Lilleshall (LiMe Sept 14 1951 p5 col 5).

Reeve, Rev Arthur Stretton *102nd bishop of Lichfield since Diuma, member of the winning Cambridge boat race 1930, crashed his car into a house at Muckley Corner.* Bishop of Lichfield 1953-74 (SLM Summer 1954 p26). The car crash was on Oct 21 1956 at about 8.45pm when approaching the brow of the hill near the Boat Inn when his car skidded. It struck a kerb and then careered into the bay window of a house at No. 3. Summer Hill, occupied by Mr and Mrs Clive Edmonds, both of whom were near the window watching TV at the time. The Bishop came into the house after the accident and was full of apologies (LiMe Oct 26 1956 p2p).

Roads *'Miss Lonsdale's holes'* How holes for new drains for the city of Lichfield were locally referred to after a protest by Miss Lonsdale, a relation of Bishop Lonsdale, to the local council and a public inquiry (SA Aug 8 1936 p11 col

2). *Legal history made*. When a jury at Lichfield Quarter Sessions in the Guildhall took three hours on Jan 21 1955 to decide unanimously that a 30-yard long stretch of Levetts Fields Road could be stopped-up for vehicular traffic, for the construction of the new Birmingham Road, after 10 objections had been lodged against its closure. Never before, it was thought, had objections been made to the proposed closing of part of a public highway (LiMe Jan 28 1955 p5).

Roman Lichfield *'the county's finest example of Roman architecture'* Roman site at Wall, according to the Staffordshire Advertiser and Chronicle May 10 1956 p6.

Sailing *Enterprize World Championship winner 2006, Fireball World Championship 4th 2005, winner 2007*. Richard Estaugh (b1959), sailor, of Birchwood Road, Boley Park. The 2007 tournament was in partnership with Bob Gardener. To summer 2008 Estaugh had achieved in sailing 10 world championships and 15 national titles (LiMe July 31 2008 p11).

Scarlett, Daniel and Lily *Longest married couple in the Lichfield area ever.* Born c1895, and c1897, respectively. Married at St Anne's, Chasetown, on Christmas Day 1916, and celebrated 72 years of marriage in 1989, 54 years of which spent in High St, Chase Terrace, later at Boney Hay (LiMe Jan 6 1989 p2p).

Selby, Anthony John *Hammerwich's saddest*. Of Burntwood Road, Hammerwich, aged 13 months, who swallowed a piece of sharp-edged coal which got lodged in his windpipe, and died at the Hammerwich Cottage Hospital on Dec 9 1941 (LiMe Dec 19 1941 p4 cols 5-6).

Selwyn, Rev George Augustus *1st Bishop of New Zealand, 97th bishop of Lichfield since Diuma, rowed in the first university boat race*. (1809-1878). Bishop of New Zealand 1841-67, of Lichfield 1867-78 (SLM Summer 1954 p26).

Seward, Anna *The 'Swan of Lichfield',*

Anna Seward

'inventress of epic elegy'. (1747-1809). Poet. She lived in the Bishop's Palace to her death. *Her best known work* is the poetical novel 'Louisa' (1784). Eramus Darwin referred to her as the 'inventress of epic elegy'.

Showmanship *Chestonian challenge cup winner 1954*. Kimline Commander owned by Mr HJ Wall of Edwards Road, Chasetown, awarded at Cradley Heath by the Staffordshire Bull Terrier (Founder) Club on Jan 9 1954 as 'dog of the year'. Kimline Commander also secured the Jim Harris challenge cup for obtaining the highest number of points during 1953 (LiMe Jan 15 1954 p5 col 5).

Shrievalty *First sheriff of Lichfield*. Gregory Stonyng, 1553 (VCH vol 14 p83); *first female sheriff*. Mary Halfpenny, 1968 (VCH vol 14 p83). *When the sheriff carried a gas mask on the Sheriff's Ride*. 1939 (SA Sept 16 1939 p3 col 7). *First member of Parliament on the Sheriff's Ride*. Major General JA d' Avigdor-Goldsmid, 1971 (LTM Oct 1971 p31ps). *First lady to lead the Sheriff's Ride*. Miss Mary Tayler, aged 16, the daughter of Sheriff, John S Tayler, because he was no horseman, and completed the ride in a Land Rover in 1951 (LiMe Sept 14 1951 p3). *First sheriff accompanied on the Sheriff's Ride by his lady*. Simon Price and his wife, Lesley, in 2009 (E&S Sept 1 2009 p13).

Siddons (nee Kemble), Sarah *Her first appearance under her married name*. Was at the Guildhall, Lichfield, 1773 (LAL p10).

Skelton, Rev Kenneth *'the courageous Bishop Skelton', 103rd bishop of Lichfield since Diuma*. Bishop of Matebeleland, Rhodesia, 1962-70; bishop of Lichfield 1975-84; thus described in Harold Wilson's 'The Labour Government 1964-1970'. He is said to have visited every parish in Lichfield diocese (SLM Sept 1983 p8p).

Skirlaw, Walter *32nd Keeper of the Privy Seal, 57th bishop of Lichfield since Diuma*. Serving as Keeper in 1382-86. Bishop of Lichfield 1385-86.

Slavery *'The last public sale of a slave in England'* This recorded remark was the belief of the auctioneer, John Heeley, of Walsall, after the sale of a negro boy aged about ten or eleven, advertised for sale in Aries Gazette, Birmingham, on Saturday Nov 30 1771 at the Baker's Arms Inn (later Wheatsheaf Inn), Bird St, Lichfield, kept by a Mrs Webb. The boy is described as 'remarkably straight, well-proportioned, speaks tolerably good English, of a mild disposition, friendly, efficacious, sound, healthy, fond of labour, and for colour an excellent fine black'. It has been suggested that a gentleman from Shenstone area bought him. Although trading in slaves was not outlawed until 1807 in a sense Heeley's was a valid claim as he knew a legal case the following year would set a precedence. In 1772 the Lord Chief Justice ruled a slave's abduction was illegal as no legislation existed in England for any person to be owned by another and that slavery therefore did not exist in England. His judgement effectively emancipated all the slaves in England (Stringer Collection, Bodleian Library, Oxford) (HOWW) (LiMe April 21 1939 p10 col 6) (John Shaw in 'Lichfield Gazette, a free magazine April 2009 Issue 7 pp22-23).

Smith George and Thomas *Strange but true!* George, employed at Manor Farm, Wall, for nearly 50 years, was buried on May 24 1950 in Wall churchyard, on the same day his eldest son, Thomas, aged 52, died in a Lichfield hospital. Thomas had been ill for some time. In WW1 he had served in the Scots Guards (SA May 27 1950 p6 col 7).

Smith, Squadron Leader Nicky *Last to fly a Wessex helicopter in RAF service.* Of Lichfield, performing a flypast at RAF Akrotiri, Cyprus, on Jan 31 2003; the Wessex entered RAF service in 1960 (E&S Jan 31 2003 p28p).

Societies *First meeting of the Staffordshire Agricultural Society.* At the Swan Hotel on May 20 1800. *2nd oldest floral and horticultural society in England 1920.* The Lichfield Floral and Horticultural Society, established in 1816, who postponed their centenary exhibition until 1920 (SA Aug 9 1902. July 10 1920 p11 col 2). *First Lichfield and District organists' Association meeting* was held at Lichfield on Feb 5 1927; the association was formed in Nov 1926 (TH Feb 12 1927 p6 col 7). *1st winners of the Staffordshire W.I. Challenge Banner.* Lichfield W.I. in 1920, with 22 certificates, of which eleven were first class. The banner was instituted by Mrs Harrison of Maer Hall (chairman of the County Federation of W.I.s). It was at first awarded annually to the Institute gaining the largest number of certificates for merit at the W.I.'s annual exhibition, later it was judged on a points system (SA Oct 2 1920 p9 cols 3-4). *'one of the oldest institutes in the Federation'.* Wall Women's Institute, being formed on April 17 1917 (LiMe April 19 1957 p5p), but Whittington W.I. is older having been formed in 1916. *The Burntwood Tapestry* is an embroidery made by Burntwood Community Group in 2003-07. It depicts 20 local scenes and hangs in Chase Town Library (TB July 12 2007 p6p).

Stavenby, Bishop Alexander *Lichfield Friary's most famous old worthy.* (d1238). Bishop of Lichfield 1224-38. Henry III was jealous of his intimacy with the Earl Marshal and charged him as a party in the Earls' conspiracy. He founded a Franciscan friary at Lichfield c1229, which became a small extra-parochial estate.

Stonier, James *The P.C. who saved Lloyd George.* (1869-1955). Formerly of Chasetown; he married at St Anne's, 1891, and his funeral took place there. He was on duty at Birmingham Town Hall on Dec 18 1901, policing a political rally, at which Lloyd George spoke opposing the Government's attitude to the Boer War. The meeting developed into a riot, and Stonier took a spur-of-the-moment decision to change clothes with Lloyd George, in order to allow him to escape the building disguised as a policeman (LiMe Nov 21 1941 p8 col 4) (BPn Nov 22 1954 photo) (Birmingham Mail March 3 1955).

Swimming *Youngest ever UK Olympian in the men's senior swimming squad to 1984, Olympic 4x200 metres swimming relay bronze medalist 1984.* Paul Howe of Cannock Road, Burntwood, aged 16 (CAd Aug 3 1984 p32p).

Swinfen-Broun, Col MA *'Lichfield's greatest benefactor of modern times'.* Of Swinfen Hall, who donated 11 and half acres of Beacon Place estate to extend Beacon Park in 1943; endowed a bed at the Lichfield Victoria Hospital in memory of his late daughter Mrs Farnham in 1935; in 1938 provided £5,000 for the hospital's Maternity Block; in WW2 he gave funds for the erection of a sports pavilion to be built after the war. His late wife, Mrs Swinfen-Bourn, had also endowed a bed at the hospital and paid for the clock tower outside the Municipal Offices (LiMe Dec 10 1943 p7p. Dec 31 1943 p7p).

Talbot, Miss Clara *3rd Bower Queen of the Greenhill Bower Festival.* Aged 18, of Beacon Place Farm, Lichfield, in 1931. The first 'Queen' was crowned in 1929 (VCH vol 14 p160) (WSL 323/41/80. Horne's Scrapbook. No. 2. p57). For the first 'Beauty Queen' of Lichfield see Shenstone.

Theatres *Unique ventilation system.* At Garrick Theatre, Lichfield, opened 2003; it uses natural ventilation instead of mechanical devices to help lower carbon dioxide levels (Staffordshire County Guide

2006/7 p53).

Thurston, Frederick *'One of the first musicians to broadcast'*. Born Lichfield 1902. In 1922 he was asked by Stanton Jefferies, the only musician on the Marconi Company's staff, to assist in getting together a small combination of players to perform at Marconi House. Their music went over the air, somewhat uncertainly, from Writtle. With the formation of the British Broadcasting Company Thurston was appointed principal clarinet, a position he held until retirement in 1946 (LiMe May 17 1946 p4 col 3).

Utilities *Staffordshire's earliest recorded windmill*. At Hammerwich, 1300; although one in Blymhill parish may be older (VCH vol 14 p267). *Staffordshire's last working windmill*. Reputedly Speedwell Mill, working to c1908/9 (BEV p180) (VCH vol 14 p267) (WBJ p25). *First pumping station of the South Staffordshire Water Works Company*. At Sandfields, 1858. *First pit in the world to be electrically lit*. Hammerwich No. 2 Pit of the Cannock Chase Colliery, alias The Cathedral and then The Fly, near Chasetown, 1883; but a pit at Hamilton (Lanarks) claims to have been lit in 1882 (VCH vol 14 pp215,216). *Most incorrect telephone bill by 1980*. £1,494,000,000 for the Blue Bell Inn, Aug 18 1975; the Post Office admitted it contained 'an arithmetical error' (GBR 1980 p202).

Water polo *Winners of the 1st Staffordshire Water Polo Championship*. Lichfield Swimming Club who won six goals to nil against Stafford Swimming Club on July 26 1892 at Stafford Public Baths; the championship continued until at least its 4th year (SA July 30 1892 p4 col 7. May 16 1896 p4 col 7).

Weighman, William *Last hung at Lichfield*. Aged 26. Of Manceter, Warws. Hung at the Gallows Wharf gallows on June 1 1810 along with John Neve, 25, of Herefordshire, and James Richardson, 39, of Red-Acre-Hill, Cheshire, for forging bank notes (SA June 2 1810) (LiMe Oct 27 1933 p7 col 1. Nov 10 1933 p7 col 3) (VCH vol 14 p85).

Wightman, Edward *Last person in England burnt at the stake for heresy*. In the Market Place, Lichfield, 1612 (Staffordshire Breaks 2006. Staffordshire Tourism).

Wood, Thomas *Brownhill's bravest*. Of Coppice Side. When aged 12 on June 10 1939, rescued from the canal Thomas Kitson, 6, who would have drowned otherwise.

He was awarded a Royal Humane Society certificate (SA Sept 23 1939 p8 col 1).

Wood, Alderman WA *'one of Lichfield's most honoured citizens'*. (1857-1935), brewer, freemason, founder of the Johnson Society 1909; Lichfield City councillor from 1902; thrice Mayor of Lichfield, in 1930, 1931, 1932, (only previously accorded to two other persons); member of the Lichfield Bower Committee for 50 years; Governor of Lichfield Grammar School; President of the Lichfield Bowling Club (LiMe April 5 1935 p5p).

Woods, Dr Edward Sydney *Hitchhiked a lift in a milk van when bishop, 101st bishop of Lichfield since Diuma*. Bishop of Lichfield 1937-53. When he visited an art exhibition at Stafford by car in 1950. Outside the Art School he dismissed his chauffeur and then found that the exhibition was at the Library. After 'thumbing' a lift in the van, Dr Woods, arrived at the Library nearly half an hour late (SA Nov 25 1950 p5 col 6).

WW2 *First place in Britain to demonstrate a new 'Black-out' system for air-raid precautions*. Lichfield on March 8 1938, with control equipment capable of switching on and off street lighting, calling volunteer firemen and wardens from their homes, and sounding sirens at six different points in the city for alarm and all-clear signals (SA March 5 1938 p3 cols 4-5). *2nd Cathedral in country visited by a WW2 U.S. Negro Spiritualist choir*. Lichfield on Sunday Oct 24 1943. The choir, composed of 50 members of the U.S. Army Engineer Dept, previously had performed only at Liverpool Cathedral, and had fulfilled engagements for the BBC (LiMe Oct 29 1943 p4 cols 1-2).

Wright, Edward *'died by the Visitation of God'*. Brother to Lichfield High Sheriff, died in 1814. His body was found in a field near to Pones Mill on May 11 1814. A Coroners inquest held the following night returned a verdict of *died by the Visitation of God*. It is supposed that he died in an apoplectic fit (SA May 16 1914 p5 col 1).

Yeo, Matthew (born c1986) of Lichfield. Manchester University undergraduate who captained his university in the BBC's quiz programme *University Challenge 2009*. Although their opponents, Corpus Christi College, Oxford, won in points (275 to 190), Manchester won by default owing to an Oxford man having graduated from the College (LiMe March 5 2009 p3p).

Little Wyrley See Norton Canes.

Longdon Longdon is Staffordshire's 58th largest parish, consisting of 4,545 acres; 57th closest parish to the county town, 9.4m SE; extremist length 3.4m; extremist width 3.9m. The parish's chief settlement The near-continuous pretty village of Longdon running into Longdon Green. What Longdon is famous for the Pagets and their Beaudesert Hall (now demolished).

Aldrich, Walter *Longdon's kindest.* He left by will dated 1758 rental to fund a bread dole every Sunday in lent for poor widows of the parish.

Altitudes The highest point of the parish is 741 feet at the boundary at Castle Ring, the highest point of Cannock Chase and covering 8.5 acres is one of the most complete encampments in Staffordshire (NSFCT 1950 p101). Lowest point is 253 feet on the east boundary following Lichfield Road.

Bailey, Henry *Assumed the name and arms of Paget.* (1744-1812). He was a descendent of Henry, 2nd son of the 5th Baron, in 1770, becoming 9th Baron Paget; Lord Lieutenant of Anglesey; created Earl of Uxbridge 1784 (SN Sept 19 1980 p8). He carried out much renovation to Beaudesert Hall and had a highway which ran in front of the house moved to its present position half a mile or more away.

Church St James' at Longdon is one of 4 such county dedications (of AP churches); 23rd= oldest county church dating from the C12 or roughly 1150. During a restoration scheme in 1950 a staircase, which it was believed had been sealed up for 200 years, was discovered leading to the rood loft on the north side of the chancel (LiMe Sept 29 1950 p3 col 5).

Crick, Rt Rev Douglas Henry *Tallest bishop in the country 1954.* Born 1885, DD, Bishop of Chester 1939-55; Suffragan Bishop of Stafford 1934-39; Rector of Stoke-on-Trent 1924-34; Prebendary of Longdon 1929-39. He stood 6 feet 4 inches (SA Oct 8 1954 p2 col 6).

Folklore *Longdon's best.* The village is famous for the proverb, said to be first recorded by Stebbing Shaw in the late C18, which alludes to its length of its main street

> The stoutest beggar that goes by the way
> Can't beg through Longdon on a Midsummer's day.

An old inhabitant at the end of the C19 had another similar saying that 'Long long' has run the beggar to death'.

The stoutest beggar cannot beg through Longdon as it is such a long village.

Forster, Charles Smith *Walsall's first MP.* Died 1850. He lived at Lysways Hall 1836- (SOS 1840 p242) (W p568) (SNWA p44).

Forster, John Henry *Record for winning the Henley Regatta, the Grand Challenge Ladies' Plate and Stewards' Cup all in one year, 'one of the best of postprandial speakers'.* John Henry Forster (1842-1904) of Hanch Hall, 2nd son of Sir Charles Forster, Bt, MP. The year was 1863, and the record had not been beaten by 1904 (SA June 25 1904 p4 col 5).

Geology The Beaudsert Hall-Upper Longdon-Brereton Cross area is Bunter; Beaudesert Old Park is Middle Coal Measures; Gentleshaw Common-Beaudesert New Park - Keuper Sandstones; Longdon and the east side of the parish is Keuper Red Marls; Longdon Green is Keuper Sandstones.

Hollinshead, Reg *He had had 1,500 racehorse winners by 2003.* Born 1924. Racehorse trainer at Lodge Farm, Upper Longdon, since c1950, in flat and National Hunt racing. He has trained Derby winners Walter Swinburn, and Willie Ryan, as well as Kevin Darley, Paul Eddery and Tony Culhane. He trained Remainder Man which finished 3rd in the Epsom Derby 1978, and 2nd in the 2,000 Guineas 1978 (Cannock & Rugeley Chronicle April 3 2003 photos).

Hunt, Joseph Geoffrey *Gentleshaw's saddest.* When aged 2 years 10 months, of near East Lodge, Gentleshaw, he was strangled to death by his insane mother Dorothy Mabel Adderley, aged 19, between March 14-15 1941. His body was found in Grand Lodge Wood (LiMe March 21 1941 p7. April 25 1941 p3. July 4 1941 p4 col 5).

May, William *Staffordshire's 15th= oldest man ever.* Of Longdon. He lived to the age of 108 in the 17th Century; his wife lived to the age of 98 and they died within days of each other, so that they were buried in the same grave on the same day (NHS p327).

Nip, Mrs *Staffordshire's 10th oldest woman ever.* Of Gentleshaw, who reputedly lived to the age of 109 or older (NHS p320).

Paget, Mrs Arthur *2nd Staffordshire girl to adorn the frontispiece of Country Life magazine.* She achieved this in the edition June 18 1898, vol 111 no. 76

Paget, Charles *Plotted against Elizabeth I.* Died c1590. Spy, brother of Thomas, worked for the King of Spain but continued to supply the English government with information. Died at Brussels.

Paget, Charles Henry Alexander *Restored and beautified Plas Newydd and studied the Welsh language.* (1885-1947). Son of Alexander (d1896). 6th Marquis; 7th Earl; 15th Lord Paget; mayor of Burton on Trent 1912. He overhauled Beaudesert Hall and replaced some of the C18 additions with work more in the original Tudor style; after a fire in Nov 1909 more restoration was carried out (NSFCT 1914 pp175-176. 1976 pp13-14) (Plas Newydd. NT Guide. 1991. p32) (SN Sept 26 1980 p52).

Paget, Clarence *Chosen to command the two vessels sent to Calais to bring Prince Albert for his marriage to Queen Victoria.* In 1840. Brother of Alfred.

Paget, George Augustus *Commanded military forces in the Crimean War.* 6th son of the 10th Baron, publishing accounts of the battles in his 'Crimean Journals' (1875).

Paget, Florence *The 'Pocket Venus', she led the cotillon at the famous ball given by the Brigade of Guards in honour of the marriage of Edward VII.* Only daughter of the 2nd Marquis, because of her beauty; she eloped with Lord Hastings on the day before her marriage to Henry Chaplin (CCF pp97-98) (LiMe May 22 1931 p5 col 2).

Paget, Henry *Captain of the Yeoman of the Guard.* (c1663~5-1743). 2nd but eldest surviving son of William (d1713). 7th Baron, in 1715; envoy-extraordinary to George of Hanover, 1714, who later in the year became George I; created Earl of Uxbridge 1714.

Paget, Henry *Died childless.* (1719-69). Succeeded his grandfather Henry in 1743. 2nd Earl of Uxbridge, 8th Baron Paget.

Paget, Henry *Married three times.* (1797-1869). 2nd Marquis and 11th Baron Paget, son of the 10th Baron. Served as Lord Lieutenant of Anglesey and a colonel in the army.

Paget, Henry Cyril *'the Dancing Marquess', 'most eccentric English aristocrat ever'.* (1875-1905), 5th Marquis, son of

Henry (d1898), 4th Marquis. He dressed in outlandish clothes, his willowy figure could be spotted walking along Piccadilly with a snow white, pink-ribboned poodle under his arm. He was so rich and self-indulgent he had

Henry Cyril Paget (d1905) -'the Dancing Marquess'.

his motor cars modified to spout exhaust gases perfumed with parchouli and 'l'eau d'Espagne'. Most outrageously he loved to perform sinuous, sexy, snake-like dances in front of astonished audiences round Europe, earning him the sobriquet, the 'Dancing Marquess'. Died 'pathetically alone' of pneumonia at the Hotel Royale, Monte Carlo (Daily Mail Oct 27 2007) . the second claim appeared as the sub-title to an article on the Marquis for an exhbition on the Pagets at Cannock Library, 2009).

Paget, Henry William *Longdon's most famous old worthy, called 'Waterloo Marquis,' 37th Field Marshall of the British Army.* (1768-1854), 10th Baron and 2nd Earl of Uxbridge (new creation), cavalry commander to the Duke of Wellington at Waterloo 1815, where he famously lost a leg, and received the Marquisate of Anglesey for his services. But earlier he aroused notoriety eloping with Lady Charlotte Wellesley, wife of Duke of Wellington's brother, causing a sensation in 1809-10. In 1812 he succeeded to his family's vast estates centred on Beaudesert Hall (in which he later installed the 'Waterloo Staircase'), the earldom of Uxbridge, and the barony of Paget. There was a Longdon popular saying *'The Marquis of Anglesey lived for forty years with one foot in the grave'* (LTM Nov 1972 p25)

Paget, Lewis *'appointed mastership of the game in Cankerwood'.* In the early C16, Cank Wood was a part of Cannock Chase near Beaudesert.

Paget, Thomas *Improved the house at Beaudesert, implicated in the Throckmorten Plot.* (1544-89~90). 3rd Baron Paget.

Paget snr, William *Sergeant of the Mace in the City of London.* Secretary of State in Henry VIII's reign.

Paget, William *Lord Lieutenant of Buckinghamshire.* (1609-78). 5th Baron Paget, royalist in the Civil War.

Paget, William *Ambassador to Vienna and then Ambassador to Turkey.* (1637-1713). 6th Baron.

Paget House Club This was a term for courtiers of Queen Victoria who were members of the Paget family - so many of the 10th Baron's children having positions as equerries or maids of honour in the royal household. In fact there were often up to eight of them around. Lord Alfred Paget, son of the 10th Baron by his second marriage was a senior equerry to the Queen. In the early years of the Queen's reign he was her favourite dancing partner, and there were even rumours that the two would marry.

Pagett, Elijah *The other Staffordshire Paget who lost a leg at Waterloo.* Of Kingswinford (1792-1878), in the 44th Regt of Foot, died at Guns Lane, and buried in All Saints churchyard, West Bromwich (TB June 1 2000 p20).

Place-name The name Longdon first appears in 1002-04, and means 'long hill' presumably the high ridge between London and Rugeley (PNSZ p369).

Poorest, Longdon's In 1821 Rugeley received money Longdon for board of its poor in Rugeley workhouse (SRO D6447/1/).

Population Longdon was 59th most-populated Staffordshire parish in 1801 with 909 people; 61st in 1811 with 1,017; 63rd in 1821 with 1,115; 64th in 1831 with 1,147; 66th in 1841 with 1183; 69th in 1851 with 1148; 68th in 1861 with 1,220; 66th in 1871 with 1,359; 68th in 1881 with 1,366; 67th in 1891 with 1,338; 67th in 1901 with 1,342. Longdon could be ranked 70th worst-affected Staffordshire parish for loss of men in WW1, with 22 lives taken.

Quote *Choicest.* Thomas Pennant in his Journey From Chester to London, 1811, passed through Longdon 'The village consists of scattered houses, extending for a vast way on each side of the lane; from whence the name... THIS village antiently was full of gentleman's seats.'

Sneade, Mistress Alice *First person in the parish register.* Widow, buried April 25 1663 (the register is the bishop's transcript).

Stokes, Capt HS *Military Cross medalist.* Of the Welsh Guards, awarded Sept 25 1915. He lived at The Brooklands, Longdon Green, and designed its garden. His garden, containing many rare birds and plants, was described as in 1938 as *'the finest of their kind in Staffordshire'.* It opened to the public to raise funds for charity in 1931 (LiMe Aug 26 1938 p2 col 5).

M-N

Marchington See Hanbury.

Mavesyn Ridware Mavesyn Ridware was Staffordshire's 106th largest parish, consisting of 2,486 acres; 51st= closest parish to the county town, 9.2m SE; extremist length 3.4m; extremist width 2.2m. The chief settlement of the parish is the fair-sized village of Hill Ridware, continuous with Rake End, whilst Mavesyn Ridware remains nothing more than a hamlet.

Altitudes The highest point of the parish is Porter's Hill at 361 feet. Lowest point is 207 feet by the Trent below Mavesyn Ridware.

Beresford children *Children that rang hand bells in belfry for Children's Hour.* Peter and Dennis Beresford, twins aged 13, and their sister Joan, aged 15, of Market Street, Lichfield, who rang a full peal of grandsire doubles of 5,040 changes

to celebrate Joan's 15th birthday. Their ringing was broadcast on the radio programme, Children's Hour, on May 31 1947 (LiMe May 30 1947 p2p).

Church St Nicholas' in Mavesyn Ridware village is one of 3 such county dedications (of ancient parish churches); 22nd oldest county church dating from 1140. *Staffordshire's clumsiest church rebuild onto the remaining W tower* Mavesyn Ridware. The rebuild, of 1782, is the nave, a brick 'box' in the Gothick/ Classical style with pointed windows. The *church with the most hatchments in Staffordshire* is Mavesyn Ridware with 10; there are 78 known hatchments in the county (Hatchments in Britain No. 8 p147). *First peal of grandsires and doubles of 5,040 changes rung on the bells* was on Saturday Aug 31 1934 by the Society of Change Ringers for the Archdeaconry of Stafford. The peal was 42 scores with ten different callings in two hours and 48 minutes. It was the first peal for treble and tenor ringers (LiMe Sept 7 1934 p4 col 6). The *most bizarre thing* is the Mavesyn Chapel with bogus C15/16 memorials of the later C18. These include, in the centre of the room, the chest tomb of Sir Robert Mavesyn, who died 1403 at the battle of Shrewbury; another tomb-chest, with incised effigies on a slab of Thomas Cawarden (d1593), and wife. On the floor incised effigies in slabs of David Cardon (d1557), and wife, John Cardon (d1485), and wife, John Cardon (d1477), and Hugh Davenport (d1473) (BOE p203). However, there are original medieval memorials - in two recesses are the effigies of two Knights, one C13 with his legs not crossed, the other cross-legged (BOE p203).

Civil war *One of the worst-affected Staffordshire parishes by low-level violence in the Civil War.* Mavesyn Ridware (info Prof Philip Morgan, 2006).

Fire *Fancy that!* In autumn 1931 when the thatched cottage occupied by Mr A Humphries, owned by Mr D Walker of Manor Farm, Mavesyn Ridware, was on fire Lichfield Fire Brigade had to form a human chain from the pump at the back of the house as no water was available for the pumps. The fire was successfully put out (LiMe Oct 9 1931 p4 col 6).

Fishing *Fancy that!* In 1785 a pike was caught in the Trent near Mavesyn Ridware which weighed 24 and half pounds. In 1772 a larger one of 31 and three quarters of a pound was caught in the same place (LiMe Aug 13 1954 p3 col 2).

Folklore *Mavesyn Ridware's best.* Is that neighbouring medieval lords Sir Robert Mavesyn of Mavesyn Ridware (b c1360), and Sir William Handsacre of Handsacre fought a combat by two oaks called Gog and Magog, before they left to fight on opposite sides in the battle of Shrewsbury on July 22 1403; Sir William was slain.

The 15th Century warring lords of neighbouring manors. In the centre are the two oaks, Gog and Magog.

Geology The Trent valley is Alluvium; Mavesyn Ridware, Blithbury villages and

the rest of the parish is Keuper Red Marls; Bentley-Stone Cottages area is Keuper Sandstones.

Greatrix, Sergt WS *Mavesyn Ridware's hero.* Originally of Hill Ridware, awarded the British Empire Medal (Military Division) for meritorious services in Italy Sept-Dec 1944, safeguarding a large petrol installation, serving chiefly with the N.F.S. (SA July 28 1945 p7 col 3).

Hancox brothers *Mavesyn Ridware's saddest.* The deaths of two brothers Daniel Hancox, 21, and Thomas Hancox, 30 of 3 Council Houses, Hill Ridware, when their motor cycle crashed into a telegraph pole on the main Oxford-Banbury road at Adderbury on July 26 1936 rocked the parish. Both were employed at a press steel works at Oxford and were returning to their lodgings at Headington. The funeral at Mavesyn Ridware was probably the largest ever seen in the village (SA Aug 1 1936 p7 col 8. Aug 8 1936 p7 col 5).

King, Agnes Gretta *Mavesyn Ridware's villainess.* She was committed to the Assizes for maliciously setting fire to the house of her employer on Nov 24 1924, she admitted to stealing clothes and household articles to the value of £5. 9 shillings. She was aged 17, of Hill Ridware, domestic servant at Mavesyn House, Mavesyn Ridware, residence of Mrs Sutton. (LiMe Jan 9 1925 p4).

Manorial business *Staffordshire's most famous pair of trees.* The ancient oaks called Gog and Magog, which stood between Mavesyn Ridware and High Bridge, which according to legend was where Staffordshire's most famous combat between neighbouring lords was fought in 1403. The oaks were cut down in the 1880s, and a fragment of one has been kept in the vestry of Mavesyn Ridware church. *Staffordshire's earliest surviving painted glass.* Mavesyn Ridware, of 1260; it went to the hall (BAST 1952 p72).

Mavesyn, Sir Robert *Maveysn Ridware's most famous old worthy.* (c1360-1403). Lord of Mavesyn Ridware, who famously fought with his neighbouring lord, Sir William Handsacre, at a certain place equidistant between their manors before the battle of Shrewsbury, as described in Shakespeare's 'Henry IV' Part II Act V Sc 3. The two had long disputed over fishing rights in the Trent. Sir William (for Hotspur) was slain, and Sir Robert (for Henry IV) went on to be killed at Shrewsbury.

Mavesyn Ridware's villains Four men (two dressed as Teddy boys) who threatened the postmistress, Bessie Kiff, at 8.30am on Aug 22 1956 at Hill Ridware at pistol point - making off with approximately £25 in notes. Previously the thieves had stolen an old Hillman Minx saloon, and when it ran out of petrol at Fosseway Lane, Lichfield, they stole a local resident's Rover Saloon. In it they proceeded to Hill Ridware; it was later found abandoned near Blithfield Reservoir (LiMe Aug 24 1956).

Place-name The earliest record of the name, is Domesday Book, 1086 for Ridware, 1236 for Mavesyn Ridware. Ridware means 'people who lived by the ford (or bridleway)'. Mavesyn is from the Malveisin or Malvoisin family who held the manor in the C12-14 (PNSZ p459).

Population Mavesyn Ridware was 96th most-populated Staffordshire parish in 1801 with 486 people; 92nd= in 1811 with 548; 95th in 1821 with 598; 98th in 1831 with 576; 105th in 1841 with 531; 104th in 1851 with 523; 109th in 1861 with 462; 108th in 1871 with 467; 109th in 1881 with 473; 113th in 1891 with 391; 107th in 1901 with 438. Mavesyn Ridware could be ranked 110th= worst-affected Staffordshire parish for loss of men in WW1, with 6 lives taken.

Philips, Kevin *England Footballer.* Born 1974. Footballer for West Bromwich Albion, and formerly for Aston Villa, and Sunderland. Had eight international caps for England by early 2008. His residence, built 2002, in Hill Ridware was for sale in March 2008 at £1.5 million (Burton Mail March 4 2008 p7pc).

Quote *Choicest.* SC Woodhouse describing a fascinating journey he made in Staffordshire, by car, in Staffordshire Life Magazine (Nov 1967) entitled 'Ramble Amongst the Ridwares' wrote 'Near the church is a fine old tithe barn, 17th or 18th Century at least. The village is small and the narrow lane by which you enter continues round a bend, past two or three farmhouses, and then soon back again on the Abbots Bromley Road.'

Sandford, Rev Daniel *Mavesyn Ridware's kindest.* Rector of Mavesyn Ridware. By will dated 1779 he gave 200L. The rental from land purchased with it to be distributed to deserving poor (not in receipt of poor relief) on Good Friday and Advent Sunday.

Newborough See Hanbury.

Norton Canes Norton Canes was the county's 65th largest parish, consisting of 4,068 acres; 59th closest parish to the county town, 9.8m SSE to SE; extremist length 4m; extremist width 3.1m. The parish's chief settlement is Norton Canes, a sprawling mining village, contiguous with Norton East and Norton Green; there is much housing and industrial comprising the west side of Brownhills town. Norton Canes is famous for the old county family of Wyrley of Little Wyrley Hall, mining, and Chasewater canal-feeding reservoir, now a pleasure lake.

Altitudes The highest point of the parish is 600 feet on Watling Street on Cannock boundary. The lowest point is 387 feet by Newlands Brook on the Cannock boundary.

Church St James's at Norton Canes is one of 4 such county dedications (of AP churches); 24th last AP county church built dating from 1832.

Bristow, Raymond *Longest serving priest in the church of England by 2006.* Born 1908. Ordained 1935. In 2006 he still held the Bishop of Lichfield's Permission to Officiate and regularly takes services at St James, Norton Canes; his first curacy was at St Mary and St Chad's, Longton (Sunday Sentinel Sept 17 2006 p22) (SLM Nov 2006 p36pc & p).

Carnival *Brownhill's first carnival.* Sept 1 1934, with a procession forming at the Warreners' Arms grounds which proceeded to the main High Street; the first Carnival Queen was Miss Lilian Harrington (LiMe Sept 8 1934 p6 col 3).

Chasewater *First time ever in the history of motor boat racing that Britain competed against France.* Was at the international motorboat race at Chasewater, Sept 3 1961; France was represented by the French champion Rene Milon, and Roger Brunet, who were both past winners of France's six-hour race (SA & Chron Sept 7 1961 p6 col 7). *Only county with a schools sailing centre in the country, 1962* was believed to be that at Chasewater, officially opened in July 1962. Gary Pliva, of 105 Crab Lane, Stafford, pupil at King Edward VI Grammar School, won the prize for being the individual champion helmsman in the Cadet class at a regatta held for the official opening (SA & Chron July 19 1962 p6p). *Pioneering attempt in an aluminium gyro-glider.* Douglas Poole, aged 33, of Mere Green, Sutton Coldfield, in his own home-made one costing £700, over Chasewater in 1971. The attempt to fly 80 feet failed. A gyro-glider was a cross between a helicopter and a glider (Birmingham Post May 24 1971). *British record for harness racing against time (trotting in one mile)* was set at Chasewater on June 21 1975 when Ted Trot driven by John Blisset achieved 2 minutes 06.8 seconds. *British record for harness racing against time (pacing in one mile)* was set at Chasewater on July 7 1975 when Bomber driven by Thomas Brown achieved 2 minutes 04.3 seconds (GBR 1981 p286).

Communications *Oldest signpost in England.* Finger post, dated 1777, at the junction of Chester Road and Watling Street; in c1879 railings were placed round it; in 1929, when it was planned to restore the signpost, it was 'said to be the oldest in England'; subsequently it has been placed in the County Museum, Shugborough (SA June 1 1929 p4p) (CCBO p52). *Last telephone exchange in the Cannock district to convert to subscriber trunk dialling (S.T.D.)* That serving Norton Canes and Heath Hayes which opened in Newlands Lane, Heath Hayes on Nov 18 1971 (CAd Nov 18 1971). *First drive-through pharmacy in UK* opened by Gurd Chahal in Norton Canes in 1995 (You and Yours. BBC R4 May 4 2005). *Britain's biggest motorway service station.* Norton Canes on M6 Toll road, opened 2004 (The Independent, Review March 25 2004 pp2-3).

The oldest signpost in England when it stood on its original site at the junction of Chester Road and Watling Street.

Eagle, Mary *Woman who made butter from her milk.* **She lived** in the C17. Of Little Wyrley. Reputedly could produce two quarts of milk from her breasts per day, besides what her child sucked. From this amount she could make 2lbs of butter per week during the months surrounding her child's birth. Dr Plot sampled some of her butter.

Elizabeth _____? *First person in the parish register.* 2nd of _____? bapt, buried in or by 1565. The first legible entry is Agnes Toncke daughter of William Toncke, baptised Jan 1 1567.

Folklore *Norton's best.* Dr Phineas Fowke is remembered for walking to Edinburgh returning to Little Wyrley Hall after his boots started hurting after 50 miles changing his footwear and setting out again. He inherited the manor of Little Wyrley in 1691.

Fowke, Dr Phineas *Norton Canes' most famous old worthy.* Baptised 1639. Died 1710. Physician. He was born Bishop Burton, Yorkshire. Queens' College, Cambridge, 1654-8 Fellow of the Col-

Dr Phineas Fowke sets out on his walk from Little Wyrley Hall.

lege 1658; practised medicine in London, residing in Little Britain; Fellow of the College of Physicians 1680. He was also learned in theology and was an admirer of Seth Ward, Bishop of Salisbury, whose views in passive obedience he strongly supported. He retired to his paternal estate, Little Wyrley Hall, and there died on 21st January. He is buried at Brewood.

Fowke, Roger and Phineas *Norton's kindest.* Of Little Wyrley. They left 15 penny loaves for the poor at the church every Sunday throughout the year, forever; the dole was still active in c1813.

Geology Most of the parish is Middle Coal Measures; the SE fringe is Upper Coal Measures.

Hewitt, John Thomas *Norton's villain.* A miner who was poaching murdered William Masfen, a farmer of Norton Canes, aged 29, on July 1 1893 by. Hewitt was hung (TB Oct 1982 p5).

Kilbride, John *First work-related disease pay-out in the Cannock-Pelsall Coalfield.* Miner of Grove (alias Brownhills) Colliery, when aged 43 Silicosis-sufferer awarded 24 shillings a week by Walsall County Court, 1932; he died from the disease 1939 (The Cannock Chase Coalfield and its Coal Mines. Cannock Chase Mining Historical Society. 2005. p175).

Little Wyrley Hall *Rare interior wind vane.* In a cupola in the roof over the entrance to Little Wyrley Hall; it told the way the wind was blowing without the inquirer having to leave the house (CCF pp88-89). '*finest collection of heads with magnificent antlers to be seen in Staffordshire'.* The collection of Frank Wallace (d1962) of Little Wyrley Hall. Wallace was a famous stalker who had hunted in all parts of the world. His first book was

'Stalks Abroad' (SA Oct 8 1932 p11p1).

Mainwaring, John Thomas *Self-proclaimed 'The King of Norton'.* Born 1877. Living in a caravan off Watling Street, at Wilkin, Brownhills, in June 1937, when he appeared on a charge stealing a carrier-bag of grocers to the value of 5s before Penkridge Police Court. He was not long in reminding the court of his regal status, beginning "I be tried here?... I am the King of Norton; you are in the presence of royalty. You are mere men, but I am a king, I am not going to be tried at all;" admitting to being resident at Norton Canes 50 years; and denying being a beggar and boozer. He was sentenced to 14 days imprisonment for stealing. In Jan 1938 he was charged again, this time for stealing fencing (SA Jan 12 1937 p5 col 6. Jan 15 1938 p8 col 3). There is a description of a man who self-styled himself the King of Norton Canes and believed the village was his domain in Jack Harrison's 'The King of Norton Canes; a sequel to the best-selling 'Above the Black Diamonds", recollections of Norton Canes in the 1920-30s, published 1990.

Manorial business *Only one change in lordship since the Norman Conquest.* Little Wyrley manor, allowing for inheritance in the female line (VB p125).

Mining *'one of the most famous Staffordshire collieries' c1890.* Wilkin Pit at the time of its closure c1890. A social club and cafe was built on the site of the pit mounds and buildings in 1935-36 (LiMe Aug 21 1936 p5 col 3).

Mistaken identity *When Norton Canes was mistaken for being in the Black Country.* In c1947 when a daily newspaper journalist claimed in his newspaper that he was writing from Norton Canes 'in the Black Country' (SA May 31 1947 p5 col 1).

Munn, Simon *Paralympic wheelchair basketball bronze medalist 2008.* Of Norton Canes.

Place-name Norton first appears in 951 for Norton, 1289 for Norton under Cannock, 1566 for Norton Canes. Norton means 'north town'; Canes is perhaps a corruption of Gain's (as in Gain's Brook), or from the surname Canes (PNSZ p413).

Population Norton Canes was 88th most-populated Staffordshire parish in 1801 with 547; 97th in 1811 with 519; 90th in 1821 with 669; 91st in 1831 with 678; 87th in 1841 with 755; 72nd in 1851 with 968; 59th in 1861 with 1,628; 40th in 1871 with 2,776; 35th in 1881 with 3,546; 35th in 1891 with 4,047; 34th in 1901 with 5,214.

Quote *Choicest.* Phil Drabble, who knew the county like the back of his hand, in The Regional Books 'The Black Country' 1952, noted dwellings long suffering from mining subsidence 'At Norton Canes, in the east, is a cluster of houses which are quite uninhabited. They have sunk below the water level and their occupiers would literally need boats to enter them. This particular lot of houses have frequently been used to bait politicians - a popular local sport - who have given signs of tongue-cheeked promises, which never amount to more.'

Wallace, Frank *'one of the world's foremost game-hunters and wild deer conservationists'.* Died 1962. Of Little Wyrley Hall (E&S Feb 17 1977 p8).

O-Q

Oakley Oakley township (the Staffordshire part of Croxall parish, Derbys) was Staffordshire's 151st largest parish entity, consisting of 739 acres; 44th= fartherest parish away from the county town, 17.3m ESE; extremist length 1.8m; extremist width 1.4m, making it 22nd= narrowest parish entity in Staffordshire. Oakley Farm is perhaps the largest of the three homesteads of the township.

Altitudes The highest point of Croxall is 246 feet on the boundary NE of Croxall, the highest of Oakley is 203 feet on the Elford boundary. The lowest points are 164 feet by the Trent for Croxall; 164 feet at the Trent and Tame confluence for Oakley.

Chetwynd Bridge *'one of the oldest bridge sites in Staffordshire'.* The site of Chetwynd or Salter's Bridge over the

Tame at Oakley (SA & Chron March 22 1956 p6 col 5).

Geology Croxall is Keuper Red Marls (most), Alluvium (Trent Plain); Oakley township is Keuper Red Marls (SE), Alluvium (Trent Plain).

Place-name The first appearance of the name, Oakley, is 1002-4, and it means 'glade where oaks grow' (PNSZ p416).

Population Oakley was 154th= most-populated Staffordshire parish entity in 1801 with 27 people; 153rd in 1811 with 27; 153rd in 1821 with 31; 153rd in 1831 with 29; 155th in 1841 with 31; 159th in 1851 with 20; 154th in 1861 with 28; 155th in 1871 with 37; 156th= in 1881 with 38; 159th in 1891 with 34; 159th in 1901 with 22.

Quote *Choicest*. Carmel and Anthony Mason in their Edingale: A Parish in Perspective, 2002, write 'Because the manor (of Oakley) was effectively split between the great families of Catton and Elford, no grand house with parks, lakes and gardens was created at Oakley since they already existed at Croxall, Catton and Elford. (Peter) Stanley supposes that the village (of Oakley) slowly faded away as its inhabitants sought employment in the grander houses nearby.'

St John the Baptist Across the border in Croxall village, Derbys, the township's parish church, is one of 11 such Staffordshire dedications, and is 48th= oldest ancient parish Staffordshire church, dating from 1200. It has an *exceptionally late incised figure slab* to George and Katherine Curzon, 1605 (LGS p118). The oldest memorial is dated 1485 and is that to Thomas Curzon and his wife Mary, he in plate armour and pointed helmet of the War of the Roses, she in a long dress and a high-crowned hat (SA & Chron March 22 1956 p6 col 6).

Ussher, Rev Richard *Author of Charles Masefield's favourite parish history*. He wrote 'An History Sketch of the Parish of Croxall in the County of Derby' (1881), which features Oakley. Charles Masefield (c1882-1917) was the author of 'Staffordshire' in the Little County Guide series.

Ogley Hay Ogley Hay was Staffordshire's 135th largest parish (extra-parochial), consisting of 1,063 acres; 81st= closest parish to the county town, 12.8 SSE; extremist length 1m, making it 11th shortest parish in Staffordshire; extremist width 2.4m. The parish's chief settlement is Brownhills, a fair-sized bustling former mining town, which sprawls into the neighbouring ancient parishes of Norton Canes, Shenstone, Walsall (det). The parish is famous for its rapid growth in the C19 from a waste heathland to a mining town.

Altitudes The highest point of the parish is Ogley Road, Brownhills, at 508 feet. The lowest point is 371 on Shenstone boundary by Crane Brook.

Church St James' in Church Road, Brownhills is one of 4 such county dedications (of AP churches); 17th last AP county church built dating from 1851.

Betteridge, Derek *Alias 'Golden Arm'*. (c1935-2009). England darts player. Of Warrens Place, Brownhills; gave regular darts performances at the old Warreners Arms Inn, High Street, Brownhills (E&S Aug 13 2009 p51p).

Birch, Jacob *Ogley Hay's villain*. He murdered his sister at their parents house in Lindon Road, almost opposite the Wheel Inn (technically Walsall parish (det)). The murder took place in the backyard before Birch went to work in c1919 (TB Nov 1968 p11).

Birch, Doug *'Mr Brownhills'*. Born 1930. Of Pelsall Road (technically Norton Canes parish), retired youth worker; chairman of the Brownhills Local Committee (founded 1996); responsible for transforming the former Brownhills Council House into the Park View Resource Centre. He was awarded the MBE in 2009 (E&S Dec 31 2008 p6pc).

Boat Inn, The *One of 1000 best pubs in UK 2005*. Walsall Road, Muckley Corner. Known as Oddfellows in the Boat by 2008. As named in Which? magazine's Good Pub Guide 2005; this was the only pub in Staffordshire, Birmingham and the Black Country in the guide (BBC news Sept 30 2004).

Cotterill, Charles Foster *Ogley Hay's most famous old worthy*. Born 1811. Speculator who "laid the foundations of the modern town of Brownhills." In 1837 he purchased the manor and waste of Ogley Hay, a former hay of Cannock Forest, and obtained an act of parliament for its enclosure. He then exploited the potential of the area, lying close to emerging transport systems, by leasing land for farming, market gardening and plantations. Although he had more success with industrial and property development bankruptcy forced him to sell all his land in 1847. After 1860 he tried to form a land company but failed to attract sufficient capital. Charles F Cotterill, a merchant, of Lichfield Street, Walsall, aged 30, occurs in the 1841 Census.

Folklore *Ogley Hay's best.* The lost Knaves Castle, a curious mound just south of Watling Street, the hide-out of highwaymen, perhaps built by them or the authorities trying to catch them. Some have thought it was of Roman origin.

Highwaymen operating on Watling Street with Knaves Castle in the background.

Foxall, Rosemary *Brownhills' villainess.* Born c1960. Jailed for two and half years in 2009 for luring children to her home in Sadler Road, and, with her husband, Martin, ten charges of making indecent videos and photographs of children and possessing 147 indecent images of them. Throughout the trial she denied any guilt. Passing sentence the judge declared "It was a monstrous breach of trust and invasion of privacy" mindful Mrs Foxall was a former dinner lady, a teaching assistant and trusted with the care of children in her community. The crime only came to light as there was a fire at Foxall's house in 2008. Mr Foxall committed suicide before he could be prosecuted (E&S July 18 2009 p6pc. July 31 2009).

Geology Brownhills village (W) is Upper Coal Measures; Brownhills village (S) is Bunter; Brownhills village (E), and the E of the parish is Keuper Sandstones.

Military defence *First annual contest of the rifle volunteers of Staffordshire.* Perhaps held at the County Rifle Association at Brownhills in 1861. The 2nd contest was held there in 1862 (SA Aug 2 1862 p5).

Place-name The earliest record of the name Ogley is 996. It means 'Hocca's or Occa's, Ocga's leah'. The place was one of the hays or bailiwicks of Cannock Forest (PNSZ p418).

Population Ogley Hay was 165th most-populated Staffordshire parish in 1801 with 5 people; 165th in 1811 with 8; 156th= in 1821 with 23; 155nd= in 1831 with 24; 133rd in 1841 with 222; 107th in 1851 with 518; 65th in 1861 with 1,357; 58th in 1871 with 1,824; 56th in 1881 with 2,040; 51st in 1891 with 2,478; 47th in 1901 with 2,677. Brownhills could be ranked 24th worst-affected Staffordshire parish for loss of men in WW1, with 144 lives taken.

Public Art *The Brownhills Miner* is a 30-foot tall iron sculpture of a miner situated in the Pelsall, Lichfield and Chester Roads roundabout (technically Norton Canes parish). It was made by sculptor John McKenna, and erected in 2006, jointly funded by Walsall Council and Walsall Borough Strategic Partnership. In 2008 it was given the name of a deceased miner Jack 'Jigger' Taylor in a competition (BBC Midlands Today Jan 9 2008).

Robinson, Jimmy *'The Pride of Brownhills'.* Born Brownhills c1934, featherweight, boxed for England as a junior, converted to Catholicism through the influence of local boxer, Bernard Hession, a Catholic. Trained at Oscott College; ordained as a Catholic priest in Dec 1971 (BPn Dec 11 1971 photo).

Perry Barr See Handsworth.

Pheasey See Aldridge.

Pipe Hill See Lichfield.

Pipe Ridware Pipe Ridware was Staffordshire's 146th largest parish, consisting of 823 acres; 63rd closest parish to the county town, 10.4m ESW; extremist length 2.1m; extremist width 1.3m, making it 14th= narrowest parish in Staffordshire. The chief settlement of the parish is Pipe Ridware, a hamlet. It is famous for the Norman Font in the church.

Altitudes The highest point of the parish is Hunger Hill at 315 feet. The lowest point is 203 feet by the Trent at Pipe Ridware.

Church St James' at Pipe Ridware is one of 4 such county dedications (of ancient parish churches); 20th last AP county church built dating from 1842. Most notable monument is in the chancel on the N wall, a stone mural monument with Latin inscription and bearing arms, to John Whitehall, a notable beekeeper, sheriff of Staffordshire 1680, of Pipe Ridware Manor House. On the floor beneath, was his grave, dated 1684 (SHOS vol 1 p165) (GNHS p149) (NSFCT 1933 p64) (JME part iv p55).

Cooper, William *Pipe Ridware's villain.* Farm servant, found guilty of breaking into the house of his master, William Leese, at Pipe Ridware, and stealing 13 cheeses on Aug 15 1844. He was sentenced to 10 years transportation at the Assizes later that year (SA Dec 14 1844 p3 col 6).

Folklore *Pipe Ridware's best.* There is the belief Billy the Kid was Billy Bonney and so the son of Rev Thomas Bonney curate of Pipe Ridware (DNB) (TB Jan 20 2000 p5).

Geology Pipe Ridware village and N is Keuper Red Marls; Quintins Orchard is Keuper Sandstones; Trent valley is Alluvium.

Hodgkinson, Miss Emma *Affectionately 'Little Emma'*. Born Oct 3 1867. Of Gold Hay Fields. Later resided at Hill Ridware. She had a notable long association with St James', Pipe Ridware. From the age of 14 and for more than 70 years she carried out the duties of cleaner at the church, toller of the bell and weeder of the churchyard paths. In addition, she decorated the church at Easter, and attended the annual vestry meeting when aged 91; and attended a coffee evening in aid of funds for the church on May 14 1959 (SA & Chron May 7 1959 p6p. June 4 1959 p4 col 5).

Miss Emma Hodgkinson in her younger days cleaning Pipe Ridware church.

Littleton, Sir Edward *Pipe Ridware's most famous old worthy.* (1727-1812). M.P. and agrarianist. Eldest son of Fisher Littleton of Pipe Ridware. Baptised in Pipe Ridware church 28 July 1727. He succeeded to the estates and baronety of his uncle of Pillaton Hall, entering parliament as member for Staffordshire in 1784, serving until his death. He was a very keen supporter of the Staffordshire and Worcester Canal, agriculture, improv-

ing the Cannock Heath breed of sheep, and foxhunting, taking over the Cannock Wood Hunt in 1774. He died at Teddesley and is buried at Penkridge.

Place-name Earliest record of the name, Ridware, is Domesday Book, 1086; 1371 for Pipe Ridware. Ridware means 'people who lived by the ford (or bridleway)'. Pipe is from the Pipe family who held the manor in the C12-14 (PNSZ p460).

Population Pipe Ridware was 140th= most-populated Staffordshire parish in 1801 with 107 people; 143rd in 1811 with 101; 143rd in 1821 with 114; 143rd in 1831 with 111; 145th in 1841 with 100; 147th in 1851 with 90; 146th in 1861 with 93; 147th in 1871 with 90; 149th in 1881 with 74; 148th in 1891 with 84; 152nd in 1901 with 63.

Quote *Choicest.* Two county magazine features sum up Pipe Ridware; SC Woodhouse in Staffordshire Life Magazine, Nov 1967, wrote 'You turn sharp right down another quiet lane, and in about a mile and a half you come to Pipe Ridware, with a small modern rebuilt church with, inside, a lovely circular Norman font.' Whilst Julian A Bielewicz in Staffordshire Magazine, Oct 1973, wrote 'On the banks of the Trent lies the small, secluded village of Pipe Ridware.'

Trent, River *Most polluted river in England 1970* (VB p191); the river flows past Pipe Ridware.

Whitehall, Bridget (c1670-1716) and **Frances** (c1668-1743). *Pipe Ridware's kindest.* Daughters of John Whitehall of Pipe Ridware Manor House. Both died unmarried and were benefactors to the poor of the parish; Frances was successful in the practice of surgery (SHOS vol 1 p165) (GNHS p149) (STMSM Oct 1973 p27).

R

Rolleston Rolleston was Staffordshire's 76th largest parish, consisting of 3,647 acres; 60th= farthest parish away from the county town, 15.5, ENE; extremist length 4.8m; extremist width 5.5m, making it 21st= widest parish in Staffordshire. The chief settlement of the parish is Rolleston, a fair-sized and very pretty village. Ans-

low township has the smaller village of Anslow. The parish is famed for the old county family of Moseley (of whom Sir Oswald Moseley, the Fascist, was one) and their Rolleston Hall.

Altitudes The highest point of the parish is 463 feet by Holly Bank, S of N Inn. The lowest point is 151 feet by the Dove at Dove Cliff.

Church St Mary's at Rolleston is one of 23 such county dedications (most common dedication in the county); 8th= oldest county church dating from 1100. *Most interesting thing* is the recumbent effigy of a priest (possibly a rector of Rolleston) on the N side of the chancel; often wrongly attributed to Bishop Robert Sherburne (d1536), founder of Rolleston Grammar School (VCH vol 10 p206). *Largest monument* is a canopy tomb for Sir Edward Mosley (d1638) (VCH vol 10 p207). In the churchyard is *Staffordshire's only wheel-cross surviving in its entirety.* However it is not in situ and belongs to Tatenhill (SA April 16 1954 p4 col 5).

Coltman, Pte (L-Cpl) William Harold *'The most highly decorated non-commissioned officer in the country' 1974.* (1891-1974). Born Rangemore. For services in WW1, winning a V.C. in Oct 1918, twice winning the Military medal and Distinguished Conduct Medal. 1/6 Batt of North Staffs Regt. Stretcher-bearer; his brassard is on display at the Staffordshire Regt Museum at Whittington Barracks. The VC was for conspicuous bravery, initiative and devotion to duty during operations at Mannequin Hill, NE of Sequehart, on Oct 3-4 1918. In later life Pte Coltman lived in Wheatley Lane, Winshill (SA Jan 11 1919 p5p. June 5 1920 p6 col 8p) (BOb Sept 22 1966 p8. July 4 1974 p3p) (LiMe June 12 2008 p11p).

Folklore *Rolleston's best.* Burnt Gate Inn at Anslow is haunted by a ghost called 'Kit-Mark' a drummer boy who appeared in the 1960s and 1980s (GLS pp17-18), and The Spread Eagle Inn in Rolleston is reputedly haunted.

The drummer boy ghost who appears in the Burnt Gate Inn at Anslow.

Geology Dove valley is Alluvium; Rolleston village and the south of the parish is Keuper Red Marls.

Law *First marriage nullity suit of its kind before a Court.* Brought by Horace Moss, a coachman of Sir Oswald Mosley of Rolleston Hall, in Nov 1896 against his wife, Lucy Archer of Suffolk. He alleged she had defrauded him into marriage by not disclosing to him prior to the marriage she was pregnant. They first met in service in Ireland in 1889 and married on Sept 29 1895 at Hintlesham, Suffolk, and afterwards went to Burton upon Trent. Lucy claimed the child was conceived when she was raped by her brother-in-law. The judge reserved his decision (SA May 22 1897 p7 col 5).

Moon, Ernest *Rolleston's villain.* When aged 30, of 76a Beacon Road, Rolleston, he pleaded guilty at Burton Quarter Sessions in 1956 to obtaining, with intent to defraud, from David Ritchie, the sum of £60 in Nov 1955, by falsely claiming he was the owner of a caravan. The prosecution said of him "This man is a thoroughly dishonest man. It is his 12th appearance on charges of dishonesty. Not only that, but during his Army career there were charges against him of theft. In addition to the present charges he is asking you to take into consideration six other offences of a dishonest nature, all concerned with obtaining money by false pretences.' Moon was sent to prison for five years (BOb Feb 9 1956 p5).

Mosley, Lady Diana (nee Mitford). *One of 'The Girls in Pearls', 'far more intelligent and dangerous than her husband'.* 2nd wife of Sir Oswald. The Girls in Pearls were Diana and her five sisters, all possessed of an eccentric brilliance and known as such in society. Evelyn Waugh wrote that 'her 'beauty ran through a room like a peal of bells'. The second quote is from WW2 intelligence case reports kept on her; she was an unashamed supporter of Adolf Hitler (The Sunday Telegraph April 6 2008 p26).

Mosley, Max *President of the Federation Internationale de l'Automobile.* Born 1940. Son (and favourite son) of Sir Oswald by his second wife, from 1993 (The Sunday Telegraph April 6 2008 p26).

Mosley, Sir Nicholas *341st lord mayor of London.* Died 1612. In 1599-1600. His son Sir Edward Mosley (d1638), bought Rolleston Hall from the Rollestons c1615 (LGS p204);

Mosley, Sir Oswald *1st President of the Burton Natural History and Archaeological Society.* (1785-1871); the Society was formed in 1842, revived in 1876 (BOb Nov 21 1968 p7).

Mosley, Sir Oswald *Model for 'John Bull'.* (1848-1915). Of Rolleston Hall. 4th Bt, whose well-known profile and love for all things English led to his use as the model for the Punch cartoon of 'John Bull'. Vanity Fair magazine (edition about

Sept 3 1898) also has a cartoon by 'Spy' of Mosley as 'John Bull' (SA Sept 3 1898 p4 col 6);

John Bull as he appears on the old 'John Bull Printing Outfit' box.

Mosley, Sir Oswald *Local people referred to him as 'The 'Tutbury Tup'.* (1873-1928), 5th Bt. His father banished him from Rolleston Hall for debauched behaviour, so he took up residence in Tutbury.

Mosley, Oswald *Worst Briton of the C20.* (1896-1980). Of Rolleston Hall. The fascist, as polled by BBC History Magazine, late 2005.

Sir Oswald Mosley (d1980) and his first wife Lady Cynthia Mosley.

Mosley, Lady Cynthia (nee Curzon). (1898-1933). *Paid more for her knickers than men got in their pay packets!* First wife of Sir Oswald. Fanny Deakin, the Silverdale socialist, said at a political rally "Lady Cynthia pays more for her knickers than what you men get in your pay packet" (ES Oct 13 2007 staying in p13).

Paxton, Rev EA *First civil and military chaplain for Khartoum.* Former curate of Stoke, Surrey, and took up his new post in 1904. He was the nephew of Rev G and Mrs Todd of Needwood, and was well known in the Needwood area, having stayed with his aunt and uncle, and preached in the area (SA Sept 17 1904 p7 col 7).

Place-name The earliest record of the name is 941. It means 'Hrodwulf's or Hrodulfr's tun (PNSZ p463).

Population Rolleston was 80th most-populated Staffordshire parish in 1801 with 646 people; 80th in 1811 with 700;

74th in 1821 with 869; 76th in 1831 with 866; 83rd in 1841 with 797; 78th in 1851 with 918; 77th in 1861 with 956; 73rd in 1871 with 1,079; 74th in 1881 with 1,140; 73rd in 1891 with 1,196; 71st in 1901 with 1,303. Rolleston could be ranked 55th worst-affected Staffordshire parish for loss of men in WW1, with 35 lives taken.

Quote *Choicest.* Michael Raven (d2008) in his A Guide to Staffordshire & The Black Country The Potteries & The Peak, 2005, says 'The centre of this large village is truly most charming. The Alder Brook is entrenched and runs through the centre of the settlement. It is fringed with willows and crossed by an old bridge with a cascade. Next to the church is the old and very large Spread Eagle pub, which has a riverside car park and an embowered beer garden.'

Richardson, Elianor *Earliest person recorded in Rolleston parish register.* She was buried?, or baptised? June 1569.

Rolleston, Nicholas de *Rolleston's longest serving vicar.* He served for 87 years, 1318-1405; however, this seems too incredible to be true, and another possibility is Roger de Rolveston 1179-1255, but his length of incumbency also seems incredible; the next longest serving vicar would be John Paget Mosley, who served 1789-1834.

Sherbourn, Rt Rev *Robert Rolleston's most famous old worthy.* (c1454-1536). Secretary and councillor to Henry VII 1496; Bishop of Chichester 1508-36. He founded the free grammar school at Rolleston, 1520, the oldest such foundation in the country. The original endowment letter, written in black letter, was kept in a wooden box in the school room. Staffordshire sources, stretching back to Stebbing Shaw, claim him as a Rolleston native, but the Dictionary of National Biography says he was born at Basingstoke.

Sherriff brothers *Anslow's villains.* Gypsy brothers convicted of the manslaughter of PC William Price of Stretton, near Burton, who they attacked on Jan 24 1903, whilst asking the brothers about the theft of some ferrets from a Mr Draper, a local farmer. PC Williams died the next day of his wounds; the brothers were caught and three sentenced to 15 years imprisonment for manslaughter (Staffordshire Police 150th Anniversary Commemorative Issue).

Sport *Pugilist fight of 31 rounds which only ended with the death of a combatant* was when Charles Beale, a farmer, of Stretton, and Stringer Tonks, a basket-maker of Repton, having quarrelled, agreed to fight at Rolleston to decide their dispute. They met on Jan 16 1811, with the constable of the parish present as stakeholder, and fought with such 'determination and courage seldom witnessed'. Tonks struck Beale a fatal blow and was tried for manslaughter (SA Jan 19 1811. Jan 28 1911 p10 col 3). *World record for British National Powerboat.* 54.58 mph in the 'flying kilometre' on Lake Windermere by Derrick Tilke, 44, of Lyndale, Bellhouse Lane, Anslow, in a boat 'Bewitched' built by himself. This was accepted as a world record by the Union International Motonautique. The event, in Oct 1970, which hosted 42 boats was the first of its kind to be held in Britain (Burton Daily Mail Oct 29 1970 p10p).

Village life *Oldest free grammar school foundation of its kind in the country.* Rolleston, founded 1520 by Robert Sherbourne, bishop of Chichester (SVB p142). *Staffordshire's 13th earliest commutation of tithes when they were dealt with under a parliamentary enclosure act.* The great and small tithes of Rolleston, by allotments of land, 1802. *Village which boycotted the Staffordshire Best Kept Village Competition.* Rolleston, from 2000, to at least 2006, because parish councillors say the notices that each competing village has to put up to promote the competition in themselves look an eyesore. Rolleston has been awarded 2nd and 3rd places and highly commended accolades (Burton Mail Feb 16 2006 p9).

Rushall Rushall was Staffordshire's 119th largest parish, consisting of 1,950 acres; 72nd farthest parish away from the county town, 14.3m SSE; extremist length 2.8m; extremist width 2.4m. The chief settlement of the parish is the village of Rushall which grew up at a road intersection nearly a mile north of the parish church and hall. Rushall parish is famous for Limestone quarries and Rushall Hall when it was a parliamentary garrison in the Civil War.

Altitudes The highest point of the parish is 512 feet on Aldridge boundary near College Farm. The lowest point is 397 feet by Ford Brook on Walsall boundary, south of Ryecroft.

Bond, Nigel *Rushall's boy hero.* Of Rushall, aged 12, awarded a testimonial on Valour by the Royal Humane Society for pulling a seven year old out of the Rushall Canal in July 1967 (The (Pelsall & Rushall) Post Dec 1992 p6).

Chatwin, Cpl E *Rushall's hero.* 1st South Staffs, born Rushall, killed in action July 1 1916, awarded the M.M. in Feb 1917. Another Rushall WW1 hero is Sgt Charles Thomas Craddock, 7th Batt South Staffs A/CSM, born Rushall, killed in action in Flanders May 6 1918, awarded the M.M. in Jan 1918 (ELSON-SS pp99,101).

Clowes, Alice *Earliest person recorded in Shenstone parish register.* Wife of Richard Clowes, buried April 5 1660.

Church St Michael the Archangel's at the north end of Leigh Road, Rushall. Is one of 12 such county dedications (of ancient parish churches); 13th= last ancient parish county church built, dating from 1856. *In the churchyard* is the tombstone of Charles While d1760 suggests he was a kindly giant.

'Within this Tomb the above Charles While doth lie,
He was six feet and full six inches high,
In his proportion Nature had been kind,
His Symphany so just none fault could find,
A Husband kind and to his children dear,
Generous to all and to his Friend sincere'

(ROR p103). There is also the grave of Alfred Moss (1860-1936), poet of Aldridge (SA Aug 8 1936 p11 col 1).

Folklore *Rushall's best.* That in the Civil War one Pitt was used to bribe the parliamentarian garrison commander of Rushall Hall, Capt Tuthill, by the royalist garrison commander of Dudley Castle, Col Leveson, who offered him a sum

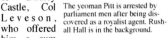

The yeoman Pitt is arrested by parliament men after being discovered as a royalist agent. Rushall Hall is in the background.

of £2,000. But Pitt was discovered, and hung at Smithfield, London, on Oct 12 1644. It is unclear which Pitt or Pytt this was: whether Francis or his son Thomas (b1619), Pitt or Pytt, a yeoman farmer of Heath Town, or Wednesbury, or Wednesfield, or Wolverhampton.

Frampton, Edward Reginald *'last of the Pre-Raphaelites'*. Born 1872. Made frescoes for Rushall church 1905-6, one depicting the four Archangels, including Michael to whom the church is dedicated, the Tree of Knowledge, the Tree of Life, and the angelic choir, representing the largest of only four surviving Frampton frescoes (TB May 6 2004 p22p).

Geology The east part of the parish is Upper Coal Measures; Rushall church, village, and the west part of the parish is Middle Coal Measures; the south part of the parish is Silurian (Wenlock) Limestone.

Leigh, Colonel Edward *Rushall's most famous old worthy.* (1602-71). Parliamentarian, Biblical critic, historian. Author of 'Select and Choyce Observations, containing all the Romane Emperours' (1657) and 'Critica Sacra', containing an engraving of him, which was acclaimed by Archbishop Usher. In the Civil War he was a Commissioner for Staffordshire in the Scandalous Ministers Act 1642; took Eccleshall Castle 1643; commanded a company of Foot and one of Horse; sat on numerous Parliamentarian committees. At the Restoration he retired from public life; died at Rushall Hall, buried in Rushall church.

Parker, Nicholas *Rushall's kindest.* By will dated 1627 he gave money from rental to the poor of Rushall in the form of shilling loaves at Christmas to widows and large families in the parish. The dole appears to have operated to at least within some years of c1813.

Peach, Pte Douglas *Rushall's villain.* He shot dead Violet Richards, 24, and Kitty Lyon, 18, both from Paddock, Walsall, on Sept 21 1941, subsequently robbing them of their handbags, as they were walking through the cattle bridge carrying the railway north of Rushall Hall. Peach was hung at Winson Green Prison, Birmingham, on Nov 26 1941 (MMMR pp79-82).

Place-name The earliest record of the name, Rushall, is Domesday Book, 1086. It means 'The halh overgrown with rush-

es' (PNSZ p470).

Population Rushall was 97th most-populated Staffordshire parish in 1801 with 485 people; 84th in 1811 with 615; 89th in 1821 with 670; 89th in 1831 with 693; 51st in 1841 with 1,609; 49th in 1851 with 1,946; 38th in 1861 with 2,842; 35th in 1871 with 3,702; 27th in 1881 with 5,809; 25th in 1891 with 6,980; 25th in 1901 with 7,943. Rushall could be ranked 46th= worst-affected Staffordshire parish for loss of men in WW1, with 48 lives taken.

Pubs *One of Britain's top 10 waterside pubs 2009.* The Manor Arms by the Daw End Branch of the Rushall Canal, Park Road, Daw End, as claimed in The Sunday Telegraph's 'Britain's finest attractions' series. The inn purports to be one of the oldest pubs in Britain, originally built in 1104 and has had a licence to sell liquor since 1248 (The Sunday Telegraph Jan 4 2009 p12). However, another source says the building was originally a farmhouse. Towards the end of the C19 the Anson family used their front room as a beer house and gained a full licence in 1895 (SNAR p62).

Quote *Choicest.* Frederick W Willmore, the Walsall historian, in his Records of Rushall, 1892, wrote 'A mile to the north-east of the town of Walsall may be seen the remains of Rushall Hall, its ivy-clad walls and fringe of young trees, with the church and graceful spire in the foreground, presenting a pleasant picture to the visitor passing towards it from the dusty highway.

Rann, John *Rushall's longest serving vicar.* He served 45 years, 1726-71; but John Ayliff may have served longer from 1456 to well into the C16.

Roads *One of the worst roads in the country.* The main road from Walsall to the Brownhills boundary, as described by a councillor in 1927 (I Remember Rushall: oral History from Walsall LHC. Victoria Wooldridge. 2002 p8). *'Rush-all the way through'* A very old jibe aimed at Rushall mindful the original village was only a place 'en route' to somewhere else (I Remember Rushall etc. p8).

Wussey, Henry *Rushall person with earliest-surviving will.* It is dated Nov 21 1524.

S

Shenstone Shenstone was Staffordshire's 22nd largest parish, consisting of 8,543 acres; 70th= farthest parish away from the county town, 14.5m SE; extremist length 5.3m, making it 27th= longest parish in the county; extremist width 5m, making it 28th= widest parish in Staffordshire. The chief settlement of the parish is Shenstone, a growing fair-sized village; there is much desirable housing at Little Aston (Sutton Coldfield suburbs). Shenstone parish is famous for its early history finds, Iron Age fort, and gentlemen's seats.

Altitudes The highest point of the parish is Castle Old Fort at 600 feet. The lowest point 282 feet by Black Brook below Shenstone Park.

Aston, Thomas *Oldest sub-postmaster in the country 1946.* (1853-1946). Of Shenstone. He was appointed the local sub-postmaster in c1894 and served until his death (LiMe Feb 15 1946 p2 col 4).

Bretherton, Carl *Irish Open (Golf) Championship winner 1919, England County Championship winner 1928.* (c1892-1976). 'one of the great golfing figures for the Midlands and Britain' 1911-76, of St John's, Shenstone. Handsworth Golf Club 1900-76 (their Bretherton Bowl, for scratch amateur competitions, is named after him); played for England against Scotland 1922-25, against Ireland and Wales 1925; in Warwickshire team which won England County Championship 1928; President of the Warwickshire Union of Golf Clubs 1936-, British Golf Greenkeepers' Association -1976, and Sports Turf Research Institute -1976 (Birmingham Post March 25 1976).

Churches St John the Baptist at Shenstone is one of 11 such county dedications (of AP churches); 15th last AP county church built dating from 1853. *In the churchyard* is the grave of John Radford Cartwright, Shenstone Woodend police constable 1936-62, noted for doing police business by bicycle, for which he was given a monthly 'cycle allowance' of 1s. 6d. to keep it in good repair. The gravestone inscription reads 'On his bicycle he kept the peace' (Yesterday's Country Village. Henry Buckton. pp126-131).

Trinity Street Methodist Church at Shenstone. 'one of the few Methodist village churches which could boast a resident minister' 1939 (LiMe Jan 20 1939 p8 col 4).

Coleire, Miss Gratiana *Shenstone's kindest.* Died 1801. Last surviving member of the old Shenstone family of Coleire. Of Lichfield Cathedral Close. She made an unusual and specific bequest to Arabella Hallen (d1813), and Shenstone churchwardens of 200L plus 150L stock to keep Arabella, Coleire's maid, and any other poor of Shenstone 'who should not receive relief as paupers'. Also a further sum of 200L to be distributed as the churchwardens think fit. The saying of morning prayer in the church throughout the year on Friday, a tradition which continued until c1968, appears to have been paid for from interest from her stock (Shenstone Parish Church and Village. D & A Davies. 1993).

Community achievements *Winners of the first co-operative display of handicrafts in UK* was Little Aston W.I. in 1937, at an event at the Borough Hall, Stafford, organised by Staffordshire Federation of W.Is. Hitherto, its annual handicraft exhibition (for the prized Challenge Banner), had comprised submissions by individuals. At the Federation's annual council meeting it was stated that with this, their first co-operative one, the county Federation were making history, from which could be inferred that this was the first co-operative handicraft display in the country (SA March 20 1937 p5 col 1. April 24 1937 p9ps). *Best kept station in the western district of the LMR Birmingham region 4th 1948, 2nd 1949, 1st 1950, 1st 1951* Shenstone (LiMe Oct 26 1951 p2 col 6).

Early man *Northernmost end of the Forest of Arden.* Could be Shenstone Woodend (SVB p111). *Most important Late Bronze Age artefacts found in Staffordshire.* The hoard of implements from a rock-cut grave at Greensborough Farm (Gainsborough Farm) (SSAHST 1967 pp1-15). *Staffordshire's earliest evidences of man.* A hand axe of the Upper Palaeolithic (pre-Ice Age) period, found 0.5m NNW of Shenstone Hall cSK 111054 (SSAHST 1972-73 p5 fig 1) (NSJFS vol 12. 1972. pp1-20) (SL p35) (MR p280).

Ellison, Alfred *Shenstone man who attempted to break the Cape Town to England flight record in 1934.* Of Footherly

Hall, managing director of Alfred Ellison Ltd, West Bromwich. His brother, George Ellison, navigated. Landing their Puss Moth aeroplane at Cairo in the dark they damaged the under carriage and so spoilt their attempt at the record (LiMe Oct 12 1934 p7 col 5).

Ellison, Miss Yvonne *First 'Beauty Queen' (Carnival Queen) of Lichfield.* Daughter of Alfred Ellison of Footherly Hall. When aged 17 in 1934. Lichfield's August Bank Holiday hospital fete and carnival organised and held the contest. Also in 1934 she held the Miss Shenstone title (SA Aug 11 1934 p12p).

Folklore *Shenstone's best.* Numerous traditions are associated with the Shire Oak, which marked the boundaries of Shenstone and Walsall parishes, near the summit of Shire Oak Hill. It was believed to be 2000 years old when the stump was removed in the 1890s. It is said to have been the rendezvous of druids, Civil War troops and highwaymen. But most famously that Dean Swift sheltered under it in a storm on a journey to or from Ireland. Under the tree Swift was joined by a tramp and his woman-friend. Their conversation revealed they had only just made love together. This so scandalised Swift he married them immediately. The woman asked for a marriage certificate, where upon Swift wrote the following:

> Beneath this oak in stormy weather
> I joined this whore and rogue together:
> And none but He who made the thunder
> Can put this whore and rogue asunder.

Jonathan Swift performs an impromptu marriage between two tramps under the boughs of the now lost Shire Oak.

Geology The Lynn-Hook Hill area is Permian belt; Shenstone, Upper Stonnall, Little Aston villages and the north of the parish is Keuper Sandstones; Shenstone Woodend and the SE is Bunter.

Golf *Inventor of the Dunlop 65 golf ball.* Samuel Graham Ball (1899-1991), resided in Thornhill Road, Streetly, at the time of his death; former Dunlop (later Dunlop Slazenger) employee. Invented 1934 after it was discovered that a ball with 332 dimples each 0.013 inches deep would give a perfect flight. '65' was chosen as it was Henry Cotton's record second round score in the 1934 Open Championship (SNAR p105).

Hospitality *Staffordshire's first 'British Welcome Club' for American servicemen in WW2.* At Cooper Recreation Room, Shenstone, which opened May 30 1944, under the auspices of the W.V.S. (LiMe June 2 1944 p3 col 2). *The country's first luxury hospital to be run by a private consortium of part-time NHS hospital doctors.* The private hospital project with 30 pay beds proposed for Little Aston Hall in 1975 (Birmingham Sunday Mercury Oct 12 1975). *(Staffordshire) Restaurant of the Year 2006.* The Mango Tree at Stonnall, in the Non-European and Asian influence category, as judged by Staffordshire Good Food Awards (SLM Dec 2006 p100).

Lea, Henry *Staffordshire's 17th= oldest man ever.* Of Shenstone. He lived to the age of 107.

Miller, Katie *Raymarine Young Sailor of the Year 2007.* Of Shenstone. Born 1988. For her three-month voyage around the British Isles in her yacht Elektra in summer 2006 (LiMe Jan 11 2007 p3pc).

Milner, _____? *Earliest person recorded in Shenstone parish register.* Daughter of Thomas Milner, who was baptised on March 1 or 16 1579.

Noy(r)es, Joan *Shenstone person with the earliest-surviving will.* It is dated April 4 1533.

Parker, Admiral Sir William *Last of Nelson's captains, Shenstone's most famous old worthy.* Admiral Sir William Parker (1781-1866). Perhaps born at Almington, Drayton-in-Hales. Rear-admiral of the UK 1862; admiral of the Fleet 1863. He purchased Shenstone Lodge 1812 to where he retired and died of bronchitis on 13th November. He is buried at Shenstone. His memorial in Lichfield Cathedral was erected by public subscription.

Place-name The earliest record of the

name is Domesday Book, 1086. It means 'beautiful stone, shining rock' (PNSZ p488).

Population Shenstone was 45th most-populated Staffordshire parish in 1801 with 1,309 people; 48th in 1811 with 1,378; 43rd in 1821 with 1,699; 44th in 1831 with 1,827; 45th in 1841 with 1,962; 47th in 1851 with 2,043; 49th in 1861 with 2,131; 51st in 1871 with 2,224; 49th in 1881 with 2,488; 45th in 1891 with 2,681; 40th in 1901 with 3,043. Shenstone could be ranked 30th worst-affected Staffordshire parish for loss of men in WW1, with 71 lives taken.

Quote *Choicest.* Rev Henry Saunders begins in his History of Shenstone, 1794, the *first published history of a Staffordshire parish*: "SHENSTONE or as it is written in ancient records *Scertestan*, is situated in a pleasant part of the county of Stafford, by all travellers admired as a beautiful and well-watered spot, that part of it especially so named; neither may we wholly except some of its districts, which in some measure deserve notice, as will be evidenced when we treat separately of them."

Rowlands, Dan *Shenstone's first WW2 casualty.* (1922-41). He lost his life on HMS Hood in late May 1941; he was described in the Lichfield Mercury June 6 1941 p6p as 'One of the best known names in the village. Full of fun, overflowing with life, a cheery grin on his round, jolly face, a mischievous twinkle in his eye'.

Rural life *First Shenstone Horticultural Show.* The first annual exhibition of the Shenstone and District Horticultural Society occurred on Wednesday, Aug 5 1896, at Shenstone Court. Winner of the greatest number of prizes was F Milner (SA Aug 8 1896 p2 col 6). *Staffordshire's first horse trials.* Lichfield Preliminary Horse Trials held at Owletts Hall Farm, Lynn Lane, Shenstone, on Aug 27 1960. The trials were run in conjunction with the British Horse Society under its rules, with the object of encouraging combined training, and better horsemanship and horsemastership (LiMe Sept 2 1960 p3p). *Extraordinary-sized duck egg.* A duck of Mr Wright of Stonnall, laid an egg in 1852 which measured four inches from end to end, and eight inches in circumference, and weighed over four ounces (SA May 29 1852. May 30 1952 p5 col 6).

Russell, Mr and Mrs *Fancy that!* Littlehay farmers, who claimed at an inquest in March 1891 their son, James Henry Russell, aged 8, had died of injuries inflicted by the master at Shenstone National School, Mr Worthy Bartlett, beating him about the head with a strap and stick in Jan 1891. The jury returned an open verdict. A post mortem showed the cause of death to be from erysipelasas; it could not be proved the wounds were due to Bartlett's severity. Bartlett was cautioned, and the school accepted his resignation (SA March 21 1891 p6 col 6).

Scribbans, Harry *'one of Birmingham's richest men' 1927.* (c1877-1935). Baker's boy, who made a fortune in WW1 when his slab cake was served out in forces canteens. He came to live at Little Aston Hall in 1927. He once spent £1,000 on a private firework display. When he died he left an estate worth £2,475,239 net personally, on which duty of £1,241,078 was paid (Birmingham Sunday Mercury Oct 12 1975).

Sims, Henry *Shenstone's saddest.* When aged 34 and chief stockman, of Pingle Fields Cottages, on a road off the main Watling Street, he lay in ambush outside his cottage and shot dead the local gardener and neighbour Henry James Woodman, in the delusion Woodman was in line for his job. Before the shooting on April 18 1929 he shot dead his wife, Elsie, 35, and son Cyril, 9 in their beds, and finally shot himself. As evidence of his intentions he wrote letters asking for forgiveness to his parents and mother-in-law. A verdict of insane mind was declared (Staffordshire Weekly Sentinel. April 27 1929 p10).

Smith, Andrew *Shenstone's bravest.* Of Shenstone. Born c1980 with a kidney disease which he endured under the control of drugs. In early 1988 his condition worsened and he was put on constant dialysis. In Sept 1988 a kidney transplant left his immune system in a poor shape. In summer 1989 he was awarded the coveted Certificate for Meritorious Conduct by his cub pack for displaying constant cheerfulness and endeavour (LiMe July 28 1989 p7p)

Social life *First savings bank in the area.* Shenstone, started in 1818; the chief depositors coming from the Black Country. *First reading room in the area.* Oddfellows Hall in Shenstone, built during the Crimean War (St John the Baptist, Shenstone. Dick & Audrey Davies. 1993. pp11,12il). *Shenstone Reading Society's first lecture.* Was given by Rev RW Essington, vicar of Shenstone, on the Crimean War, at the National School room on Dec 14 1854, when the Society is described as recently formed. The second lecture was given by a Mr Brown on 'On the Atmosphere' on Dec 29 1854 (SA Dec 16 1854. SA Dec 17 1854 p2 col 3. Jan 6 1855). *One of the 10 worst places in country to find a single lady to court.* Shenstone, where young single men far outnumber single women (BBC 1 Midland Today Sept 17 2007).

Spray, Steve *ACU 750cc Supercup series winner 1989, British Formula One Motorbike Champion 1989, Powerbike International winner 1989.* Of Shenstone, born c1963, rider for JPS Norton team (LiMe Oct 6 1989 p72. Oct 20 1989 p64p).

Stevenson, Edward *Shenstone's villain.* Highwayman, alias Little Neddy. He operated at Shenstone (LiMe June 12 2008 p4).

Streetly inhabitants *Last people in the Midlands to pay 3d. delivery charge for post* were the inhabitants of Streetly before it was built up, according to a newspaper of 1881 (TBS p24).

Sutton, Mrs Lucy *Staffordshire's oldest woman 1945.* Of Ivy Cottage, Shenstone. She died on April 15 1945 aged 102. Up to a few days before her death Mrs Sutton was in her usual health and weeding in her garden, but had a fall from which she did not recover. She had lived practically all her life in the Shenstone district, and had been widowed for over 30 years. She had all her faculties, except eyesight; did her own housework and looked after an elderly invalid daughter (SA April 21 1945 p6).

Talbot, Connie *Britain's Got Talent runner-up 2007.* Born 2000. Of Streetly. Appeared in this TV contest when she attended Blackwood Primary School (E&S Oct 26 2007 p17p).

Waters, Mrs Valerie *The 'Shy Saboteur'.* In 1977 when aged 45, of Roman Road, Little Aston, she became a cause celebre, being imprisoned on a legal technicality, that of refusing in court to be bound over to keep the peace. On Nov 13 1976 she went with fellow Hunt Saboteurs' Association members to Atherstone Hunt to put hounds off their scent, where it was claimed she was assaulted by hunt supporters. At the subsequent court case she gave evidence as a prosecution witness, but refusing to be bound over to keep the peace was jailed for a month; the accused went free. To the dismay of many the Home Office Minister, Brynmor John, claimed he had no power to intervene.

During her imprisonment at Risley Remand Centre, Lancs, The Sunday Times, Aug 21 1977, described her as 'a mildmannered, respectable housewife and mother', the wife of successful Birmingham tailor, Tom Waters (Birmingham Post Aug 10 1977. Aug 25 1977) (The Sunday Times Aug 21 1977) (Birmingham Mail Aug 24 1977).

Willoughby, Mrs M *'Maggie Jacques', 'the Derbyshire Nightingale'.* Died 1953. Leading soprano, originally of Buxton, lived at Shenstone from 1920 (LiMe Jan 23 1953 p7 col 5).

Statfold Statfold was Staffordshire's 158th largest parish, consisting of 455 acres; 11th farthest parish away from the county town, 21.3m SE; extremist length 1.3m, making it 15th= shortest parish in Staffordshire; extremist width 0.8m, making it 9th narrowest parish in the county.

Altitudes The highest point is 310 feet N of Statfold Farm. The lowest point is 243 feet by the junction of Statfold and Tamworth roads. The chief settlement is Statfold, essentially is one property, Statfold Hall, long and still the seat of the old county family of Wolferstan.

Folklore *Statfold's best.* In the later C17 Dr Plot was told - though he might have been duped - that when men came to remove the spire from the chapel a toad was found in the hole in the top stone, but on being revealed to the air, died (NHS p247).

A 17th Century workman discovers a toad in the spire of Statfold chapel.

Geology All the parish is Keuper Marls.

Gilman, David *Silver Lapwing Trophy holder 1992, Ashley Trophy holder 1994.* Of Statfold Farm. The first is the coveted Country Life (magazine) Farming and Wildlife Award, consisting of £1,000 prize money. He was nominated by FWAG (Staffs Branch) for his efforts to farm with nature, not against it. The second, organised by Staffs CC environment division (the competition has a different theme each year), was awarded in recognition of effort to restore hedgerows (TH Feb 14 1992 p5. Nov 18 1994 p18).

Pipe-Wolferstan, Lieut-Col Egerton Stanley *Statfold's hero.* (1861-1937). Of Statfold Hall, JP, Staffs CC. He was awarded the Queen's Medal and Khedive's Star for service in Sudan 1882, awarded the Queen's medal with one clasp and the King's medal with two clasps for service in the Boer War 1900-02; adjutant 1896-1906, then commander 1908-12, of the 4th (Militia) Battalion of the North Staffs Regt; commander of the 10th Batt Prince of Wales' North Staffs Regt 1914 (SA Feb 27 1937 p11p).

Pipe-Wolferstan, Samuel *Statfold's most famous old worthy.* (1750/1-1820) Antiquarian who kept a diary. Son of Rev Samuel Pipe and Dorothy, daughter of Statfold Wolferston, through whom he inherited Statfold Hall. A great friend and helper to Rev Stebbing Shaw and William Pitt in their several Histories; and also to Rev Thomas Harwood's 1820 edition of Erdeswicke's History. In 1776 he assumed the surname and arms of Wolferstan in lieu of his own.

Place-name First appearance of the name is c1226, and it means, probably, 'studfold' (PNSZ p510).

Population Statfold was 154th= most-populated Staffordshire parish in 1801 with 27 people; 154th in 1811 with 25; 154th in 1821 with 29; 151st in 1831 with 41; 153rd in 1841 with 45; 152nd in 1851 with 38; 156th in 1861 with 26; 150th in 1871 with 55; 151st in 1881 with 61; 155th in 1891 with 53; 160th in 1901 with 21.

Statfold's chapel Is one of only three undedicated ancient parish churches; 13th= oldest county church dating from 1120. Restored 1869, re-equipped and rededicated 1906, still used for worship in 1934 (SA Sept 1 1934 p6 col 5). The *most interesting things* in the earlier C20 were two female effigies under arches on either side of the chancel. The one in the S wall was a woman, of c1375, in a pointed arch 3 feet 11 inches high. She is six feet long, her feet rest on a headless dog. The other, in the N wall, is of a woman, c1390. She is six feet 3 inches long. She is either a widow, or member of a religious order, her feet rest on a dog (GNHS p169) (JME part 1 p21) (LGS p220).

Streethay See Lichfield.
Streetly See Aldridge.
Stretton See Burton.

T

Tamhorn Tamhorn was Staffordshire's 149th largest parish (extra-parochial), consisting of 793 acres; 39th farthest parish away from the county town, 18.05m SE; extremist length 1.4m, making it 20th= shortest parish in Staffordshire; extremist width 1.8m. The chief settlement of the parish is a tiny canal side estate hamlet focused on Tamhorn Park Farm. Tamhorn is famous for MOD shooting range of Whittington Barracks.

Altitudes The highest point is 318 feet on the Hopwas Hay boundary. The lowest point is 190 feet by the Tame. **Geology** The Tame valley is Alluvium; the SW and centre of the parish is Bunter; the centre west fringe of the parish is Keuper Marls.

Place-name First appearance of the name Domesday Book, 1086. It means 'the horn-shaped land near the river Tame', or possibly '(the estate at) the bend of the river Tame' (PNSZ p528).

Population Tamhorn was 163rd most-populated Staffordshire parish in 1801 with 10 people; 163rd= in 1811 with 9; 159th in 1821 with 16; 165th in 1831 with 7; 165th in 1841 with 5; 162nd in 1851 with 10; 157th in 1861 with 23; 156th in 1871 with 31; 158th in 1881 with 33; 160th in 1891 with 21; 161st in 1901 with 20. Tamhorn's most famous old worthy is Sir Thomas de Tamhorn (c1340-1421). Lord of Tamhorn. Sheriff of Staffordshire 1380; M.P. for Staffordshire 1377 (the second sitting), 1382.

Quote *Choicest.* General William Dyott of Freeford in his diary July 1827 referring to the coverts etc of Tamhorn Park says 'I have passed many pleasant days at Tamhorn, and shall greatly feel the disappointment of being deprived of the excellent sporting it afforded me.'

Tamworth Tamworth was Staffordshire's 41st largest parish, consisting of 6,384 acres; 28th= farthest parish away from the county town, 19.2m SE; extremist length 5m, making it 31st= longest parish in the county; extremist width 4.7m. The parish's chief settlement is Tamworth, a market and corporate town.

The parish is famed for a castle, politics, Sir Robert Peel, and the Tamworth Pig. *Staffordshire's earliest commutation of tithes when they were dealt with under a parliamentary enclosure act.* The great and small tithes of the manors or prebends of Comberford and Wigginton, by allotments of land, 1770.

Abelwhite, Alison First *'The Star of Merit' award holder in Tamworth.* Of Dosthill Vicarage. She received this award in the 1st Dosthill Company of Girl Guides, for her 'initiation, devotion to duty and great courage, often under suffering'. It is the highest award which can be presented to any Guide. She was born with two holes in her heart (Lichfield & Tamworth Magazine. Oct 1972 p35).

Altitudes Highest point for Tamworth (Staffs) is 312 feet near Bangley Farm on Watling Street; for Tamworth (Warws) is 362 feet on E boundary, SE of Lodge Farm (Amington Lodge). The lowest point for Tamworth (Staffs) is 184 feet by the Tame at Comberford; for Tamworth (Warws) is 195 feet by the Tame and Anker confluence.

Angling *Ladies' National Angling Champion 1967.* Mrs May Mulvey, wife of the proprietor of a fishing tackle shop on Watling Street, Wilnecote, making her Britain's top woman angler for that year, and achieving a first for Tamworth (TH July 7 1967 p1 cols 5-6p).

Anglo-Saxon and Norman Tamworth *'For its magnificence the wonder of the age'.* King Offa's palace at Tamworth (Staffordshire County Handbook c1958). *2nd mill-site of the Anglo-Saxon period to be found in England.* The water mill found in 1971 in Bolebridge Street, Tamworth. The other excavated mill-site of this period is at Old Windsor, on the River Thames (The West Midlands in the Early Middle Ages. Margaret Gelling. 1992. p148). *Biggest omission of the Staffordshire Domesday Book.* Tamworth, a significant settlement, went unmentioned. *Foremost royal residence of the Mercians.* Tamworth (PNSZ p11).

Animals *Rare ones.* A burbot caught in the Tame at Fazeley Bridge, 1654 (NHS pp240-241 tab 22 fig 4). An albino frog called 'Tom Tom' found at Tamworth on Sept 13 1994. *Purest, least interbred British pig, most common pig breed on British farms* 'Tamworths', in the early 1960s, but had dwindled to only 150 sows in Britain by 1997 (The Oldest: In Celebration of Britain's Living History. J Calder

& A Bruce. 2006) (The Times. March 29 1997 p8p). Apparently there is this old rhyme about the pig:-

Ah, Tamworth Pig is a very fine Pig,
The best you ever see.
Tamworth Pig's the best of all,
The Pig of Pigs is He!

(TH Feb 20 2003 p14). *Tamworth Pig's first showing at Staffordshire County Show* was in 1960 (SA & Chron June 2 1960 p8). *Best animal lovers in the Midlands 1990.* The people of Tamworth were then best at taking in stray animals, according to The National Animal Rescue Association (TH Oct 10 1990 p27). *Record bid for pair of Irish elk antlers.* £47,000 at auction in 2000. The 10,000-year old antlers once belonged to Sir Robert Peel (E&S March 14 2003 p41). *Dog with insatiable appetite for human underwear.* Taffy, a Springer Spaniel, belonging to vet Eubie Saayman of Tamworth, who had 'eaten' 40 underpants and 300 pairs of socks to 2007 (BBC 1 Midlands Today Nov 27 2007).

A Tamworth Pig sleeping at the Staffordshire County Show, 2009.

Argyle, John F *'The man who put Tamworth in the movies'.* Died 1962. Son of a Tamworth lawyer, who set up his own film company, Argyle Arts Pictures Co, in 1930. He often used local locations for instance, his own home Dryden House, Comberford Road. In 1932 he moved to London and set up a new movie company, Argyle Talking Pictures Ltd. His 'Flames of Fear' (1931), related to a man's fear of working in the coal mines, was shot at Pooley Hall Colliery (TH Oct 11 2001 p14p).

Athelstan *First Saxon king to be acknowledged as King of England.* (899-939). Crowned at Tamworth in 925 (TH Oct 1 1999 p14).

Athletics *TBS English Schools Combined Events Champion 1994.* Marc Newton of Tamworth AC (TH Sept 23 1994 p96).

Barnes, Thomas *Staffordshire's most successful foundling.* He was found in a barn at, and adopted by, Hopwas. He became a wealthy London merchant and endowed a school in his native village, 1717.

Bonner, C *One of Tamworth's three V.Cs* (TH Jan 9 1915 p8 col 5. Oct 13 1917 p3

col 4. Jan 19 1918 p3 col 3).

Bowls *British Ten-pin Bowling Association National Champion 1995.* Julie Pritchard of Tamworth, claiming top 20 overall position (TH April 7 1995 p104).

Brassington, Jon *Solo harmonica player national champion 1993.* When aged 26 of Houting, Dosthill, and a member of the trio known as 'Reed Combination' who also received awards at the event organised by the International Harmonica Organisation (TH July 30 1993 p9).

Briggs, Robert H *Tamworth's villain (modern times).* Tamworth Town Clerk 1919-1928, native of Leigh, Lancs, born c1892, embezzled the sum of £438 meant for a philanthropic scheme by the town council to advance money to people who were about to build houses in Tamworth under the Housing Act 1923. Sentenced to 9 months imprisonment (TH July 2 1928 Special edition. March 11 2004 p14).

Brindley, RP *Possibly Tamworth's longest-serving bell ringer.* He retired in 1937 after 65 years (TH June 12 1937 p5 col 5).

Briscoe, Bill *Strange but true!* Born Two Gates. He retired as landlord of the Boot Inn, Lichfield St, Tamworth in 1970 aged 76, after 55 years, having never had a drink; he came to the inn with his family in 1915 (TH Oct 9 1970 p8 cols 4-7).

Buildings and housing *First fireproof housing in the country.* Probably terraces in Mill Lane, Fazeley, with brick roof-vaults and floors, built in association with Robert Peel's cotton mill, 1795. *Tamworth's first public library.* Opened on Jan 19 1841 by Sir Robert Peel. It stood at the top of Coleshill at its junction with Lower Gungate, later to be known as 'Miss Blight's School', demolished in 1938 (TH Oct 7 1944 p4 col 3). *Tamworth's worst C19 slums.* The tiny cottages that were once in Peel Street and Brewery Lane, and were themselves the oldest part of the town. In the vicinity had stood the old Staffordshire Town Hall (TH Nov 19 1999 p14). *First reservoir in the country in which the concrete is consolidated by the vibrated shuttering principle.* Hopwas Wood (covered) Reservoir built above Hopwas pumping station by Tamworth Waterworks, officially opened Sept 16 1936 (SA Sept 19 1936 p3 col 7). *"one of the ugliest and most inappropriate frontages you can see anywhere in the town"* The replacement of Church Street, Tamworth, a street of charming old timber-framed shops demolished 1968 to make way for a modern shopping arcade (TH Aug 27 1999 p14ps). *An original Staffordshire Conservation Area.* Tamworth in 1969, one of three approved by the Council of British Archaeology (BOb Aug 7 1969 p1). *'one of the 'greenest' towns in the Midlands' 2006.* Tamworth, producing just 5.4 tonnes of carbon dioxide emissions per person, compared to Stafford - one of the worst - producing 10.9 tonnes per person, according to the Department for the Environment (Birmingham Mail. Nov 21 2006 p18). *Britain's greenest hotel 2008* Premier Inn, which opened on Dec 8 2008, at Tamworth. Endorsed by the Carbon Trust, it combined green building materials and an array of groundbreaking technologies unmatched anywhere in Britain (The Observer. Dec 7 2008 p4). *First Gregory type 'People's houses' in the Midlands* A hundred such houses built by Tamworth Town Council on the Gillway estate at Tamworth. The first recipients of one were Mr and Mrs Geoffrey Griffin on Nov 17 1952. The homes sought to curtail the rising cost of building by providing accommodation in blocks of four self-contained flats, and three-bedroomed houses, of varying designs to suit differing aspects in a traditional styles, but cutting out waste space and unnecessary out buildings (SA Nov 21 1952 p1 col 9).

CHURCHES St Editha In central Tamworth is one of two such county dedications (of AP churches); 23rd= oldest county church dating from the C12 or roughly 1150. *One of the finest churches in the country.* St Editha's, listed in top 100 churches in England in Tim Tatton-Brown's 'The English Church' (2005) (SLM Nov 2005). *One of the most interesting parish churches.* St Editha, according ot Pevsner (BOE p274). *One of the largest parish churches of Staffordshire.* St Editha's at about 190 feet long (BOE p274). *Largest medieval parish church in Staffordshire.* St Editha (CHMS p53). *Longest church entry in Pevsner's 'Staffordshire'.* St Editha's at 96 lines (BOE pp274-277). *Most impressive Decorative church as a whole in Staffordshire.* St Editha's (BOE p22). *One of only three double spiral staircases in English churches* A double - ascending and descending - cochlea flight of stone stairs in one cylinder well, both winding round the same pillar in the SW corner of the steeple at St Editha. There are two entrances (one inside and one in the churchyard), and two exits at the top; one flight has 106 steps, the other 101. Plot called it 'the most unusual piece of Stonework, and the most extraordinary of any Ecclesiastical building,' he had ever met with. The other examples are at Much Wenlock, Salop, and Pontefract. The famous example is at the chateau of Chambord, France (NHS pp369-371) (SHOS vol 1 p425) (SLM Autumn 1957 p13 p of close up of the platform to the other spire) (CHMS p53) (SGS p167) (COS p49) (MR p322) (GLS p93-94). 'finest object inside the church' Perhaps, according to Henry Thorold, the splendiferous baroque monument under the tower to Sir John Ferrers (d1680): two knelling figures - Sir John and his son Humphrey (d1678) - support the base, cherubs adorn the sarcophagus with luxuriant garlands of fruit and flowers, and an urn stands above. It was commissioned from Grinling Gibbons, but probably carved by Arnold Quellin (BOE p276) (SGS pp166p,167). *Perhaps unique in England.* The tippet drawn over the head of the effigy of Baldwin de Witney (d1369), Dean of Tamworth; he restored the church after the fire of 1345. The effigy lies in the founders arch in the N wall of the N chapel; the feet rest upon a dog which was headless by the mid C20. Masefield says the tippet is a very unusual arrangement, whilst Staffordshire Life Magazine thinks it could be unique in England (LGS p230) (JME part i pp18-19) (CHMS p53) (SLM Autumn 1957 p15). A stained glass window to WW1 dead is the *1st proposed such window for a church as a WW1 memorial in Staffordshire.* Tamworth parishioners met to discuss this at College Lane School as early as Dec 17 1918 (SA Dec 21 1918 p7). *First peal ever rung exclusively by Tamworth men.* The Tamworth Branch of Staffordshire Association of Bell Ringers on Feb 13 1888 at St Editha, a peal of Grandsire Triples rung in 3 hours 8 mins, Tayler's six part, 5,040 changes, tenor 22cwt 1 quarter in E flat (TH Feb 18 1888 p5 col 1).

St Editha Amington. Alias *'the Church on the Green'* built in the 1860s (TH Sept

The top of the double spiral staircase in the SW corner of W tower of St Editha's church, Tamworth, 2009.

11 1998 p26).

St Martin in the Delph at Stoneydelph. *Tamworth's first woman deacon* was Miss Diana Brewer, who took charge at St Martin's in 1988 (TH July 29 1988 p9).

Unitarian Chapel *Oldest free church in Tamworth.* In the later C20 it became the base for the Royal Naval Association Tamworth branch (TH May 15 1998 p26p).

Civic affairs *Tamworth's first mayor* was Robert Nevill, 1836. *Tamworth's first woman mayor* was Miss Alice Evelyn Argle (1877-1950), the first woman to be elected a member of Tamworth Town Council, Nov 1930, and the borough's first female mayor, 1937 (SA Aug 19 1950 p4 col 3). *Tamworth's first honorary freeman* was Frederick George Allton of 'Standon' Ashby Road, Tamworth, born Lichfield 1864, created May 2 1951; baker; elected to Tamworth Town council 1900; to Tamworth RD 1901, representing Fazeley parish (LiMe May 11 1951 p3 col 2. Dec 31 1954 p2 col 7). The 2nd honorary freeman was Alderman George Henry Jones, miner, OBE, JP, Mayor 1932-33, in appreciation of his services to the council; son of a collier, born Brindley Heath, Hednesford (SA Jan 7 1955 p1 col 3). *Tamworth borough's first council house* was No. 28 Lichfield Road in 1901 (TH Oct 9 1970 p8); *its first post-War* was at Fazeley, opened Jan 1 1947 (TH Jan 4 1947 p3 cols 4-5); *it's 5,000th* was No. 139 Caledonian, Glascote, for Mr and Mrs Sidney Meredith, in 1970 (TH Oct 9 1970 p8). *First Rural District in the country to sell a council house.* Tamworth R.D.C. who sold 41 East View, Glascote, to its tenant, William Thomas Perry, miner at Birch Coppice Colliery, for £1,225; sale agreed on Dec 19 1952 (TH Dec 26 1952 p5 cols 6-7). *Tamworth's first 'overspill' housing estate* 1,700 houses on The Leyfields estate for Birmingham's overspill population. The initial project - for which work began in 1961 - housed 556 families. Officially opened in May 1962 (TH Feb 8 2001 p14ps). *'Worst Architecture in the World'.* Leyfields estate, according to Alderman Tom Kennedy at a Tamworth borough council meeting, in March 1966. He said the houses on it were ugly and horrible and had become slummy. The council gave approval to the first stage of an improvement scheme to give a 'face lift' to the estate (TH March 11 1966 p1 col 2). *Last Tamworth borough council meeting* was on March 5 1974; Tamworth District Council came into being from April 1

1974 (TH March 8 1974 p1 col 1-4).

Clarke, Sir Charles Mansfield *Doctor to Queen Adelaide, wife of William IV.* Of Wigginton Park, the seat of his older brother John Clarke (d1818) (TH Jan 10 2002 p14).

Clegg, Dr David *Tamworth's 'Peter Pan' of GPs.* Born c1927. General practitioner in Tamworth 1958-90, moved to the Hollies Practice at Tamworth Health Centre 1969, chairman of the Aldergate Practice (TH Sept 28 1990 p3).

Communications *Tamworth's first telephone exchange.* The National Telephone Company opened an exchange in George Street, Tamworth, in the Coventry division, on June 3 1897 (TH June 5 1897 p5 col 6). *Tamworth's first radio programme.* Perhaps that on May 8 1925 entitled 'Tamworth Tower and Town', a wireless talk from Birmingham by John Hingley, lasting 15 minutes (TH May 16 1925 p6 cols 3-4). *First wireless S.O.S. message relating to Staffordshire.* perhaps the announcement made from the BBC's London Station (2LO) on Monday evening March 8 1926 asking Albert Wilkins to go to 27 Bradford St, Tamworth, where his father lay dangerously ill. Wilkins of Birkenhead was listening and notified the BBC's Liverpool staff who passed on his whereabouts to the London Station who in turn communicated with Police Inspector G Jeffrey of Tamworth by phone; but his father had died before the broadcast was made (TH March 13 1926 p8 col 7).

Community achievements *National Brass Band Competition winners 1921, 1923, one of the leading brass bands in the country 1921-39.* Amington Band, also winning the Junior Cup (1921), and the Senior Award (1923), and Grand Shield (1923) (TH June 7 2001 p14p). *'most internationally-minded school in the Midlands' 1950.* The Girls' Secondary Modern School, Croft St, Tamworth, for having numerous associations/ links with international events/ bodies (TH April 15 1950 p4 cols 5-6). *Staffordshire County Show Best Farm 1948.* Hopwas House farm, run by Charles Wylie, in the large farm category, over 200 acres; 1948 was the first year of this prize (SA July 24 1948 p5 col 7). *'Most successful mobile library in the country'.* Tamworth, introduced in 1988 to Amington and Stonydelph estates (TH Dec 16 1988 p23). *Fancy that!* 1,000 inflatable bunnies from Info. Publishing, Ladybank, Tamworth, were used in the video for the 1989 Christmas hit single 'Jivebunny' (TH Dec 8 1989 p2). *Best Large Town in Heart of England competition winners 1988, 1989, 1991.* Tamworth (TH July 21 1989 p1. Aug 2 1991 pp1,2). *Strange but true!* Warren Roberts, manager of Cloud 10 night club in Tamworth, took the Club's lap-dancers into the air in a specially-commissioned hot air balloon to perform in 2005-06 (BBC news Dec 12 2005). *5th top tourist centre in Heart of England Region 1995.* Tamworth, out of 60 other centres in the region's tourist board's annual assessment (TH Oct 6 1995 p3). *BBC Gardener of the Year 2006 venue* were five new terraces at Tamworth.

Contest *Britain's representatives in the European version of TV's 'It's a Knock Out' 1976.* Were from Tamworth. *'biggest event of its kind in the UK'* The Man v. Horse v. Bike race, a unique event, which came to Hopwas Woods on April 19 1992, involving 500 runners, riders and cyclists (TH April 17 1992 p104). *UK Strongest Man finalist 2004, 2005.* Dave Meer of Tamworth (ES May 10 2006 p12).

Cordell, Gregory *Britain's first couple who never met before their wedding.* Of Tamworth. On Jan 25 1999 when aged 27, he and Carla Germaine of Sutton Coldfield, Warws, 23, married having had no contact with each beforehand; by July they had separated (Daily Telegraph Jan 26 1999 p3ps) (Daily Mail July 17 1999 pp26-27).

Cotton milling *Tamworth's rarest trade token.* Harding Calico Printing Company 1799, one of only six in existence, went to the Tamworth Castle Museum in 1971 (TH June 4 1971 p1 cols 5-6). *Sir Robert Peel's first cotton mill at Tamworth.* Lady Meadow. *His largest cotton mill at Tamworth.* Fazeley, at the junction of The Birmingham and Fazeley and Coventry Canals Fazeley, 1790s (BOE p132) (SL p116) (MR p149).

Cowland, James William *Amington's villain.* When aged 66, of Decoy Cottage (originally of London), and working as a stockman at Amington Hall Farm he shot dead Mrs Joan Guild, aged 26, of 13 Sheepcote Estate, Amington, land worker at the same farm, on July 29 1951, and then took his own life. However, Cowland's motive for murdering Mrs Guild, remained rather puzzling (SA Aug 3 1951 p4 cols 3-4. Aug 17 1951 p1).

Cricket *Tamworth FC's earliest recorded cricket match* was against Appleby Grammar School 1858 (LTM Jan Feb

1972 p35).

Crime *The Tamworth bomb hoax.* When 20 parcels were sent off from Tamworth railway station on Dec 1 1894 by Charlie Dent, a painter and decorator, and Frank Cannock, a mechanic at Cookes Clothiers. The parcel sent to the Lord Mayor of Liverpool went off and alerted the authorities. The men had done it to win a prize of £250 offered by a new periodical as an award for the best publicity stunt to advertise their magazine. But the magazine roundly condemned them. However, 224 Tamworth inhabitants signed a petition asking for them to be pardoned. They were each fined £20 (TH Dec 22 1894. Dec 17 1999 p18). *Staffordshire's biggest cash haul.* Perhaps the nearly £2 million stolen from a Nat West bank depot in Tamworth in the night of Oct 18 2006 (BBC 1 Midlands Today Oct 19 2006).

Davis, Mr B *Britain's?, Midlands' oldest working barber 1955.* Born c1866. Of Silver St, Tamworth. He worked to his death, aged 89. Born Aston, Birmingham; came to Tamworth in 1905 (TH Sept 23 1955 p7 col 3).

Day, Priscilla *Staffordshire's 15th= oldest woman ever, Tamworth's oldest female citizen ever (probably).* 1886-1992. Former caretaker at Tamworth old Girls' Grammar School (TH July 17 1992 p11).

Doyle, Nicholas *Dosthill's villain.* Born c1975. He roasted alive a pet gerbil in a microwave and tortured two other gerbils to death, all belonging to Philip or Lee Wood after a night drinking on Aug 7 1993. His parents of Cottage Farm Road, Dosthill, subsequently disowned him. After his sentence to four months youth custody the JPs chairman, Mrs Jane O'Brien, said: 'The story that has unfolded in this court today is horrendous. The callous and brutal treatment of these animals is beyond comprehension' (TH Aug 13 1993 p1. Sept 10 1993 p3. Oct 8 1993 p13).

Eastaff, Derrick *Appeared in first wedding televised from the Tamworth district.* Aged 23 he married June Hanbury, aged 19, of Hockley, at Wilnecote parish church on Saturday June 14 1958. The wedding was of interest as Derrick, a miner at Amington Colliery, had been injured in a pit fall three years earlier and was wheelchair-bound, and June was a former Beauty Queen (TH June 20 1958 p7 col 8).

Farr, W *Staffordshire's oldest man ever.* Of Tamworth. He lived to the age of 144.

Fasher, William *Staffordshire's 7th oldest man ever.* Died 1785, aged 118 (W p616).

Florendine, Thomas *'Grand Old Man of Amington'.* Born Glascote 1840. He served on the District Council 1901-, Board of Guardians, and JP in Warws to 1933. Moved to Amington in 1877 before when he was the landlord of the Gate Inn. When he retired in 1899 he built 'Ashleigh' on the corner of the Glascote Road and was still living there in 1934 (TH Oct 6 1934 p5 cols 4-5).

Folklore *Tamworth's best.* In C10 Polesworth Abbey, Warws, was founded by a West Saxon King, who made a relation, Editha (later St Editha), abbess. The grasping then lord of Tamworth Castle Sir Robert Marmyon expelled the nuns from the Abbey. So one night in 1139 St Editha's ghost visited Sir Robert at Tamworth Castle threatening to punish him if the Abbey was not returned to the nuns. The ghost threatened to strike him with her crozier and told him his wounds would not heal unless he restored the nuns to their convent.

Football *The father and son on West Bromwich Albion books at the same time.* Hubert 'Jack' Pearson born Kettlebrook, Tamworth, and his son "Keeper" Harold Pearson in 1925 (TB April 13 2006 p24). *Only footballer to receive a 'benefit' during WW2.* Harry Hibbs of Wilnecote, who served his apprentice with Tamworth Castle in the mid 1920s, and was goalkeeper for Birmingham City from 1924-25; he retired from football in 1945-46 (TB May 4 2006 p34). *When two Tamworth goalies were in one Wembley final!* The FA Cup Final of 1931 when Birmingham City's Harry Hibbs (of Wilnecote) and West Bromwich Albion's Harold Pearson were at opposing ends of the pitch. The final score was 2-1 to Albion (TH May 18 2000 p14ps). The situation was repeated when Dosthill's Gavin Ward, Leicester City goalkeeper, faced Mile Oak's Martin Taylor, Derby County goalkeeper, in the Endsleigh League Play-Off Final at Wembley on May 30 1994 (TH May 25 1994 p104). *Football's 'Gentleman Cowboy'.* William 'Billy' Goffin (1920-87), born Amington. Worked for the Glascote foundry of Messrs Thompson & Southwick aged 14; played football for Tamworth prior to WW2. After WW2 played for Aston Villa to early 1950s (TH Dec 16 1960 p20) (Wikipedia, 2009). *Most people given a Red Card in football in Staffordshire, possibly in UK.* When Dave Warwick, referee, sent 50 spectators off the ground at an under-11s cup match between Bedworth Eagles and Gillway Boys at St Edith's Field in 1995. The incident began when he sent an Eagle player off for punching an opponent. Then a club official, remonstrating with him, got a Red Card. This led the two sets of supporters to yell obscenities at each other. Warwick then ordered the entire crowd away from the pitch, pending the game's abandonment. The crowd complied for the sake of completing the game (E&S Dec 3 2005 p8).

Geology The Anker valley area is Alluvium; the Amington Hall area is Keuper Marls; the Rye Hills area is Keuper Sandstones; Amington-Stonydelph villages is Lower/ Middle Coal Measures; west of the Anker is Keuper Marls; Keuper Sandstones (Bolehall village), Lower/Middle Coal Measures (Glascote village and S); Castle Liberty is Alluvium (all); Fazeley is Alluvium (Fazeley village and Tame valley), Keuper Marls (rest); Syerscote, Tamworth is Keuper Marls (all); Wigginton is Keuper Marls (Hopwas village, Wigginton village, lodge and Comberford), Alluvium (Tame valley and Coton); Wilnecote is Lower/Middle Coal Measures (most), Keuper sandstones (NW).

Glazier, Colin *'one of the world's greatest war heroes', Tamworth's hero.* (1920-42). Able Seaman. Of Two Gates. On HMS Petard when he gave his life recovering vital Enigma codes from a sinking German U-boat, so by foreshortening WW2. His

The relief portrait of Colin Glazier which appears on the memorial erected to his memory in Church Street plaza, central Tamworth.

feat of heroism, and that of colleagues Lt Tony Fasson, and Tommy Brown, was a story line in the boys' own magazine, The Hornet, 1969, but was generally little known until c2000. A memorial was erected to his memory in Church Street plaza on Oct 27 2002 (TH Oct 31 2002 p1. March 6 2008 p6) (Sunday Express Nov 11 2007 p48) (The Real Enigma Heroes. Phil Shanahan. 2008).

Golf *Phil Dingley Cup winner 1991* was Jonathan Whitehall, aged 15, Wilnecote High School pupil, scoring 69 rounds of 72 (TH June 21 1991 p94). *National (English) Public Golf Course Ladies Champion 1992* was Helena Rean of Tamworth Golf Club; they hosted the event, which was organised by the National Association of Public Golf Courses (TH Sept 8 1995 pp92,96).

Guy, Thomas *Tamworth's most famous old worthy.* (1644-1724). Philanthropist and printer. Bookseller 1668-, amassed a fortune through printing Bibles. In 1707 he built and furnished three wards of St Thomas's Hospital, London, and founded the hospital in Southwark which bears his name, 1722. Although he was born in London, the son of a lighterman and coal-dealer, his mother was a Tamworth native, and he endowed almshouses there in 1678, and represented the town in parliament 1695-1707. He died unmarried on December 17th.

Hart, Alderman William Francis *'one of Staffordshire's best known farming personalities' 1960.* (1888-1960). Of Holmcroft, Comberford, Tamworth, member of the Staffordshire Agricultural Executive Committee in WW2; prominent NUF member; Staffs CC 1949-; Alderman on Staffs CC 1955-; moved to Tamworth from Eccleshall in 1916 (SA & Chron Feb 4 1960 p7).

Headquarters *Great Britain's 'HQ' town.* By 1994 the trend was noted for national and international firms and groups to base themselves in Tamworth (TH March 25 1994 p28). In 2008 No. 42 Heath Street, Tamworth, was the *national home* of these trade organisations: Door & Shutter Manufacturers Association, alias Door & Hardware Federation (DHF, 1970); of the British Local Manufacturers' Association (1898, dormant in 2002); Fabricated Access Cover Trade Association (1995); Power Fastening Association Ltd (PFA, 1978); Performance Textiles Assoction Ltd (PERTEXA, 1919). Tamworth was also the national home of the Chief Fire Officers' Association (CFOA, 1974), at 9-11 Pebble Close, Amington; and the Laboratory Animal Science Association (LASA, 1976), who promote welfare of animals in laboratory science. *National home (2002) of the Association of British Introduction Agencies (1981).* Market Street, Tamworth.

Healthcare *'no other town in the Midland counties showing greater improvements than Tamworth... a Cottage Hospital and Dispensary, a Free Library and Baths... besides which the town had been* repaved... (and enjoyed) the grandest water that was ever known'. Tamworth Herald, April 23 1887 p5 cols 5-6 on the achievements for Tamworth of Rev William MacGregor (see below, Tamworth's kindest) (Midland History 1999 vol xxlv). 'the largest acute General Hospital in the only Hospital Group in the country which was staffed entirely without Resident Doctors'. Tamworth Hospital, Hospital Street, in Group 23 Lichfield Sutton Coldfield and Tamworth. It eventually became the case after the founding of the hospital in 1880 as consultants were appointed one by one (A History of Tamworth Hospital. Dr Charles Goodliffe. 1976. p101). First Staffordshire Red Cross detachment to gain certificates for advanced knowledge of First Aid. Possibly Mrs N Davis, cadet officer (joined 1953), and Mr AF Thompson, an instructor (joined 1958), members of Tamworth detachment (TH Dec 22 1967 p3 cols 6-8).

Hewitt, Pte Phillip One of Tamworth's Iraq War heroes. Aged 26, with Pte Leon Spicer, lost his life in the war (E&S March 20 2008 p24).

Kinross, CT One of Tamworth's three V.Cs (TH Jan 9 1915 p8 col 5. Oct 13 1917 p3 col 4. Jan 19 1918 p3 col 3).

Leach, Mrs Susannah Oldest person to be confirmed in Staffordshire. She possibly could claim this when aged 81, at, and when residing at Guy's Hospital, Tamworth, by the Bishop of Lichfield in autumn 1897, as she was too infirm to attend church (SA Nov 6 1897 p7 col 4).

Lees, James Tamworth's first WW1 fatality. Of Wilnecote, aged 27, 2nd South Staffs Regt, killed in action at Moussey on Sept 15 1914. Lees could probably claim this, also Bombardier George Brookes of Two Gates, of 31st Battery Royal Field Artillery, who died on the same day of wounds received at the battle of Aisne (TH Oct 24 1914 p6 ps col 4).

Lester, Mrs CM First women to sit on the magistrates' bench for Wilnecote, Warws. Died 1957 aged 81. Along with Mrs JVL Grant, from Oct 23 1934 (TH Jan 18 1957 p5 col 2. Jan 25 1957 p5 col 6).

MacGregor, Rev William Tamworth's kindest, 'Tamworth's greatest philanthropist'. (1848-1937). He resided at Bolehall Manor. On his retirement as vicar of Tamworth in 1887 a memorial address signed by 1,200 townspeople described him as 'one of the best men and greatest benefactors that the parish of Tamworth ever had.' He helped found Tamworth Cottage

Hospital, had erected the Public Baths, partially restored St Edith's church, designed Hopwas church, and through his exertions caused the building of a Free Library and Reading Room. The second claim was made by Mabel Swift (SA March 6 1937 p11p) (Lichfield & Tamworth Magazine Oct 1972 pp25-27p) (TH June 8 2000 p14p. March 17 2005 p40).

Rev William MacGregor - Tamworth's kindest.

Martial Arts Welsh National Open Judo (young) Champion in under 34 kgs 1994 Luke Dennis of Bolehall (Jan 14 1994 p96). By 1994 Richard Weston, aged 21, the National Thai boxing champion had moved to Fazeley (TH Nov 25 1994 p96).

Mason, William Tamworth workhouse's oldest inmate ever. Perhaps William Mason who reached the age of 101 on March 1 1922 (TH March 4 1922 p8 col 3).

Military defence First meeting of the Tamworth Rifle Volunteers Took place on Nov 30 1859 (SA Jan 14 1860 p5 col 4). First annual rally of No. 6 South Staffordshire County, of the British Legion took place at Tamworth, Sunday July 1 1934; there was a service in the parish church and a March Past in the grounds of Tamworth Castle. No. 6 branch was made up of Armitage, Brereton, Colwich, Great Haywood, Lichfield, Longdon, Rugeley, Shenstone, Whittington and Tamworth (SA July 7 1934 p11ps).

Mineral extraction Royal Albert Hall is decorated with Glascote terracotta using clay hewn at Gibbs and Canning's Glascote Heath pit, operating by at least 1847 to 1950; in addition, their terracotta was used for the internal and external surfaces of the Natural History Museum in Kensington, the Savoy Hotel, the head offices of Prudential in Holborn and the Picture Gallery in Whitechapel (TH June 21 2001 p14p). First demonstration of the Tamworth District of Amalgamated Association of Miners was a procession of 1,500 men led by the Tamworth Rifle Corps Band from Hall End, Wilnecote via Two Gates, Fazeley, Tamworth, and Bolehall in a show of strength on July 28 1873 (TH Aug 2 1873). 1st Tamworth miner's gala was on June 12 1954 in Tamworth Castle pleasure grounds. This was the first to be organised by the

Midland Area Council of the NUM. Five Midland colliery bands headed the procession (SA Feb 5 1954 p1. SA & Chron Feb 3 1955 p1 cols 7-8). *'Dosthill should be Dusthill!'* A correspondent to Tamworth Herald complained in 1994 Dosthill should be Dusthill after all the dust generated by the 'Stoneware Dump' on Rush Lane (TH March 11 1994 p6).

Motor-racing *British Formula Three Champion 1993, Macau Formula Three Grand Prix bronze 1993* Kelvin Burt of Tamworth (TH Sept Sept 10 1993 p88. Nov 26 1993 p93. April 21 1995 p88. Sept 1 1995 p80).

Parkes, Samuel *Tamworth's forgotten hero, one of the 600, first Private soldier to receive the V.C.* He was christened at Tamworth church, received the V.C. (established Jan 1856) in 1857; took part in the Charge of the Light Brigade, 1854 (ES June 20 2006 p6. Jan 4 2007 p14).

Payne family *The family who have lived as Red Indians since c1977.* Of Belgrave, Tamworth (Central News Jan 22 2007).

Place-names First appearance of the name 675-92. It means 'enclosure, homestead on the river Tame' (PNSZ p529). Comberford (meaning 'the ford of the valley'), in the north of the parish, is a rare placename in the Midlands (DUIGNAN).

Poorest, Tamworth's In the earlier C18 there was a poorhouse opposite Church Street, in Colehill (later taken in as the town post office), erected by the Earl of Northampton. In 1750 Lords Weymouth and Middleton had a new workhouse erected between Lady Bank and the river Tame, later known as Brewery House. Another institution was built on Wigginton Road after the 1834 (TH May 12 2005 p36). In 1888 there was a proposal to form a new Poor Law Union centred on Wigginton, for Tamworth townships and parishes neighbouring them in Staffordshire (SA March 24 1888 p5 col 5).

Population Tamworth was 23rd most-populated Staffordshire parish in 1801 with 2,722 people; 22nd in 1811 with 3,188; 21st in 1821 with 3,901; 24th in 1831 with 3,915; 25th in 1841 with 4,202; 25th in 1851 with 4,502; 25th in 1861 with 4,693; 25th in 1871 with 5,047; 34th in 1881 with 3,572; 28th in 1891 with 6,194; 28th in 1901 with 6,817. Tamworth could be ranked 20th worst-affected Staffordshire parish for loss of men in WW1, with 200 lives taken. According to the 1991 Census Tamworth had

the largest proportion of younger people countrywide in the up-to 17 years old age bracket; in Staffordshire it had the highest unemployment rate (10.4% of males and 5.2% of females that could be economically active), highest proportion of single parent families, and highest number of cohabiting couples (TH Feb 19 1993 p19. May 7 1993 p15).

Pringle, Bryan *Opened the first Meadows Festival (Edinburgh).* (1935-2002). Actor. Born Glascote in 1975. When aged 3 his family moved to Bolton, Lancs, where his father was vicar of St Bede's, Morris Green. His acting career took off with a part in the film 'Saturday Night, Sunday Morning' (1960), since when he has appeared in Ken Russell's films, and TV's 'Inspector Morse', and 'EastEnders' (SA & Chron March 17 1960 p10) (Wikipedia, 2008).

Pubs, dining and entertainment *Tamworth's oldest pub.* The Old Stone Cross, Church Street; there may have been an inn on this site as early as 1290, when one 'Isabel' was caught three times for giving short measure at her an alehouse at the 'Cross'. Vaulted cellars appear to be coeval with the crypt of St Editha's church; Mick Jagger, of the Rolling Stones rock group, was famously banned from the pub in 1963 (TH Dec 1 2005 p40pc). *One of the oldest coaching inns in England* was The Queen's Head Inn, Wilnecote village, reputedly dates back to the C14; Dick Turpin, highwayman, reputedly frequented 'Dick's Room', a snug little tap room here (TH Sept 27 2001 p14ps). *Tamworth's oldest theatre* was in Church Street (formerly that part known as Butcher Street) - Sarah Siddons performed there in the C18. The building became a malthouse and then a Baptist chapel, before being converted to the Arts Centre in 1975 (TH March 10 2000 p14). *Tamworth's first cinema* was Clifford Thornburn's Palace Cinema, squeezed in at the side of his George Street shoe shop, 1910. The first film shown was 'The Portuguese Rebellion' followed by a feature film 'Robert the Silent' (TH June 15 1935 p6. Feb 14 2002 p14p). In 1935 the new Palace Cinema was described as *'one of the finest and most delightful entertainment houses in the Midlands ... if not the whole country'* by William Jackson, chairman of the directors and the principal contractor (TH June 15 1935 p6). *Tamworth's first Chinese restaurant.* The Sing Hong, Lichfield St, opened in 1965 (TH Sept 17 1965 p16 col 3): *Indian restaurant;* Royal Bengal, Lichfield St, opened June 1 1972 (TH June 9 1972 p3 cols 5-7). *Tamworth's first major public bonfire* was on Nov 5 1970 at Castle Pleasure Grounds, attended by 8,000 people, run by Tamworth BC (TH Nov 13 1970 p17 col 1-5).

Quote, choicest Tamworth was a Staffordshire town Daniel Defoe did see, and in his A Tour Through The Whole Island of Great Britain 1724-6, he writes 'From Litchfield we came to Tamworth, a fine pleasant trading town, eminent for good ale and good company, of the middling sort; from whence we came into the great road again at Coleshill in Warwickshire.'

Rail *There is no doubt that Tamworth, in its strategic position, should become the central railway station for the whole country!'* Edmund Peel of Drayton Manor, chairman of the Birmingham and Derby Junction Railway, at a board meeting at a formative stage in the company's history, from the late 1830s (TH March 8 2001 p14). *First locomotive on the Birmingham to Derby railway line*

Aftermath of Tamworth's first rail crash in 1870, as depicted in the Illustrated Midland News of the time.

'Tamworth' on July 1 1839 (TH May 23 2002 p14). *Tamworth's first rail crash* occurred at 3.57am on Sept 14 1870 on the LNWR with the derailing of an Irish Mail train, which was shunted onto a siding, three people were killed - Samuel Taylor, the engine driver, Thomas Davis, the fireman, and Fr Healey, a Catholic priest (Illustrated Midland News Sept 25 1870 il) (TH June 25 1999 p14il). *Pioneer in first-aid for railway passengers*. HC Paterson (1898-1968), born Kilsythe, near Glasgow; his interest in first aid began with membership of St John's Ambulance Brigade. He resided on the Gillway Estate to 1965 (TH April 19 1968 p9 col 8). *UK trainspotter's favourite station* used to be Tamworth for locomotive engine types, because of its position on the main lines of both the Midland and Western divisions of the London Midland Railway; indeed, its popularity grew so much that spotting facilities had to be withdrawn in the interests of efficiency and the comfort of passengers, c1948; spotters, mostly boys,

then started to use the Station Fields as an observation point, and 'this spot became famous in the trainspotter world as Tamworth Field' (Railway Station postcard collection at National Monument Record Centre, Swindon) (TH March 8 2001 p14. Aug 9 2001 p14).

Reading, Donald *Boy Wilfred Pickles visited in hospital.* When aged 13, of Wilnescote Parish church choir, the famous broadcaster visited him on Good Friday 1951 in Tamworth Central Hospital, during a good will tour of the Warwickshire Coalfield, visiting miners' clubs at Tamworth, Belgrave, Baldesley and Atherstone (TH March 31 1951 p4 cols 3-5).

Reliant Robin *1st 3 wheeler Reliant 'vans'* Were licensed on Jan 1 1935, the creation of Tom 'Laurie' Williams (1891-1964), originally built in his back garden at Kettlebrook. He retired as managing director in 1964 (TH Feb 14 1964 p13. Sept 9 2004 p14). *Reliant's 1st passenger wheeler* The Regal Mark 1, which appeared in 1953. *Britain's first flowline production light alloy motor vehicle engine* The 600cc overhead valve unit on a Reliant Regal 3/25, Oct 1962. *First 4 wheeled vehicle by Reliant* Was the Sussita shooting brake designed and developed for Autocars Ltd of Haifa in 1958, this further developed into a sports car known in Israel as the Sabra and the Carmel an economy family saloon (LTM Sept 1971 p23). *Biggest order in its history to 1964* £1 million from Autocars Ltd, Haifa, Israel for 4,000 cars and commercial vehicles in Jan 1964 (TH Jan 17 1964 p1). *Israel's biggest-selling motor vehicle 1964* The Reliant Sussita, with 10,000 supplied by the company (TH Jan 17 1964 p1). *First mass-produced car in Turkey* A Reliant Saloon 4/5 seater designed by Reliant was expected to be in production from late 1966 (TH Jan 28 1966 p12 cols 3-4). *Biggest and most experienced users of glass fibre in the European motor industry, manufacturing the world's biggest range of fibre bodied vehicles* Reliant in 1971 (LTM Sept 1971 p24). *2nd largest Brit-*

A Reliant Robin car.

ish-owned motor manufacturers Reliant at Tamworth producing 20,000 vehicles a year. (Staffs Illustrated June 1969. Staffs Scene). *10,000th Robin Reliant* Was registered and took to the road in the week Oct 6-11 1974 (Oct 11 1974 p19). *1st ever 'Del Boy' Derby* Was at Goodwood Motor race circuit, Sussex, in 1992. The idea of the race came after reports of a court case involving a Reliant Robin owner caught speeding on a motorway at 94 mph (TH March 6 1992 p27).

Rhead, Harold *Tamworth's 'finest actor'* According to the Tamworth Herald. Of Rosy Croft, Tamworth when he died 1995. Known for his booming voice; played Abraham in Lichfield's 'Mystery Plays'. Equity member since 1981. Tamworth Town Crier 1985 (TH May 26 1995 p2).

Road *Tamworth's first car* was a Cubitt, made in Aylesbury, owned by William Griffiths of Invermay, 33 Wigginton Road, Tamworth, owner of Griffiths Engineers' Forge and Castle Cycle Works, Gungate (TH June 22 2000 p14). A motor car was first seen on the streets of Tamworth on Monday afternoon, Nov 23 1896 (TH Nov 28 1896 p5 col 3). *Tamworth's first bus conductor* Joseph Willdig of Prospect St, The Leys, Tamworth, on Tamworth's first bus, before WW1 (TH Jan 5 1968 p6). *Staffordshire's only voluntary ambulance service to 1953* Based in Mile Oak and operating for Tamworth 1941-53 when superseded by a Staffs County Council new station in Tamworth, opened in Jan 1953 (SA April 3 1953 p1). *One of the last horse-drawn vehicles to pass along Church Street.* In 1958 (TH Feb 21 1958 p7 cols 4-6p). *First woman bus driver for Midland Red in Tamworth.* Mrs Pauline Hand of Polesworth in 1971 (TH Sept 10 1971 p1 cols 6-9p). *Tamworth firm which made the Chitty Chitty Bang Bang car for a stage production.* Midland Hydraulic Services at Mariner on the Lichfield Road Industrial Estate, costing £13,000, for a production opening at Blackpool Town Hall on Nov 18 1989 (TH Nov 10 1989 p27). *When the original Chitty Chitty Bang Bang car visited Tamworth.* On May 20 1969 coming to the town's Co-operative Societies Supermarket, Church Street, to promote Ambrosia canned milk puddings; there was a competition to win the car (TH May 23 1969 p1 cols 1-3).

Rose, Henry *Staffordshire's longest organist at one church (perhaps).* (1864-1955). ARCO, organist and choirmaster at St Editha's 1886-1950, formerly organ-

ist at Lichfield Cathedral, and Broadstairs (TH Jan 7 2000 p14p).

Shopping *Prettiest shop in Tamworth c1900.* G Griffin & Sons, watch repairer, on the north side of George St (TH Nov 24 1967 p5 cols 4-5p). *'best florist in Britain' 1994.* 'Julie Anne' Florists of 26a Market Street, Tamworth, opened c1981, run by Julie White, which won the national award for Britain in the Flower Council of Holland's Retail Florist of the Year Competition (TH Feb 11 1994 p29).

Simkins, Harry *The 'Bonehill Poet'.* He wrote a 182-line rhyming verse about Tamworth, dated June 1873 (TH Jan 3 1969 'Chronicle Herald' p3).

Skating and skiing *Royal Navy ski champion 1963.* Harry King, aged 18, born in Austria, raised in Tamworth (TH Feb 15 1963 p22 col 4p). *MK Ice Dancing winner 1994.* Craig Ash, aged 13, of High St, Dosthill, with his dancing partner Stephanie Monoghan of Stetchford, Birmingham (TH Feb 18 1994 p2).

Smith, Mrs Violet *First Staffordshire Dancing Masters' Association International award winner.* Probably could be claimed by Mrs Smith. Of Tamworth. She obtained this award dancing with Mr Avinal at the Derby Examination Centre on Jan 8 1950. She was the first from Tamworth to receive it and only 30 such awards had been made in Great Britain to 1950 (TH Jan 28 1950 p3 cols 5-6).

Snow Dome *Europe's first indoor skiing centre, UK's first indoor ski slope with real snow.* The snowdome which opened 1994 (Staffordshire County Guide 2006/7 pp33,57). *UK's only children's snowplay* (Staffordshire Breaks 2006. Staffordshire Tourism). *World's first indoor snowmobile track, only indoor snow track* (Staffordshire Breaks 2006. Staffordshire Tourism) (Snowdome leaflet 2006).

Societies *First delivery man for Tamworth Co-operative Society.* J Hawkin (d1926) of Amington (TH Oct 23 1926 p5 col 3). *'one of the few (building societies) in the country whose directors are unpaid' 1951.* Tamworth Building Society (SA May 25 1951 p1 col 3).

Spicer, Pte Leon *One of Tamworth's Iraq War heroes.* Aged 21, with Pte Phillip Hewitt, lost his life in the war (E&S March 20 2008 p24).

Steele-Bodger, Henry William *President of the British Veterinary Association.* (1897-1952). Of Lichfield Street, Tamworth. Born Peterborough, began his practice in Tamworth in 1922, president of the association 1939-41. When on the council 1939-51 he was instrumental in creating the Association's committee concerned with a nation wide survey of diseases in food producing animals (LiMe Jan 18 1952 p3 col 5).

Stott, Mrs G *Champion Woman Town Crier of the Midlands 1963*. When aged 67, of 13 Blythe St, Tamworth, she appeared in a contest organised by Independent Television companies, going on to be placed in the first nine nationally; she made a television appearance on 'Lunch Box' (TH March 22 1963 p15).

Swimming *Great Bitter Lake record swimmer.* Corp Pulcella Swan, aged 21, son of Mr and Mrs Pulcella of 37 Manor Rd, Bolehall, in 4 hours 43 mins, beating the previous record by 26 mins. The Lake, in the Suez Canal Zone, is 7 and half miles long (TH Sept 9 1950 p5 col 8).

Tamworth Castle *One of the finest examples of herring bone walling in the country.* That in the lower portions of the curtain wall at Tamworth Castle, 1070-1100 (WMLB pp89,91) (TNE p261). *Rare cut halfpenny of Edward the Martyr.* Found in the Tamworth town ditch, 1960. *'earliest (scissors) ever discovered'.* A pair of early C15 origin found during excavations at the Castle, 1972; scissors were thought to have not been invented until the C15 (TH Aug 8 1972 p1p). *King's Champion.* The Marmions of Tamworth Castle held Scrivelsby manor, Lincs from the king by the service of being armed on the day of coronations for the defence of realm, a service which became known as acting King's Champion. *Hatchment with the most quarterings in Staffordshire.* That of 4th Marquess Townshend at Tamworth Castle with 16 (Hatchments in Britain No. 8 p147). *Only family in Britain other than the royal family entitled to own swans.* Townshend family, once of Tamworth Castle; strictly the head of this family and the monarch (Daily Mail Jan 11 2008 p9). *'Castle' bicycles.* Made

by Griffiths Engineers' Forge and Castle Cycle Works, Gungate, Tamworth. There was an example of a 'Castle' bicycle in Tamworth Castle Museum in 2000 (TH June 22 2000 p14).

Thompson, Miss Edith *Tamworth's first Carnival Queen.* Of Glascote in 1931, at Tamworth's first carnival; the procession was headed by the Amington Band (TH June 15 2000 p14p. July 28 2005 p40p).

Titterton, Ernest *Observer to all 12 British atomic tests carried out between 1952-55.* Atomic scientist, former Tamworth Grammar School pupil. In 1943 he joined British scientists sent to work on the Manhattan project in New Mexico; a couple of years later he advised on instrumentation at the Bikini weapons test; director of the School of Physical Sciences at the University of Canberra, 1968-; knt 1970 (TH Aug 1 2002 p14p).

Townshend, George *20th Field Marshall of the British Army.* 1st Marquess Townshend, of Tamworth Castle, 1796.

Trade claims *One of only three in UK and six in world NAMAS accredited calibration laboratories.* Acquired for Sline Masters of Lichfield Road Industrial Estate, Tamworth, in 1990, costing £1m (TH July 27 1990 p24). *World first.* The production of a 32-page broadsheet newspaper by Tamworth Herald in the week for Oct 22 1971, on the Goss Suburban web off-set printing press (TH Oct 29 1971 p1). *One in every four men in UK wear underwear produced in Tamworth!* 1991 Claimed by Thistle Trading Co Ltd on Amington Industrial Estate, founded 1990. By 1991 they were producing over 1 million pairs of jockey shorts and briefs for the country's leading high street chains (TH Oct 11 1991 p27). *'most improved plant' award winner 1991 UK.* Corrugated Ltd of Tamworth (later Smurfit Corrugated) in the 10th Safety Competition sponsored by the British Fibreboard packaging Association at the International Paper Board Industry journal, launched 1982 (TH Dec 6 1991 p33). *Ford Motor Company's Car and Commercial Parts National Award winner 1994.* Hamer Ford of Bitterscote (TH June 24 1994 pp30,31).

Trade unionism and exhibitions *First branch of the Amalgamated Engineering Union to introduce an apprentice award scheme.* Tamworth branch; the first ball and prize giving was on Nov 2 1951 (TH Nov 10 1951 p4 col 5). *Tamworth's first industries exhibition.* Opened at the Assembly Rooms on July 24 1951 by Walter Higgs, a Birmingham industrialist and former president of the Birmingham Chamber of Trade, who said he could think of on other town in the the Midlands which had such a diversity of industry as Tamworth, and went on:- "It is more Tamworths we want in Britain rather than more Birmingham." (SA July 27 1951 p5 cols 1-2).

Ward, Bill *Strange but true!* Actor who appeared as the villain, Charlie Stubbs, in ITV's 'Coronation Street' c2006. He was so loathed by viewers of the soap opera he was assaulted by a member of the public. This was in a Tamworth shopping centre (Bill Ward on Channel 4's The Paul O' Grady Show. Oct 2 2007).

Watercraft *SS Tamworth* was a small merchant navy vessel built 1924 which carried coal from Newcastle to London throughout the WW2. She often carried the Convoy Comodore and his staff. In 1947 she was sold to Malta and renamed the 'Eastern Trader', she was probably sold later, and broken up (TH Aug 24 2000 p14il).

West, Harry *Amington's bravest.* When aged 31, an LNWR platelayer of Amington, along with Ernest Bailey, 19, MR employee, tried to save the three Wood children from drowning in the Anker on April 30 1904, whilst they were gathering flowers on the north river bank. The Royal Humane Society were informed of Bailey's bravery, whilst for West, who lost his life, a subscription fund was got up to help maintain his widow (SA May 7 1904 p7 col 7. July 9 1904 p4 col 6).

Williams, Arthur *'Grand Old Man of Hopwas'.* Of Bridge House, Hopwas, fireman, market gardener, chorister, sidesman at St Chad's, Hopwas, member of the old Tamworth Volunteers; originally of The Bodnets, in Tamworth parish, died aged 92 in 1952 (TH Nov 21 1952 p5 col 3. Nov 28 1952 p4 col 4).

Williamson, William Harold *Bolehall's bravest.* When aged 38 he successfully rescued Elaine Anne Spencer, 13, of Bolebridge Street, from the Anker on March 12 1950 and received the Royal Humane Society's certificate (SA Aug 5 1950 p5 col 7).

Wilson, Eve *Tamworth's Citizen of the Year 1989.* Founder of Special People in Need charity (S.P.I.N.) founded March 1988, organised by Tamworth Herald (TH July 14 1989 pp1-2).

Wood, Henry *Tamworth's historian.* (1898-1980). Born Fazeley. Town Clerk from 1928, and saved the borough's ancient records from decay in Tamworth Castle. Author of 'Medieval Tamworth', 'Borough By Prescription'. On his retirement in 1959 he was made a Freeman of the Borough (TH May 14 1999 p14p. Feb 19 2004 p14ps). Also Henry Charles Mitchell (1872-1947), stone-

Henry Wood: Tamworth's Historian.

mason, author of 'Tamworth Tower and Town' (1936), honorary curator at Tamworth Castle, contributor to TH. Buried Wigginton Road cemetery (TH Sept 6 2001 p14ps. June 17 2004 p14ps).

Woodcock, Alderman TF *One who helped achieve perhaps the country's live-longer-as-a-parish-clerk record.* He was aged 93 when he retired as clerk of Fazeley PC in 1941. William Banton (b1868) of Bolehall, succeeded him and was still clerk in 1958 - then thought to be oldest clerk in the country (TH Jan 3 1958 p4 col 6).

Wright, Robert *Tamworth's villain.* He was one of the Gunpowder Plotters, friend of Edward Devereux (brother Robert, Elizabeth I's favourite), one of the two MP's for Tamworth 1588. Executed for treason Jan 31 1606 (TH Nov 1 2001 p14).

Tatenhill Tatenhill was Staffordshire's 14th largest parish, consisting of 10,100 acres; 73rd= farthest parish away from the county town, 14.2m due E; extremist length 6m, making it 18th= longest parish in the county; extremist width 4.6m. The chief settlement is Barton-under-Needwood, a large village, none of the other townships have ever had settlements to compare. The parish is famous for the Wychnor Flitch custom.

Altitudes The highest point is 442 feet at Callingwood Gate. The lowest point is 157 feet by the Trent.

Ashworth, Roy *He bought the Batman and Robin Car used in T.V. series.* Of Tatenhill. Director of Burton Coin Machines Ltd. He bought the car for £1,050 in 1969 when aged 45 (TH Feb 14 1969 p1 cols 7-9).

Blount, William *Introduced Sir Thomas More to Erasmus.* Of Barton-under-Needwood, later 4th Lord Mountjoy, in winter 1497. More went on to inspire and encourage Erasmus to write 'Praise of Folly' (1511); to More the book is dedicated (SA

Oct 26 1935 p10 col 6).

Bronze Age *Rare flat Bronze Age ceme-tery, outside southern England* was found at Graycar Business Park, Barton (ES Jan 18 1997 p11).

Casterton, Rebecca *Barton's saddest*. Of Holly Road, Barton. When aged 13 she lost her life in a car accident with her best friend Lauren Brooks, aged 12, of Forest Road, Burton, whilst return-ing from riding lessons on Jan 20 2006. The girls had attended John Taylor High School, Barton, pupils lined the streets of the village during the funeral procession, and the school erected a memorial garden to them in 2007. The two were described as 'little angels' with 'hearts of gold' in messages placed in the floral tributes at the accident site on the southbound A38, close to the Clay Mills junction. The lorry driver, Robert Murray, who had caused the accident, by talking on his mobile phone whilst driving, was jailed for four and half years in 2007 (Burton Mail Jan 23 2006 p1pc. Feb 4 2006 pp1pc, 3ps. Jan 24 2007 p3. May 11 2007 p5).

Churches St Michael and All Angels' at Tatenhill is one of 12 such county dedica-tions (of ancient parish churches); 80th old-est AP county church dating from 1296.

St James' at Barton-under-Needwood was built 1517-33 and is the *most note-worthy Perpendicular church in Stafford-shire* (BOE p22). It has *'one of the oldest church chests in existence'* and itself has three locks.

Buildings and the built-environment *Oldest house in the parish 1971*. Blaken-hall (BOb Oct 28 1971 p7). *Last village in the county to get piped water*. Perhaps Dunstall, from 1954 (East Staffordshire Official Guide. 2005?). *Tutbury RDC's 500th post-war house*. No. 69 St James Road, Barton-under-Needwood, officially opened on May 4 1954 (BOb May 6 1954 p1ps). *Britain's 3rd best pub 2004*. The Middle Bell Inn, Barton-under-Needwood, as ranked by a trade magazine (BBC news Aug 12 2004). *One of the AA's 1001 Great Family Pubs*. Horseshoe Inn, Main Rd, Tatenhill 'Probably five to six hundred years old, this historic pub retains much original character, including evidence of a priest's hiding hole' (book of the above title, 2005). *England's finest parsonage 'west' region winner*. The Old Rectory, Tatenhill, in a contest sponsored by Savills estate agent in 2008, out of 100 nomina-tions nationally. The house was built for the Dean of Lichfield in 1710 (Burton Mail

Sept 15 2008 p14).

Clarke, Simon *324th richest in Britain 2005, 318th richest in 2006*. Son of Sir Stanley Clarke (d2004), of the Knoll and Barton Hall, Barton-under-Needwood (UAd April 26 2006 p5).

Clarke, Sir Stanley *Owner of Grand Na-tional winner 1997*. (1933-2004). Of the Knoll and Barton Hall, Barton-under-Needwood, with the horse Lord Gyllene. Founder of the prop-

Stan Clarke

erty developing company St Modwen; Northern Racing Group president and owner of Uttoxeter Racecourse (BBC Midlands Today Sept 20 2004).

Coltman, L-Cpl William Harold *Tatenhill's hero*. (1891-1974), D.C.M. M.M., 1/6th Batt North Staffs Regt (T.F.), born Tatenhill Common. He was awarded the V.C. for conspicuous bravery, initia-tive and devotion to duty, during opera-tions at Mannequin Hill, NE of Sequehart on Oct 3-4 1918 as a stretcher-bearer res-cuing men from behind enemy lines (SA Jan 11 1919 p5 col 6).

Communications *'one of the oldest sur-viving road signs in Staffordshire' 2006*. A finger post sign, dating from 1896. It was moved to its present position, opposite the Shoulder of Mutton Inn, Main Street, Barton-under-Needwood, in 1919 to make was for the War Memorial. In 2006 it was restored by Barton Civic Society (Burton Mail Feb 9 2006 p11p. April 27 2006 p11p). *First telegram to be received and delivered by Burton Post Office* was delivered sometime in the earlier C20 on horseback by George Needham (d1973) to Byrkley Lodge; Needham was 'Bur-ton's last horse-drawn cab owner' (BOb July 5 1973 p7).

Countryside *'A view that is ever Eng-land'*. The landscape of Callingwood (History of Tutbury) (BOb Nov 15 1956 p2). *Staffordshire's only enclosure mainly of open field arable under General Act of 1836*. Catholme Meadow; 91 acres Awarded 1844 by Act of 1836 (A Domes-day of English enclosure acts and awards. WE Tate. 1978). *Unique thorn tree*. A thorn whose leaves every spring are 'as yellow as straw' and then turn green by St James' tide in Wychnor Park garden, near John Offley's sundial. It has grown like this for centuries, so it is unlikely to be diseased. The original thorn grew in a hedgerow near Wychnor chapel, then six saplings were taken from it. The other only known specimen is at Kew (Staffs Illustrated. Nov 1969).

Davidson, David and Jean *Their first Travelodge stayed in.* Serial Travelodge guests. The first Travelodge the Davidsons stayed in was that at Barton-under-Needwood in 1985. They liked the experience so much they gave up their flat in Sheffield and have since lived entirely in Travelodges in Newark and Grantham (The Daily Telegraph Sept 11 2007 p8).

Dunstall Hall *'The richest commoner in England' 1814* Charles Arkwright (1786-1850); he purchased Dunstall Lodge (alias Dunstall Hall) estate (SHC 1912 p293) (Daily Mail Dec 10 2002 p11). *Oldest art treasure in the house, 1912* was a short pillar of dark-green marble, apparently came off an Egyptian temple. *Oldest statuary in the world* are figures of lions at Dunstall Hall, believed to be sculpted at Athens 400 to 500 BC (NSFCT 1912 p193). *Only Staffordshire country house with a genuine Roman floor mosaic.* Dunstall Hall; said to come from Tivoli; Cerberus is represented in the centre. *Last three successive members of the same family to serve the shrievalty of Staffordshire* perhaps the Hardys of Dunstall Hall - Sir John Hardy in 1878, his son Sir Reginald Hardy in 1893, and his son Major Bertram Hardy (1877-1953) in 1925 (SA Aug 18 1934 p9p of Sir Reginald). *'one of the youngest Masters of Hounds in the United Kingdom' 1904* Bertram Hardy (1877-1953), son of Sir Reginald Hardy, chiefly associated with the Atherstone. He led the Staffordshire Yeomanry when they won the Territorial Challenge Cup at the International Horse Show at Olympia in 1910 (SA Aug 27 1904 p4 col 4) (BOb Sept 17 1953 p1p).

Endeavours *1st= parish registers transcribed and published by Staffordshire Register Society.* Barton-under-Needwood, 1902-03 in 2 vols. *What Barton-under-Needwood did for the Millennium* Barton Civil Society produced 'A Promenade through historical Barton-under-Needwood' a village guide by Jeff Pattison, 1999. *When BBC Radio 4's 'Any Questions?' came from Barton-under-Needwood.* The programme was broadcast on Sept 21 2007 from John Taylor High School, to celebrate the 50th anniversary of the school. *UK's largest independent re-manufacturer of power train products 2008.* LH Croup Service

of Barton-under-Needwood (Burton Mail July 25 2008 p7).

Farming *Wychnor Admiral, Wychnor Monarch, Wychnor Spark* were Hackney stallions flourishing in 1918 in the Wychnor Stud of WE Shuker advertised in Staffordshire Advertiser to pregnate local mares (SA June 1 1918 p2). *First Tatenhill Horticultural Show* was on Sept 26 1970 at Tatenhill Memorial Hall (BOb July 30 1970 p1). *0.001 in 1 chance* Healthy surviving twin foals born to a mare 'My Sharon' in 1971 on Brankley Farm, Dunstall, belonging to Mr DM Grewcock, according to 'The Veterinary Handbook, 1969' (BOb May 27 1971 p1p). *Reggio Emilia International Pig Fair gold medalist 1971.* One of the pigs of Mr Mercer, pig breeder, of Wychnor Bridges. The fair was then considered 'the biggest pig show in Europe' (BOb April 26 1973 p1). *Australian Terrier Club of Great Britain 75th Anniversary Show Best in Show winner.* Britmartz Fire on Ice (Lou), owned by Velma Hodgson and Chris Seaton of Barton (LiMe Aug 7 2008 p24).

An illustration by Don Osmond from Kathleen Lawrence-Smith's 'Tales of Old Staffordshire', courtesy of Countryside Books, showing a couple being awarded the Wychnor flitch of bacon, after proving to the lord of the manor they have lived in harmony for a year and a day.

Folklore *Tatenhill's best.* Each former township, except Dunstall, has folklore, each as legendary as the other. For *Tatenhill* there is the tradition Robert de Ferrers I offered Callingwood, a wood, for brave conduct at the battle of the Standard (1138) and that is was 'claimed' by one of his men. However, the truth is it was called in English 'Challenge' wood (later spelled as Calling), as its ownership was disputed in the earlier 1120s. For *Wychnor* there was the medieval custom of a married couple, who were tenants, being able to claim a flitch of bacon from the lord of the manor if they could swear they were still happily married a year and a day after their wedding. No recipient has ever been recorded, although, apparently there was a claimant in the 1720s. Until recently a wooden effigy of a flitch hung over the fireplace at Wychnor Park hall. The custom was described by D.G. Harnaman as the *'most extraordinary' of the Staffordshire tenure of manor customs* (SA Dec 31 1954 p7). For *Barton* there is the story of Catherine Mewis (1802-28), the young girl of Barton who could only see on a Sunday, totally blind the other six days of the week. This was interpreted by some as a Providential sign.

Gardner, Steve *British Powerlifting Championship winner 1989, European Powerlifting Championship silver 1989, World Powerlifting Championship bronze 1989.* Policeman of Barton-under-Needwood. In the super heavy weight category. At the world championship he broke two European records (LiMe July 21 1989 p64p).

Geology The Trent plain area is Alluvium; that of Barton, Dunstall, Tatenhill villages and the west of the parish is Keuper Marls.

Gilmour, Miss EM *First female chairman of Tutbury RDC.* Of 82 Wales Lane, Barton-under-Needwood, in 1962-64, daughter of Rev Edwyn Gilmour, first vicar of All Saints', Burton; awarded OBE in 1974 (BOb May 30 1963 p5. June 20 1974 p8).

Harrison, Lieut-Col WE *'one of the keenest agriculturists in the Midlands' 1934.* (1875-1937). Of Wychnor Park, chairman of Staffordshire County Council from 1927, breeder and exhibitor of Shorthorn, British Friesian, and Blue Albion cattle, also an enthusiastic gardener (SA April 7 1934 p9p. March 27 1937 p7p).

Holland, Miss Mary *'one of the first women to be made a Justice of the Peace for the county of Stafford'.* Of The Grove, Barton-under-Needwood; she moved to Barton in 1903 with her family, who claim descent from Richard de Holland, living at Barton in 1314 (SA Sept 30 1933 p9p).

Lowe, Miss MD *Barton's historian.* Of Radhurst Lodge, Barton. She was described in The Burton Observer's series, Our Rural Heritage, as 'an authority on the history of the village' (BOb Oct 28 1971 p7). Latterly there has been Steve Gardner, author of 'Under the Needwood

Tree' (1995), and 'Life and Times in Barton' (2001).

Martin, Louis *Broke four British weight lifting records at John Taylor School.* MBE, world record holder in the Staffordshire & Worcestershire Weightlifting Championships on Feb 4 1967, in the under-14 stone categories:- Bodyweight 195.75, Snatch 291.5, Jerk 382.25, Press 320.25 (Burton Mail Feb 6 1967 p5p).

Place-name The first appearance of the name, Tatenhill, is 941. It means 'Tata's hill' (PNSZ p530).

Population Tatenhill was 40th most-populated Staffordshire parish in 1801 with 1,430 people; 37th in 1811 with 1,754; 39th in 1821 with 2,059; 40th in 1831 with 2,180; 41st in 1841 with 2,229; 40th in 1851 with 2,329; 42nd in 1861 with 2,500; 43rd in 1871 with 2,593; 45th in 1881 with 2,722; 44th in 1891 with 2,722; 49th in 1901 with 2,552. Tatenhill could be ranked 31st worst-affected Staffordshire parish for loss of men in WW1, with 70 lives taken.

Price, Rev Humphrey *'the good parson of Needwood Forest'.* Curate of Barton 1798-1809, when he became perpetual curate of Christchurch-on-Needwood. He still had the living in 1851 although for many years he had resided at Tutbury. He was known as this because he defended the poor carpet-weavers of Kidderminster, and suffered a year's imprisonment for his outspokenness. Thomas Cooper (1805-92), occupied the same day-room as him in Stafford Gaol. His son, Edward, (b1801), was an artist (SLM Spring 1956 p8).

Sport *Staffordshire's earliest polo club* was possibly that a Barton, in existence at Barton in the 1880s, only a few years after the formation of the fist such club in England in 1872 (VCH vol 10 p244). *Most times a 425kg weight has been lifted 22 feet in the air in an hour, first tug of war club to take two medals in one weight class at the national championships, World 4+4 660kg Gold medalists 2004, English Tug-of-war Association Championship 720 kilos silver medal 2008, catch weight bronze medal 2008.* Holland Tug of War team of Barton-under-Needwood, formed at Red Lion Inn in 1970, moving to Holland Sports Club in 1974. In 1996 the club won 50 trophies in a year. Their weight lifting record feat of 80 times, acknowledged by GBR, was achieved by them in June 2000 using their training rigs; it sets a benchmark for tug of war endurance and is one of the club's proudest moments; it was still remained unbroken in 2006. Their two-medal take occurred in 2000, with a silver and a bronze in the 620kg mixed class (Burton Mail April 24 2006 pp8-9ps. June 25 2008 p29pc. July 10 2008 p37). *Barclays England Schools Girls' under-14 basketball champions 1989*. The Baby Bullettes of John Taylor High School, Barton-under-Needwood (LiMe March 24 1989 p80). *Home of the National Football Centre* was proposed for a site at Byrkley Lodge, Rangemore in the early 2000s but as yet (2006) uncompleted. It will include state-of-the-art training facilities with upwards of 14 pitchs, sports medicine and sports science centres. Given the go-ahead in 2008 (BBC website, 2006) (Burton Mail June 4 2008 p1).

Statham, Anne *First female hung at the New Gaol at Stafford*. Of Wychnor Bridges. When aged 28, after murdering her illegitimate baby boy. Executed 21 March 1817.

Taylor, Dr John *Tatenhill's most famous old worthy*. (c1480-1534). Priest, ambassador, and benefactor. Eldest of triplets born to poor parents at Barton under Needwood. Triplets were then rare and the sign of the Holy Trinity. Henry VII whilst hunting in Needwood Forest was so impressed with them he paid for their education. John rose to prominence over Rowland and Nathaniel, becoming a doctor of Canon Law; Archdeacon of Derby and Buckingham; Prolocutor of the House of Convocation, 1515; Master of the Rolls 1527-34; chaplain to Henry VIII; English ambassador to France. He built Barton church, 1517-33, which contains in several places his initials and coat-of-arms (three babes' heads and two Tudor roses). The local high school is named after him.

Thornewill, Miss Jane *'the best woman bridge player in England'*. Of Rangemore, daughter of Edward Thornewill of Dove Cliff, sister of Lady Burton of Rangemore House. She was a favourite bridge partner of Edward VII (SA March 13 1920 p9 col 3) (ESNF pp23p, 91p of the library).

Walmesley, Gilbert *He first met with his future wife, Magdalen Aston, at Wychnor Hall*. Died 1751. Diocesan registrar, and one of the Lichfield 'Lions' a loose literary circle resident or native of Lichfield in the C18. The hall was then the seat of the Offleys.

Wyatt, Job *Patented a screw-making machine*. Of Tatenhill, brother of William Wyatt of Burton-on-Trent. It appears as No. 642 in the alphabetical index of patentees c1760 (Newcomen Society vol 22 p80) (Origin and Manufacture of Wood Screws. HW Dickinson) (VCH vol 2 p142).

Thorpe Constantine Thorpe Constantine was Staffordshire's 139th largest parish, consisting of 961 acres; 7th farthest parish away from the county town, 21.9m ESE; extremist length 1.9m; extremist width 2m. The parish's chief settlement Thorpe Constantine, is no more than an estate hamlet focused on Thorpe Hall. Thorpe Constantine is famous for the woman who honoured Lady Mary Wortley Montagu (see below).

Altitudes The highest point of the parish is the parish church at 305 feet. The lowest point is 232 feet on the N boundary by Harlaston brook.

Burt, William Thomas *Royal Agricultural Society long service certificate holder and medalist*. Shepherd for Mrs Inge at the Home Farm, Thorpe Constantine, for 50 years from Oct 1 1888. In 1938 he was still in charge of the show sheep (TH Dec 17 1938 p9 col 3).

Capewell, Charles *Thorpe Constantine's villain*. When aged 21, he formed part of 'a formidable gang of poachers at Tamworth' with John Deeming, aged 26, who were charged with maliciously assaulting Thomas Harrison, an under gamekeeper of Capt Inge, with intent to kill and murder him on Dec 13 1843. They were found guilty of assault with intent to do grievous bodily harm. Together with another charge of poaching at Clifton Campville they were sentenced to 10 years transportation each (SA Dec 30 1843 p2 col 3).

Church St Constantine's at Thorpe Constantine is the only such county dedication (for AP churches); 61st= oldest AP county church dating from the C13 or roughly 1250, but the nave and chancel were rebuilt in 1883; the architect was J Oldrid Scott (BOE p281). Most interesting thing in the old church is a brass in the floor of the chancel, of a female, half of the effigy was in good condition in the C19, but the canopy, escutcheons etc were gone (GNHSS p28).

Crop maize *'A remarkable crop of maize'*. Reported on the estate of Mrs Inge at Thorpe. It was sown in early May 1934, and had reached an average height of about 10 feet by mid Oct (SA Oct 20 1934 p11p).

An unexplained block of ice, two metres
square, landed at Thorpe Constantine in 1975.

Folklore *Thorpe Constantine's best*. In
March 1975 an unexplained block of
ice, two metres square, fell from the sky
to land at Thorpe Constantine (MMSE
p288) (The World Atlas of Mysteries.
Francis Hitching).

Geology All the parish is Keuper Marls.

Inge, William *7th Chief Justice of the
King's Bench of England*. Judge, serving
from March 1316 to June 15 1317 (Wikipedia, 2008).

Inge, William *'a scholar and antiquary'*. (1669-1731). Son of William
(d1690) of Thorpe Constantine. M.P.
for Tamworth 1715-22. Rev Stebbing
Shaw described him as 'a scholar and
antiquary'.

Inge, William *'Mr Inge's abilities, im-
partiality and integrity would have been
an ornament to any bench'*, *'best justice
of any country gentleman in England'*.
Died 1785. Of Thorpe Constantine. The
first quote is from Lord Chief Justice
Mansfield (SA Feb 24 1838 p3 col 2),
the second from Thomas Pennant in his
Journey From Chester to London. Thomas Pennant. 1811. p163.

Inge, Henrietta *The woman who honoured the woman who introduced small
pox inoculation to England*. Died 1790.
Of Thorpe Constantine. Wife of Theodore William Inge (who died of small pox
in 1753), unveiled the memorial to Lady
Mary Wortley Montagu (d1762) in the
north aisle of Lichfield Cathedral, 1789;
she introduced the inoculation from Turkey (TB April 18 2002 p7).

Marlborough, Duchess of *Most famous visitor to Thorpe Constantine to
1992*. When she visited her sister, Lady
Elizabeth Inge of Thorpe Hall, to give her
condolences on the death of her daughter
in early April 1836 (SA April 9 1836.
April 11 1936 p9 col 2). On June 26
1992 Anne, Princess Royal, attended the
50th anniversary celebrations of Nether-

seal and District Young Farmers' Club at
Thorpe Hall (TH July 3 1992 p28).

Mermagen, Rev Carl Friedrich
Thorpe Constantine's saddest. Rector
of Thorpe Constantine (from 1914), and
incumbent of Statfold (from 1915), aged
64, who committed suicide near his garden on Aug 30 1934, a single-barrelled
gun lay by his side. The rector had suffered stress since the death of his wife,
Evelyn, in June 1934, and had been involved in a motor accident a few days
previous to his death, which had upset
his nerves (LiMe June 22 1934 p5 col 4.
Sept 7 1934 p5 col 2).

Place-name First appearance of the
name Domesday Book, 1086 for Thorpe,
c1245 for Thorpe Constantine. Thorpe
means 'outlying farm'; Constantine is
from the Costetin family who held land
here in 1212 (PNSZ p535).

Population Thorpe Constantine was
146th most-populated Staffordshire parish in 1801 with 62 people; 148th in 1811
with 54; 150th in 1821 with 40; 149th
in 1831 with 49; 154th in 1841 with 42;
148th in 1851 with 58; 149th in 1861
with 54; 152nd in 1871 with 49; 152nd
in 1881 with 57; 147th in 1891 with 87;
148th in 1901 with 84.

Quote *Choicest*. The parish was one
of those Stebbing Shaw got round to
in his History of Staffordshire, vol 1,
1798, "Thorp, according to our antient
etymologists signifies a pretty village,
which justly answers to its present state,
there being only five houses in the parish; but it was much more considerable
formerly."

Scroope, Lord Henry *Henry V's favourite*. He left Thorpe Constantine church a
vestment worth 26s. 8d. on condition the
priest should pray for his soul on Sundays, and in all his masses. Scroope was
beheaded for his plot against Henry V;
and his will, before his treason was discovered, is a curious piece of hypocrisy,
says Shaw (SHOS vol 1 p407).

Tutbury Tutbury was Staffordshire's
67th largest parish, consisting of 4,001
acres; 81st farthest parish away from
the county town, 13.5m ENE; extremist
length 5.9m, making it 21st longest parish
in the county; extremist width 6.4m, making it 12th widest parish in the county.
The parish's chief settlement is Tutbury, a
small market and burghal town. The parish is famous for Tutbury Castle.

Altitudes The highest point of the parish
is 459 feet in Hanbury Park. The lowest

point is 171 feet by the Dove near Tutbury Mill.

Brook, Benjamin *First pastor for Tutbury's Congregational Church.* (1776-1848). Famous for his works on Nonconformist history. He served at Tutbury 1802-30 (BS p81) (SA Jan 10 1948 p7) (VCH vol 10 p112).

Church St Mary's at Tutbury is one of 23 such dedications (the most common dedication in Staffordshire); 4th oldest county church dating from 1080. *Earliest instance of the use of alabaster in an English church* is most likely that at Tutbury, in the innermost moulding of seven orders of the doorway, of c1160 (Burton Observer Dec 1 1955 p1). *In the churchyard* is the grave of David Buxton, killed Sept 27 1678. This was the first burial at Tutbury in wool under the 1678 Wool Act for burial in a woollen shroud (PR). The *first proposed monument in a churchyard as a WW1 memorial in Staffordshire* was that discussed by Tutbury parish council in early Dec 1918 as reported in Staffordshire Advertiser (SA Dec 14 1918 p5 col 3).

Colclough, Miss June *Miss Staffordshire 1950.* Post office clerk. In 1950 when aged 20 she was made Miss Tutbury; she was the 12th Miss Staffordshire ever (SA July 22 1950 2p).

Farming and built-environment *Strange but true!* In 1884 Mr T Greensmith of Tutbury lost a valuable horse which unexplainably died suddenly. A post mortem revealed it had eaten two stones, one weighing 2 lbs, found embedded in its stomach (BOb April 16 1959 p3). *Largest farm on the Needwood estate of the Duchy of Lancaster 1957.* Lower Castle Hayes Farm, possessing 372 acres. It was apportioned additional acreage after the Fauld explosion; Elizabeth II visited it for 20 minutes on a visit to Tutbury and Burton in March 1957. The second largest was Agardsley Park Farm (BOb April 4 1957 p6). *An original Staffordshire Conservation Area.* Tutbury in 1969, one of three approved by the Council of British Archaelogy, and one of seven approved by Staffs CC Archaeology & Historic Property Sub-committee (BOb Aug 7 1969 p1).

Folklore *Tutbury's best.* Mary, Queen of Scots, was kept prisoner at Tutbury Castle on four occasions between 1569 and 1585. She complained the Castle was ill-furnished, cold, stank (owing to infrequent emptying of the privies), and her exercise garden was fit only for pigs. But that certain treasonable letters were conveyed to her in beer barrels here (Burton-on-Trent being close by), has become legend.

According to legend Mary, Queen of Scots, imprisoned at Tutbury Castle, tried to secret letters to her supporters in beer barrels (left).

Gaunt, John of *Tutbury's most famous old worthy.* (1340-99). Influential royal peacemaker and most famous occupant of Tutbury Castle. Fourth son of Edward III, who was granted Tutbury in 1361 and the duchy of Lancaster in 1362. He rebuilt the castle principally as 'a comfortable castellated residence' and through his second wife Constance, Princess of Castile, introduced to it some continental innovations such as a vineyard, a garden and bull-running.

Geology Most of the parish is Keuper Marls; Hanbury Park is Rhætic. *'incomparably the best' alabaster quarry.* Dr Plot on the quarry at Castle Hayes Park (MR2 p162). *Earliest known use of alabaster in England* is in the west doorway of Tutbury Priory church, c1160-70 (HOS 1998 p96).

Glass production *One of only five remaining crystal glass makers in UK 2006.* Georgian Crystal of Tutbury, founded 1981 (BBC Midlands Today Nov 23 2006). Tutbury Crystal, founded 1980, moved to Stoke in June 2006 (Burton Mail July 6 2006 pp16-17).

Greenslade, Michael *His last work for the VCH.* The Staffordshire Victoria County History editor (1961-95; longest-serving and its greatest) was working on Tutbury (for volume 10) when he died in 2005.

Halliday, Rebecca *Newchurch's villainess.* Born c1966. Fitness instructor, of The Sanctuary (the former Christ Church), Newchurch, who between April 2003 and Feb 2006 cheated the Benefits Agency out of £14,000 tax credits, claiming to be a single person when she was actually living with the man she later married. When

H.M. Revenue and Customs investigated they also found she had also made two fraudulent mortgage applications with inflated income figures. In 2009 she was ordered to repay £53,749, or serve an 18 month prison sentence, and ordered to carry out 200 hours of community service (Burton Mail Jan 9 2009 p4).

Mackenzie, Michael *He played Romeo in the nude*. Aged 27, actor, son of Dr IAR Mackenzie of Croft House, Tutbury, in a production of Shakespeare's Romeo and Juliet at Worthing, Sussex, in April 1970; Juliet, played by Susan Penhaligon, 20, was also to appear nude in the love scene (BOb April 9 1970 p1p).

Moore, Ann, nee Pegg *Tutbury's villainess, Staffordshire's biggest female fraudster*. (1761-c1827). She came to Tutbury, and claimed she had eaten nothing between 1806-13, when a committee exposed her as fraud.

Norman Tutbury *One of only three towns in Staffordshire where some sort of urban life existed by 1086*. Tutbury (SL pp77,146). *Only Staffordshire market recorded in DB*. Tutbury (NSJFS 1971 pp51,52).

Oakden, Capt TH *Tutbury's hero*. DSO. Of Tutbury received the M.C. for meritorious conduct in the field 1918 (SA Nov 16 1918 p7 col 3).

Pattenson, Lesley Ann *'Million to one chance'*. Of 78 Holts Lane, Tutbury. When aged four months she died in 'million to one chance' circumstances according to a doctor at the inquest, returning a verdict of 'misadventure'. She died of asphyxia between 4am-8.15am on Aug 30 1958, but not of the normal type of suffocation, as the baby was in the early stages of acute infection of a lung which had placed an increased strain upon the heart muscles. Lesley had had to go into an unnatural breathing position placing more strain on the heart - no prior examination would have revealled the Lesley's condition (BOb Sept 4 1958 p1).

Place-name First appearance of the name Tutbury is Domesday Book, 1086, and means 'Tutta's, or Stut's burg' (PNSZ p548).

Population Tutbury was 55th most-populated Staffordshire parish in 1801 with 1,004 people; 51st in 1811 with 1,235; 51st in 1821 with 1,444; 51st in 1831 with 1,553; 46th in 1841 with 1,835; 51st in 1851 with 1,798; 53rd in 1861 with 1,982; 53rd in 1871 with 2,149; 54th in 1881 with 2,306; 56th in 1891 with 2,057;

59th in 1901 with 1,974. Tutbury could be ranked 44th= worst-affected Staffordshire parish for loss of men in WW1, with 49 lives taken.

Powell, Pte J *Tutbury's bravest*. Of Sherwood Foresters, one of the five brothers who served in WW1, of Castle Street, Tutbury, was awarded the M.M. for conspicuous bravery in bombing a German pillbox in Sept 1917 (SA Aug 17 1918 p7 col 4).

Quote *Choicest*. Dr Robert Plot in his Natural History of Staffordshire, 1686, said 'During the time of which ancient Earls and Dukes of Lancaster, who were ever of the blood Royal, great men in their times, had their abode, and kept a liberal hospitality here, at their Honor of Tutbury, there could not but be a general concourse of people from all parts hither; for whose diversion all sorts of Musicians were permitted likewise to come, to pay their Services:'

Religion *George Fox's first (Quaker) meeting in Staffordshire*. Bushell Park, 1651, probably identifiable with what is now called Bushton House, between Tutbury and Anslow, according to Denis Stuart in his Phd thesis 'Early Quaker Movement in Staffordshire' (2001) p57, after his evangelising in Burton. *First public celebration of Mass in Tutbury since the Reformation* was on a Sunday in May 1938? at Tutbury Institute (BOb May 9 1963 p5).

Riley, Annette *Tutbury woman who went on national TV to tell of abuse by her husband*. Born 1963. She featured on the talk show 'Trisha' on Channel 5 in 2006 talking about the domestic abuse after her ex-husband Nicholas Forrest, aged 58, inflicted on her whilst driving along the A38 in Oct 2003. In May 2004 he was convicted at Stafford of assault occasioning actual body harm. After being released a year later he had the temerity to move to Tutbury a few doors away from his victim (Burton Mail April 28 2006 p13. May 4 2006 pp17-18ps).

Transport *'Tutbury Jinnie's' last run*. The famous train of this name left Burton at 8.12pm on June 11 1960 driven by Leslie Wildgoose of Oak St, Burton, and it was due to return from Tutbury at 8.37pm, but left a few minutes later, arriving back at Burton at 9.05pm (it was due to arrive back at 8.49pm) (BOb June 16 1960 p1). *Fancy that!* On Jan 8 1967 Special Constable William Smith of Park Lane, Tutbury, sustained severe facial injuries when his motor cycle crashed into a hole, 23 feet long, 12 feet wide, 20 feet deep, in a road at Rangemore Hill. Neither Staffs CC or Staffs Police could fathom how the hole had come into existence (BOb review of 1967).

Tutbury Castle *Largest hoard of coins ever found in the UK*. Some 20,000 or many more in the Dove at Tutbury, 1 June 1831, originally lost in the baggage train of Thomas, Earl of Lancaster of Tutbury Castle as he fled Edward II, 1322 (GBR 1974 p203). *'Old John of Gaunt, time-honoured Lancaster'*. John of Gaunt of Tutbury Castle, referred to by Richard II, opening William Shakespeare play 'King Richard II' (Staffordshire Handbook c1966 p44). *Unique court to keep order over the musicians in England.* The medieval annual Court of Minstrels of the Honour of Tutbury (MR p344). *'The last of the Tutbury Minstrels'* Henry Coxon, a clerk, d1739, as described on his memorial in Tatenhill church (UTR pp67-70) (IVNF). *2nd earliest record of bull baiting in the UK*. Tutbury bull running, recorded 1374, after its introduction from Spain by John of Gaunt and his wife Constance, daughter of Pedro the Cruel of Castile. The custom involved a bull chased, caught, slayed and feasted upon in Tutbury on the afternoon and evening of the morrow of the Assumption (Aug 16) until it was abolished in 1778 due to over-roudiness. *Mary Queen of Scots' first incarceration at Tutbury Castle.* Feb 4 to April 1569 when she was removed to Wingfield Manor, Sheffield (LGS p241). *Tutbury Castle's first gala day* was on May 15 1976. *'one of the most haunted castles in the UK'* Tutbury, according to its own website, 2008. The castle has featured on Living TV's 'Most Haunted' and 'World's Biggest Ghost Hunt' The infamous 'King's Bedroom' is often closed to the public due to the above average paranormal phenomena inside. *Largest-ever ghost walk.* Tutbury Castle, with 2000 people, more than doubling the previous record (BBC Midlands Today Aug 18 2005). *Rare species of dwarf elder.* Danewort in the castle grounds, only found elsewhere in the county at Wootton near Eccleshall (NSFCT 1885 pp69-70).

Tutbury's unluckiest The runaway wife of a Tutbury resident in 1850. On her return, her house was harangued by a lynch mob over night until her husband released her into their hands the following day. They put a rope round her waist 'and trailed her round the village, blowing cows' horns, ringing bells, shouting and other noisy accompaniments.' On arriving at Little Dove towards a cold nightfall, they dragged the woman into the water and committed all kinds of barbarities; all the while her husband was watching (SA March 23 1850. March 25 1950 p6 col 6).

Venables, Piers *Tutbury's villain*. Along with his gang, likened to Robin Hood and his men. They so terrorised the tenants of Tutbury they petitioned Parliament in 1439 to have them dealt with. Venables was Aston, near Sudbury, Derbys. The petition really came from Scropton, although his men came from neighbouring villages in Derbys and Staffs (RHH pp147,150, 151).

Walker, Samuel *'Grand Old Man of Staffordshire Agriculture' 1920.* (1836-1920). He resided at Chapel House, Tutbury, from 1864. Born Wootton Park, Ellastone (SA May 22 1920 p2p).

U-Z

Weeford Weeford was Staffordshire's 57th largest parish, consisting of 4,626 acres; 59th farthest parish away from the county town, 15.7m SE; extremist length 4.6m; extremist width 3.8m. The parish's chief settlement is at Swinfen where the Youth Offender Institution, Hotel and Hall amount to more than the hamlet of Weeford.

Altitudes The highest point in the parish is Weeford Park at 535 feet. The lowest point is 262 feet by Freeford brook in Swinfen Hall grounds.

Anglo-Saxon Weeford *'the most notable instance in the West Midlands of a -low place-name which may refer to an*

Anglian burial'. Off Low, a burial mound near Whitehouse Farm, at SK 123059, according to the famous etymologist, Margaret Gelling, in her 'Signposts to the Past: Place-names and the History of England' (1978) p155. It gives its name to the hundred of Offlow.

Church St Mary's at Weeford is one of 23 such county dedications (most common dedication in the county); 27th last AP county church built dating from 1802. *Most interesting feature* is a window in the south transcept containing old French glass showing a painting of Pontius Pilate in his judgement seat washing his hands. It was originally in the private chapel of the Duc d'Orleans, near Paris, and was stolen at the time of the French Revolution, 1793 (SA & Chron Feb 2 1956 p4 cols 8-9).

Farming *'biggest single haul of farm animals to have taken place in Britain'* to 2009 was believed to be when 500 recently-weaned free-range pigs worth £20,000-25,000, were taken from Packington Hall Farm at 3am on April 1 2009. Perhaps a rogue farmer had taken them as professional expertise would be required to round up, transport, and conceal the pigs. In 2008-09 there had been a 50% rise in the value of a fully grown pig, following the campaign over pig welfare by the TV celebrity chef Jamie Oliver (BBC Midlands Today April 1 2009) (The Times April 4 2009 p32).

The Bishop's Stones that once lay on Weeford Heath.

Folklore *Weeford's best*. Heaps of opaque pebbles known as the Bishop's Stones that used to lie in the hollow way between hills on Weeford Heath in the vicinity of Weeford Park were thought to commemorate a murdered bishop of Lichfield and his entourage, killed by thieves and placed exactly where the dead bodies had been found. However, the true story is that in c1540 John Vessy, then bishop of Exeter, native of Sutton Coldfield, had had a road which passed here smoothed to help to travellers and heaped the offending stones by the wayside.

Geology The north fringe of the parish is Keuper Marls; Packington Hall, Moor, hamlet is Bunter; Swinfen Hall is Keuper Sandstones; Weeford village, Manley Hall and the south of the parish is Bunter.

Kendrick, Edward *'one of the most highly-respected farmers in Staffordshire'* 1920, *'one of the ablest cricketers in the locality' c1872*. (1852-1920). Of Weeford House; the Kendricks have been resident at Weeford since the C16 (SA Feb 28 1920 p10p).

Manley, Isaac George *Capt Cook's principal companion on his first voyage round the world*. Died 1837. Of Manley Hall, on the 'Endeavour'; Lieutenant on board the 'Prince George' in Lord Rodney's celebrated victory over the French in 1782; in 1791 he married the second daughter and co-heiress of Charles Pole of the Redbourne family, Derbys, causing the Christian name Shawe to be introduced in the names of his descendants; promoted to the rank of Admiral of the Red 1837 (TH June 16 1928 front page).

Manley, Major Robert George *Weeford's hero*. Of 6th Inniskillen Dragoons who headed the first troop which crossed sabres with the Russian Cavalry in the Charge of the Heavy Brigade at Balaclava, in the Crimea War, Oct 25 1854. He was loudly cheered on his entering Lichfield returning home on Jan 2 1856; given a dinner in his honour at Swan Hotel, Lichfield, and the article about him in The Staffordshire Advertiser was entitled 'Welcome of a Staffordshire Hero' (SA Jan 5 1856 p7 col 3).

Natural history *First observance of the fuss ball fungi* was by Walter Ashmore of Tamworth near Packington (NHS p200 tab 14 fig 3).

Place-name The first appearance of the name, Weeford, is Domesday Book, 1086. It means 'ford by the heathen temple' (PNSZ p566). *Unique derivation for a surname*. Swinfen will be from Swinfen in this parish (PDS).

Population Weeford was 110th most-populated Staffordshire parish in 1801 with 393 people; 118th in 1811 with 377; 114th in 1821 with 440; 111th in 1831 with 470; 112th in 1841 with 426; 114th in 1851 with 425; 118th in 1861 with 399; 116th in 1871 with 395; 114th in 1881 with 405; 111th in 1891 with 417; 114th in 1901 with 385. Weeford could be ranked 96th= worst-affected Staffordshire parish for loss of men in WW1, with 9 lives taken.

Quote *Choicest*. Thomas Pennant in his *Journey From Chester to London*, 1811, came through Weeford 'A LITTLE farther, the great Watling-street crosses the road nr Weford, or the ford on the way. This is seated on Blackbrook, a small stream, now furnished with a bridge. The stream runs through a beautiful tract of narrow but rich meadows. Prettily bounded by low and fertile risings.'

Roads *'one of the most dangerous road junctions in the Midland counties' 1938*. Weeford Tollgate Crossroads, where the A5 intercepts the Lichfield-Coleshill road. On two consecutive Saturdays in Sept and Oct 1938 a total of nine people were injured and one killed. Many accidents at this spot had been witnessed by the Rector of Weeford. In Nov 1938 CC Poole, MP for Lichfield, brought the matter to the attention of the Minister of Transport in the House of Commons (LiMe Oct 7 1938 p5p. Nov 18 1938 p3 col 4).

Steadman, Ben *Woodvale Indian Ocean Race competitor 2009*. Senior prison PE officer at HMYOI Swinfen Hall, aged 32, originally from Weymouth, with another oarsman, an officer at another prison. The race is from Western Australia to Mauritius, 3,700 miles (E&S Feb 25 2009 p14ps).

Swinfen Hall *A legal precedence set* That a barrister cannot sue for his fees. This was established in the case of Charles Broun of Swinfen Hall against Charles Rann Kennedy (d1867) at the court of Common Pleas; Kennedy, a barrister, having tried to sue Broun's wife for costs incurred at previous trials (ILN July 9 1859) (CCHCB pp108-133) (GMH p27).

Swinfen-Broun, Col MA *Weeford's longest serving rector's warden*. He commenced his 53rd year in the post in 1940 (LiMe April 12 1940 p5 col 2).

Thickbroom Hall *County Archivist, Thea Randall's favourite lost country house in Staffordshire*. Thickbroom Hall, as Thea states in her lecture 'Staffordshire's Vanished Country Houses'.

Wyatt, Benjamin *The builder, steward to Lord Uxbridge*. (1709-72). Of Blackbrook, 5th son of John Wyatt I. Farmer and timber merchant and practised as a builder. The house that brought him repute as an architect was Swinfen Hall, built 1755. He had seven sons, six of whom practised architecture.

Wyatt, Benjamin *Began the North Wales Wyatts*. (1744-1818). Son of Benjamin (d1772). Migrated to north Wales in 1780. Of Lime Grove, Llandegai, Caernarvon.

Wyatt, Benjamin Dean *Built Drury Lane Theatre*. (1775-1850). A son of James Wyatt (d1813). Of London.

Wyatt, Charles *Architect who worked in India*. (1758-1813). Son of William (d1782).

Wyatt, James *The neo-Classicist, 'The Destroyer', Weeford's most famous old worthy, Royal Academy's first architect President*. (1746-1813). Born at Blackbrook Farm, son of Benjamin (d1772). He achieved fame with his Neo-classical design for the London Pantheon, Oxford Street, 1772. He became surveyor to the Board of Works, 1796; restored several cathedrals (including Lichfield), and designed many country houses, including halls at Beaudesert, Canwell, Hagley, and Little Aston in Staffordshire. His best-known work is the Gothic revival Fonthill Abbey, 1796-1807. His critics nicknamed him 'The Destroyer' (SA May 10 1947 p5 col 6).

Wyatt, Jeffrey *The neo-Gothicist and specialist in 'Tudor collegiate'*. (1766-1840). Son of Joseph (d1785). His masterpiece was Windsor Castle which he remodelled for George IV 1824-37; the King authorised the changing of his name to Wyatville to differentiate himself from other members of the family. His remodelling of the Castle has been described as the boldest and most solid example of Wardour Street Gothic (SA May 10 1947 p5 col 4).

Wyatt I, John *Spawned a dynasty of architects, inventors and builders, sculptors, painters and carvers* (MR2 p348). (1675-1742). Of Thickbroom. Great-great-grandson of Humphrey Wyat, fl1540, of Weeford.

Wyatt II, John *The inventor, made first machine to spin by rollers moving at different speeds, first perfection of the compound lever weighing machine*. (1700-66). Eldest son of John Wyatt I. Born Thickbroom. The roller machine was patented 1738. It was set up at Birmingham, but was superceded by Arkwright's spinning-jenny (KES p224) (Birmingham Gazette

March 7 1950).

Wyatt III, John *The surgeon.* (1735-97). Son of Benjamin (d1772). Member of the Royal College of Surgeons, FRS.

Wyatt, Joseph (1739-1785). Son of Benjamin (d1772). Of Burton-on-Trent. Executed masonry and made new drives at Beaudesert.

Wyatt, Matthew Cotes *Favourite of George III and his Queen.* (1777-1862). Youngest son of James (d1813). Sculptor; he executed portraits and historical pictures, which he exhibited at the Royal Academy (SA May 10 1947 p5 col 4).

Wyatt, Philip *Helped his brother in alterations at Apsley House.* Died 1836. Brother of Benjamin Dean Wyatt (d1850).

Wyatt, Samuel *The craftsman.* (1737-1807). Son of Benjamin (d1772). Of Chelsea.

Wyatt, William *Estate agent and Commissioner of Enclosures.* (1734-82). Son of Benjamin (d1772). Of Burton. He became an architect and designed Soho House.

Whittington Whittington was Staffordshire's 93rd largest parish, consisting of 2,921 acres; 55th= farthest parish away from the county town, 15.9m SE; extremist length 3.4m; extremist width 2.8m. The parish's chief settlement is Whittington, a large village with an attractive core of old villas; it expands on the east side to the Coventry Canal with new housing; there is also a large population at the barracks on Whittington Heath. The parish is famous for Whittington Barracks.

Altitudes The highest point of the parish is Whittington Heath on the Weeford boundary at 338 feet. The lowest point is 171 feet by the Tame.

Bradbury, Mrs Edith *'Mother' of the South Staffordshire Regiment.* (1873-1939). Wife of Capt S Bradbury of S Staffs Regt, was known as this. She was for many years secretary of the Old Comrades' Association. Her 'heart and soul were in the Army, with which she had been connected since her birth'. In 1919 her husband took over the Bell Inn, Whittington (LiMe Feb 17 1939 p10 col 5).

Church St Giles' at Whittington is one of 4 such county dedications (of AP churches); 61st= oldest AP county church dating from the C13 or roughly 1250. The pipe organ in the balcony with a WW1 roll of honour is the *first proposed furnishing for inside a church as a WW1 memorial in Staffordshire* (SA Dec

14 1918 p5 col 3). *Staffordshire's longest flute player in one church* is perhaps William Bass who played the flute in the choir from 1800 to 1867 (VB p36). *In the churchyard.* The oldest grave is dated 1631 (TH Sept 9 1988 p37). There is the grave of Thomas Spencer (d1905) of Marks & Spencer. There is a grave to the wife of a vicar which reads: 'The best of friends and wives, whose rectitude of life and manners made her an ornament and her death a loss to social life' (TH Sept 9 1988 p37). A grave to Marie Cecil Birch who survived her husband, Major Birch, by 53 years, which Vivian Bird noted was a remarkable widowhood (VB p36).

Community life *First Staffordshire Women's Institute.* Whittington, formed Oct 11 1916 (LiMe Oct 19 1956 p9). The first institute in the country was formed 1915 (SA June 4 1921 p9 col 6). *1st pancake race at Whittington.* Shrove Tuesday 1954. The idea for it originated from the vicar Rev RWD Peck; eight housewives took part; the first 'home' was Mrs Cecily Owen, aged 42, of 2 Passes Road in 2 mins 30 secs (SA March 5 1954 p1). *When 'Mrs Archer' opened Whittington Spring Fayre.* Miss Gwen Berryman, 'The Archers' actress playing Mrs Dan Archer in the radio soap opera, came to open the Spring Fayre on Saturday April 12 1958 (LiMe April 11 1958 p4 col 3). *An original Staffordshire Conservation Area.* Whittington in 1969, one of seven approved by Staffs CC Archaeology and Historical Property Sub-committee (BOb Aug 7 1969 p1).

Farming *First Staffordshire case in the 1900 Foot-and-mouth outbreak.* Brookhay Farm on Oct 6 1900, occupied by Thomas Tideswell (SA Oct 13 1900 p5 col 5). *'one of the most outstanding herds of British Friesian cattle in the country to-day' 1951.* The herd at Huddlesford Grange of Mr TH Cope, founded in 1937, which won the Staffordshire Agricultural Society Cup for best herd (over 100 head) in Staffordshire 1946, 1949. The stock bull of the herd, Terling Ferdinand, Register of Merit, purchased 1941 for 700 guineas, was rated 'one of the leading sires of the breed' 1951 (SLM Jan 1951 pp30-31p).

Folklore *Whittington's best.* The physical assault in 1747 on the Duke of Bedford, a leading Whig, by a pro-Jacobite dancing master, called Joul, at Lichfield Races on Whittington Heath has passed into folklore. Joul was part of a Tory (pro-Jacobite) rent-a-mob brought to the heath to hustle a group of leading Whig race-goers, in protest against the outcome of that year's county parliamentary elections.

Friendly Society *Most people from one family initiated into the R.A.O.B. during one ceremony by 1933.* When Messrs Samuel, Richard, Edgar, Joseph and William Bradbury, sons of Capt S Bradbury (see below) were all initiated into the Royal Ancient Order of Buffalos at the Bell Inn, Whittington, on March 27 1933 (LiMe March 31 1933 p6 col 3).

Gardening *First Staffordshire garden to open in the National Garden Scheme.* Appears to be the Old Hall, Whittington, residence of Edmund R Corn, on Sundays May 23 and Aug 22 1937, with music by the Amington Prize Band, admission 6d. The Scheme was founded in 1927 to raise money for the (District) Nurses of the Queen's Nursing Institute. Sandon Hall garden, near Stafford, opened to the public from 1934 in aid of local charities; from 1935 it was in aid of local charities and District Nursing, but it does not appear to have been fully in the Scheme. Sandon Hall and Weston Park did open their gardens in the Scheme in Sept 1937 (SA June 2 1934 p6 col 4. May 4 1935 p6 col 3. May 23 1936 p7 col 8. May 15 p6 col 4. Aug 14 p6 col 2. Aug 21 1937 p6 col 3).

Geology The Huddlesford and the north parish is Keuper Marls; Whittington Heath is Bunter; Whittington village, Darnford is Keuper Sandstones.

Larkins, Matthew *Whittington's bravest.* Born c1971. Of Sherwood Cottages, Main Street, Whittington, who lost his life trying to save Mark Allen, aged 9, from drowning in the very stormy sea off Porthminster Beach, St Ives, Cornwall, on July 14 1990. He was posthumously awarded for his bravery by the Penzance Coroner's Office. It was questioned whether or not coastal guards or the Life Boat service could not have tried harder to rescue Matthew (TH July 20 1990 p9. Nov 30 1990 p52).

Leedham, Betsey Maria *Whittington's saddest.* When aged 65 she was murdered by her husband, George, 57, at Longwood Farm, Fazeley, on Feb 29 1936. They had farmed at Whittington to c1932. The couple had seemed very happy together, but had had bad luck and were possibly being evicted from the farm. Mrs Leedham was found with her face blown away by a gun, lying outside the farmhouse and near the front door. Mr Leedham had seem-

ingly forced his way into the house and shot himself in the head. He was found clasping his double-barrel gun to which was attached a toasting fork (SA March 7 1936 p2 col 7).

Lloyd, David *'the Personality of ATV Today'.* He came to live in Whittington in 1965 and was shortly co-opted onto the fete committee of St Giles' church. He was instrumental in bringing a host of ATV personalities to the fete in 1966 (TH June 17 1966 p8 cols 5-7).

Marchant, Jane *Golf Foundation Award winner 1987.* Member of Whittington Barracks Golf Club, for her exceptional progress in golf in such a short space of time (LiMe Jan 6 1989 p60).

Morland, Patrick *John Leslie Eaton Challice Prizeman.* S.R.N. Of Whittington. For the best practical and theoretical male nurse of the year, awarded 1955 (LiMe Nov 4 1955 p7 col 6).

Muret, Mary *5th Concours International de Bouquets (flower arranging) Gold Medalist 1972.* Of Whittington. At the 1972 International Flower Competition at Monte Carlo (Lichfield & Tamworth Magazine Sept 1972 p12p).

Neal, Sarah *Whittington's kindest.* Of Lichfield, widow. By indenture dated 1741 left property the rental from which to found a free school at Whittington.

Newberry, Joseph *Whittington's villain.* When aged 21, along with Joseph Taylor, aged 18 and 'very juvenile in his appearance', was found guilty and sentenced to death for burglary, attempt to murder, and arson at the house of Mr and Mrs Charles Wood of Huddlesford on Nov 23 1838, making Mrs Wood and her servant drink a phial of lotion; Mrs Wood made an escape from her bedroom window, breaking her arm and spraining both ankles, then hiding in a hedge. Both men were described of 'low stature' (SA Dec 8 1838 p3 col 3. March 16 1839 p2 col 4. March 23 1839 p2 col 4).

Place-name The first appearance of the name, Whittington, is 1182. It means 'Hwita's tun' or 'white tun' (PNSZ p575).

Population Whittington was 81st most-populated Staffordshire parish in 1801 with 611 people; 87th in 1811 with 602; 87th in 1821 with 707; 84th in 1831 with 766; 82nd in 1841 with 799; 84th in 1851 with 809; 87th in 1861 with 819; 81st in 1871 with 869; 57th in 1881 with 2,009; 57th in 1891 with 2,033; 53rd in 1901 with 2,392. Whittington could be ranked

76th worst-affected Staffordshire parish for loss of men in WW1, with 16 lives taken.

Seckham, Capt Lionel Bassett *Whittington's hero.* Only son of Col Bassett Seckham of Whittington Old Hall, who won the M.C. for gallantry at Gallipoli, during the memorable landing of his regiment, the Lancaster Fusiliers (CL Nov 20 1915 p673).

Spence, Mr NA *Man who achieved 97.6 miles per gallon while averaging 30 miles an hour.* Of Whittington in 1968 setting a new record in the national economy campaign 100 miles to the gallon challenge (Staffs Illustrated June 1969. Staffs Scene).

STAFFORDSHIRE MILITIA & WHITTINGTON BARRACKS South Staffordshire **Regiment.** *First British Infantry Regiment to fight from all three elements - land, sea and air* are what become the South Staffords. Land they achieved immediately; the second element was achieved when the 1st Battalion took part in what must have been the first amphibious operations in 1707. The third was when the 2nd Battalion trained as Airborne Troops, and were the first to invade Sicily in July 1943, whilst the 1st Battalion was one of the units forming the Chindits (the Longe-Range Penetration Force) in Burma, who descended from the air into the jungle to beat the Japanese (SA & Chron March 17 1955 p4). *First known use of a tropical uniform.* Possibly a sort of sacking found locally, used by the South Staffords in the West Indies 1707-64 for waistcoats, and to line tunics (The Staffordshire Regiment Info Handbook 1980/81 p35). *'not pretty to look at, but devilish good fighters'* South Staffords in the words of a soldier's comment when to the fore in the engagement near Festubert on May 16, 18 1915 (CL Nov 20 1915 p675). *First South Stafford and 4th Territorial given the death sentence in WW1.* Lance Corp Frederick Hawthorne for refusing to raid German trenches 1916 (ES July 1 2006). *Amongst the first to break through the Hindenburg Line (seizing the St Quentin Canel).* Infantry units of 1/5th and 1/6th N. Staffords, and 1/5th and 1/6th S. Staffords in the 137th Brigade (which included other units) on Sept 29 1918. *Most decorated Non-Commissioned Officer in Britain* see Rolleston. *First British glider-borne troops in a major operation.* Airborne landings of the 2nd Batt South Staffords in Sicily on night of July

9-10 1943 (The Staffordshire Regiment Info Handbook 1980/81 p35). *Amongst first Allied troops to re-enter German-occupied France 1944.* South Staffords (The Staffordshire Regiment Info Handbook 1980/81 p35). *The South Staffords' 'Waterloo'* was the defence of Oosterbeek near Arnhem in Operation Market Garden, Sept 1944 (BBC2 June 2 2007). *Finest V.C. of WW2* has generally been considered that awarded to Major Robert Henry Cain (1909-74), South Staffords, for his defence of Oosterbeek, Sept 1944; he was the first Manx man awarded the V.C. (BBC 2 June 2 2007). *Last colonel of the South Staffords (1954-59) and first of the amalgamated Staffordshire Regiment (1959-).* Major General AW Lee.

North Staffordshire Regiment. *Longest tour of duty in the subcontinent by any regiment in British Military history.* North Staffords in India 1903-22 (ES Your Week July 8 2006 p11). *Greatest loss by the Staffords in a single encounter,* North Staffords' blackest day perhaps the 5th North Staffords who lost more than 500 men on Oct 13 1915, during the battle of Loos (ES Your Week Aug 18 2007 p5). *First British troops to enter the city of Rome in WW2.* The North Staffords, May 1944 (ES Sept 27 12008 p27). *The North Staffords' proudest battle.* The Anzio Beachhead in Italy, 1944 (ES Staying In Dec 1 2007 p13). *'The North Staffordshire' railway engine.* A Royal Scott class engine officially christened on June 13 1936 by Mrs LJ Wyatt, wife of Brig-Gen LJ Wyatt, Col of the N Staffords, at Stoke-on-Trent railway station (SA June 20 1936 p4p).

Staffordshire Militia to 1882. *Longest overseas service by a British regiment.* The 38th Foot in the West Indies for 58 years, 1707-65 (SA & Chron Aug 1 1957 p6 col 2). *Youngest man to ever win the Victoria Cross.* Drummer T Flynn (1842-92), born 'in the regiment' at Athlone, enlisted in the 64th (1855). Won his V.C. at 15 and 3 months at the seige of Cawpore 1857; but he competes with Andrew Fitzgibbon (of the Indian Medical Establishment, attached to the 2nd Hampshires in China 1860). However, the *'first two V.C's. in the regiment'* are said to have been gained in the Zulu War, 1878, where the 80th Foot formed the front of the British square which broke the Zulu power at Ulundi (SA & Chron Aug 1 1957 p6 col 2): One of these would be Pte Samuel Wassall (d1927), who could claim to be the *Staffords' 2nd V.C. recipient* (if Drummer Flynn is first). A dyer by trade he enlisted in the 80th Foot 1874. It was for 'his gallant conduct in having, at the imminent risk of his own life, saved that of Pte Westwood, of the same Regiment' (SN Jan 24 1992 p9). *First British regiment to land in Egypt to quell the revolt led by Ariba Pasha.* The 38th Foot, in 1882. (It was at the scene of his final defeat at Tel-el-Kebir that the 1st Battalion (38th-80th) served in 1954). Afterwards the 38th took part in the expedition up the Nile to Khartoum, and this was to be the last occasion for the regiment in which the colours were carried in action and the scarlet tunics were worn in battle (SA & Chron Aug 1 1957 p6 col 2).

Staffordshire Regiment mascot, Staffordshire Bull Terrier, Colour Sgt Watchman IV, with his handler Colour Sgt Malcolm Bower. Watchman IV's Retirement Ceremony at Whittington Barracks on May 20 2009 was the first time a retiring mascot and replacement mascot have ever attended the same ceremony, as most dogs die before retiring. The Staffordshire Regiment mascot tradition began in 1882 with the S. Staffords' in Egypt and their pet 'Boxer', a Stafford, who leapt from a moving train and made an heroic 200-mile track across desert to rejoin his regiment. In recent years mascots have included: Watchman I 1949-59; Watchman II 1960-67; Watchman II 1988-98; Watchman IV 1998-2009; Watchman V 2009-.

Staffordshire Regiment (after amalgamation). *Last British unit to serve in British East African colonies.* Staffords (Uganda gained independence on Oct 9 1962, Kenya on Dec 12 1963) (The Staffordshire Regiment Info Handbook 1980/81 p31). *British Army's overseas posting record for most soldiers sent abroad on foreign tours by 2005.* Staffords (TB Jan 13 2005 p19). *Last commanding officer of the Staffordshire Regiment.* Col Tim Sandiford, before the regiment became 3 Mercian (ES Sept 24 2008 p4). *BBC Midlander of the Year 2005.* Staffords for services in Iraq (ES April 29 2006 p7).

Whittington Barracks. *First military school for the A.T.S.* opened at Whittington Barracks in early June 1941 for A.T.S. N.C.O.'s, being the first of its kind in the country (LiMe June 6 1941 p7p). *Never

missed an annual dinner of the Regimental Association of the South Staffords in 41 years.* Edward Charles Thornburrow, aged 72, who had by 1952 attended every dinner at Whittington Barracks since the founding of the Association in 1911. At the 1952 dinner he was awarded the Meritorious Service Medal (SA Oct 10 1952 p3 cols 1-3). *First regular passing out parade at Whittington since WW2.* The first all-regular platoon (Gheluvelt) since WW2 passed out on Feb 11 1961 (SA & Chron Feb 16 1961 p8 col 3). *Fancy that!* Privates Neil and Helen McCreadie of Gillingham, Kent, both 27, 'passed out' together of the same 12-week basic training course at Whittington Barracks in 2001; marrying only seven weeks before joining the Army. Capt Sharon Findlay, commander of their training platoon, said "I have never had a married couple before..." (Daily Telegraph Aug 3 2001 p11p). *Largest curry ever* was a vegetable curry weighing 3,106.5 kg (6,848 lb, 1102) was served at Whittington Barracks on 17 July 2000. It fed about 7,500 people and the event raised an estimated £4,500 for charity. It was cooked by Abdul Salam of the Eastern Eye restaurant, Lichfield (GBR 2004 p111).

Yoxall Yoxall was Staffordshire's 52nd largest parish, consisting of 4,961 acres; 75th closest parish to the county town, 11.9m E; extremist length 5m, making it 31st= longest parish in the county; extremist width 3.7m.

Altitudes The highest point of the parish is 426 feet at Newchurch. The lowest point is 187 feet by Yoxall Bridge.

Astle, Thomas *Owned the finest private library of manuscripts in England, Yoxall's most famous old worthy.* (1735-1803). Archivist and collector of books and manuscripts. Born Yoxall Lodge on December 22nd. Compiler of an index to catalogue the Harley manuscripts in the British Museum 1761; FSA 1763; FRS 1766. Horace Walpole wrote of him in 1775 "In the paper-office there is a wight, called Thomas Astle, who lives like moths on old parchments." His most celebrated work is 'The Origin and Progress of Writing' 1784. He died on 1st December at his home Battersea Rise, Surrey, and is buried St Mary's Battersea.

Churches St Peter's at Yoxall is one of 15 such county dedications (of AP churches); 48th= oldest AP county church dating from 1200. The winter months curfew bell stopped in 1938, when the mechanism was found to be unsafe, and it was hoped to be resumed in 1952 (SA April 11 1952 p5 col 7). *Most interesting monument* is an alabaster table tomb in the N aisle with the effigies of Humphrey Welles (d1565), of Hoar Cross, and his wife Mary (d1584), daughter of William Chetwynd. It is probably the work of the Royleys (SHOS vol 1 p100) (GNHSS p23) (LGS p260) (CHMS p57) (JME part II pp24-25 pl 11 (a)).

Holy Angels at Hoar Cross is a luxuriant Neo-Gothic building inside and out. It was the most lavish work of its architect George Frederick Bodley (1827-1907), who worked in partnership with Thomas Garner (d1906) (A Dictionary of Architecture. Penguin. 1977). Is *'claimed to be the finest of its kind in England'*, *'the most beautiful modern church in England' 1938*, *'one of the most beautiful 19c churches in England' 1977*, *'Bodley's masterpiece'* The 2nd quote is from SA Oct 29 1938 p7p; the 1st quote is from SLM Winter 1954 p15; the 3rd and 4th are by Henry Thorold in SGS p108. Built 1871-77 by Mrs Meynell-Ingram in memory of her husband Hugo Francis Meynell-Ingram (d1871) of Hoar Cross and Temple Newsam. *Third longest church entry in Pevsner's 'Staffordshire'* Holy Angels, at 66 lines (BOE pp148-150).

Holy Angels church, Hoar Cross - the finest of its kind in England.

Community and built-environment *'considered to be the oldest village in England'*. Yoxall, according to Geoff Blore in his 'Dicky Blood's War' (2003) (see above) and presumably according to his 'Yoxall link' local searcher, Liz Guy; the village was originally carved out of the once great forest of Needwood. *Only known aisle hall remaining in Staffordshire*. Reeve End Cottage at the north end of Yoxall village; it dates from pre-1350 (SVB p186). *One of the last communities to get mains water*. Hoar Cross, 1952 (County Museum, Shugborough). *One of the AA's 1001 Great Family Pubs*. The Crown Inn, Main St, Yoxall 'In a picturesque village, this pub is reputedly over

250 years old: its name possibly deriving from its former use as the local courthouse' (book of the above title, 2005). *One of the finest examples of yew topiary in England*. Yew Tree Walk at Hoar Cross Hall (KES ps facing p97) (CL May 10 1902 pp594, 598). *Highest value street in Staffordshire 2008*. Weaverslake Drive, Yoxall, with houses worth an average of £1,08 million, according to property website Zoopla! (Burton Mail July 30 2008 p8pc) (ES Aug 4 2008 p19).

Durvall, Edwin *Yoxall's most gruesome find*. The headless body of Edwin Durvall, retired publican. Mr Durvall was reported missing from his home, The Almshouses, Colton, in Dec 1948, aged 79. His body turned up in a meadow at Yoxall in early Dec 1951. It was thought to have drifted down the Trent from Colton, and could only be identified from his hobnailed boots, laced in military fashion (BOb Dec 6 1951 p1) (SA Dec 7 1951 p1).

Farming *Yoxall Prince, Yoxall Harold and Yoxall Hero* were all stallions of Samuel Archer of High Hall Hill who were toured c1901 to sire with mares (SA April 15 1899 p8 col 7. May 4 1901 p8). *Extraordinary-sized pig* was that reared by 1838 by J Levett of Hollybank, near Yoxall, weighing 40 score, with a very admirable compactness of frame, and symmetry of proportion. It went to Mr Draper of the Oak Inn, Stafford (SA Dec 15 1838. Dec 17 1938 p10 col 3).

Featherstone, Dr Henry Walter *Founder/ first president of the Association of Anaesthetists of Great Britain*, *'one of the best known medical men in the Midlands' 1967*. (c1894-1967). Occupied Yoxall Lodge; anaesthetist at General Hospital, Birmingham, 1919-; subsequently honorary anaesthetist to the Maternity, Children's, & Ear, Nose and Throat hospitals in Birmingham (mems in Newchurch church) (Birmingham Post April 24 1967).

Fletcher, Ellie *2008 British Gymnastic champion at grade level 3*. Of Hadley End, Yoxall, of East Staffordshire Gym Club (Burton Mail May 8 2008 p44pc).

Folklore *Yoxall's best*. A blacksmith's apprentice, ill-treated by his master, committed suicide whilst his master was at church. Ever since, horses at the spot where the lad ran himself through with a spear have been startled and shy, although there is no effect to humans. Perhaps the apprentice had a special affinity with horses and this evokes a sense only known to them (SVB p187).

Horses take fright at a certain spot in Yoxall village, possibly scared by the spirit of a kindly blacksmith's apprentice who was bullied by his master.

Geology The Darley Oaks area is Rhætic; Trent valley area is Alluvium; Yoxall village and most of the rest of the parish is Keuper Marls.

Kirk, Mrs E *Yoxall's heroine*. A farm bailiff's wife, who rescued Christopher Warren, farmer, from a raging young bull, who on Aug 11 1921, butted him backwards in the direction of the village brook. The bull badly mauled him and got on top of him, but he caught it by the nose-ring in his thumb, meanwhile Mrs Kirk, who had seen the incident from her bedroom window, came to his aid and beat the animal with a stick (SA Aug 20 1921 p4 col 7. Aug 27 1921 p7p).

Lester, Alfred 'Pop' *Set up Yoxall's first garage, 'Oldest cricketer in England'.* Born 1870. Blacksmith. As claimed by Yoxall Cricket Club for whom he played on a regular basis until the early 1950s, at the age of 84, and considered the 'Grand Old Man' of local cricket. In 1956 he had been with Yoxall CC since 1884. He was still an active cricketer in 1959. He set up the garage with his son-in-law. In WW2 he

Alfred Lester of Yoxall still putting on the whites aged 82.

was never late and never missed a single parade when in the Home Guard, and was awarded a certificate for devoted service from General Officer Commanding of Northern Command (SA April 14 1945 p6 col 6) (LiMe July 4 1952 p4 col 4) (SA & Chron May 24 1956 p10ps) (BOb June 4 1959 p5p) (TB June 1994 p18p).

Place-name The first appearance of the name, Yoxall, is Domesday Book, 1086. The first part means 'yoke, yoke of oxen', the second part 'a small valley' or 'a

piece of low-lying land by a river' (PNSZ p598). *Unique derivation for a surname* Yoxall will be from Yoxall in this parish (PDS).

Population Yoxall was 46th most-populated Staffordshire parish in 1801 with 1,300 people; 49th in 1811 with 1,345; 50th in 1821 with 1,463; 50th in 1831 with 1,582; 54th in 1841 with 1,535; 60th in 1851 with 1,496; 63rd in 1861 with 1,443; 65th in 1871 with 1,419; 69th in 1881 with 1,301; 71st in 1891 with 1,283; 73rd in 1901 with 1,160. Yoxall could be ranked 43rd worst-affected Staffordshire parish for loss of men in WW1, with 50 lives taken.

Quote *Choicest*. In 2003 the memories of Richard Blood of Birmingham recounting his time as a child evacuee in Yoxall were published, written up by Geoff Blore. Richard was aged 10 when he arrived in the village, and his brother, Douglas, aged 7. He left in Feb 1944 on his 14th birthday, when legally old enough to start work. The chapter 'Change' detailing his arrival begins:- 'The new surroundings, the seemingly vast countryside bereft of factories, large building complexes, traffic, people, smoke and noise. The many different species of trees, hedges and occasional tiny cottages here and there on the narrow, twisting lanes writhing through countless fields of various shape and size, most of which contained cattle or produce. The occasional lowing of cows. The distant chugging of a tractor. ....The rural activities, farming, milling, saddle making and watching the magic wrought by the blacksmith.'

Raworth, Miss Margaret *Miss Staffordshire 1938*. Of Hadley End, aged 16, laundress (BOb May 12 1938 p7) (SA May 7 1938 p6p).

Snape, John *Yoxall's longest-serving bell ringer (probably)*. Born 1762, a ringer from 1782 to at least 1849, and 'never absent from his bell on Christmas morn' (SA Jan 13 1849 p8 col 4).

Spateman family *Yoxall's kindest*. A dynasty of Spatemans gave generously to the poor of Yoxall. Rev John Spateman by will dated 1727; his son, Francis, and his other son, Thomas.

Thompson, James *Yoxall's hero*. (1829-91). Born Yoxall, but grew up in Walsall. Private in the 1st Battalion, 60th Rifles, the forerunner to the Royal Green Jackets. At the seige of Lucknow, July 1857, he saved the life of his commanding officer Capt Wilton, by springing forward to his aid during a period when the officer was completely surrounded by the enemy. In a ferocious attack on the beleagued British position, the mutineers fought with a savage intensity, but Pte Thompson stood firm, killing two assailants at close quarters and continued to defend the ground until reinforcements arrived. His V.C. is on display at the Royal Green Jackets' museum in Winchester. His gravestone in Queen St Cemetery, Walsall, has since decayed and is lost (TB Feb 21 2008 p27p).

Women's Institute *2nd winners of the Staffordshire W.I. Challenge Banner.* Hoar Cross W.I. in 1921, with 31 certificates. The banner was instituted by Mrs Harrison of Maer Hall (chairman of the County Federation of W.I.s) (SA Oct 8 1921 p7 cols 1-3). *Largest W.I. gathering ever held in Staffordshire.* Possibly the rally of the Staffordshire Federation of Women's Institutes held at Hoar Cross on July 13 1950, with an expected 2,000 members and friends attending; the event was last held in 1946 (SA May 27 1950 p6 col 2) (SLM July 1950 p147). *Yoxall W.I. president who had a shawl she knitted accepted by Elizabeth II.* Mrs M.E. Norman of 'The Orchard', Yoxall, in 1959; it was a gift of Staffordshire Federations of W.I.'s for the royal baby (BOb Nov 19 1959 p12).

Some key abbreviations

BOb Burton Observer
BOE Buildings of England: Staffordshire. N Pevsner 1974
BPn Birmingham Post
E&S Express and Star
GBR Guinness Book of Records. 1955 -
LiMe Lichfield Mercury
LTM Lichfield and Tamworth Life Magazine. Sept 1971 - March 1973
MR2 A guide to Staffordshire & The Black Country The Potteries & The Peak. Michael Raven. 2004
NSFCT North Staffordshire Field Club Transactions
PNSZ The Place-Names of Staffordshire. David Horovitz. 2005

SA The Staffordshire Adveriser (after 1952 Staffordshire Advertiser and Chronicle)
SGS Shell Guide to Staffordshire. H Thorold. 1978
SHOS History of Staffordshire. Stebbing Shaw. Volumes 1, 2 1798 1801
SLM Staffordshire Life Magazine
SN Staffordshire Newsletter
SNAR Street Names of Aldridge, Rushall, Streetly & Pheasey. Betty Fox. 1996
SNBC Street Names of Brownhills, Clayhanger, Shelfield & Walsall Wood. Betty Fox. 1999
SSAHST South Staffordshire Archaeology and History Society Transactions. 1959 -
TH Tamworth Herald
VCH Victoria County History

Lightning Source UK Ltd.
Milton Keynes UK
11 August 2010

158217UK00001B/8/P